Praise for The Cadwaladr

★★★★★

It's been a constant battle finding an engaging read that will not only keep them interested in turning pages but will also compliment their preparation for grammar/ independent school entrance exams. This book ticked all the boxes. It's a fantastic story with a very clever and unique way of explaining the antonyms and synonyms within the text. This helped so much with my dyslexic son who reads very well but often misinterprets the meaning of the vocabulary. I would 100% recommend this book regardless of age and educational journey.

– *Mum of three boys*

★★★★★

S L Ager combines the use of effective and useful vocabulary with an in-built dictionary all in one book. Definitely a winner!!!

We introduced this book to our Year 5 students at our tuition centre last year when we read it as a group… The children loved it and wanted the story to continue… This book is now on our recommended list of books to prepare children for the 11+ exams.

– *Mrs Win*

★★★★★

My son loved reading this book, he couldn't put it down!! Excellent vocabulary list and perfect for those studying for 11plus exams. I highly recommend it. He's been asking for the second book *(Race for Gold)* EVERYDAY since he finished this one which we just purchased too! You won't regret purchasing this book.

– *Nomi_smiles*

THE CADWALADR CHRONICLES

11+ VOCABULARY

BOOK 1: TRAP

S. L. AGER

Developmental editor: Anna Bowles
Copyeditor and proofreader: Louis Greenberg
Cover design and interior formatting: Mark Thomas / Coverness.com

ISBN 978-1-913753-06-1 (paperback)
ISBN 978-1-913753-07-8 (ebook)

www.slager.co.uk

FOR ALL CHILDREN,
REGARDLESS OF DIFFICULT EXAMS

SPECIAL THANKS

I want to say a big thank you to some exceptional readers who helped me to develop *The Cadwaladr Chronicles.*

Thank you,

Janya Agarwal,

Arjun Pasumarti

and

Aaron Smith.

Table of Contents

Preface ..... *i*
How to Use This Book ..... *iii*
Top Reading Tips ..... *v*
Key to Abbreviations of Word Type ..... *vii*
Parents, Get FIVE Free Comprehension Exercises ..... *ix*
Introduction to the Key Characters, Items and Locations ..... *x*
Map of Catrin Castle ..... *xiii*
Chapter One: *The Pages* *1*
Chapter Two: *Slingshot* *12*
Chapter Three: *The Tower* *20*
Chapter Four: *Peggy* *32*
Chapter Five: *The Ring* *41*
Chapter Six: *Escape* *48*
Chapter Seven: *Forbidden Friends* *55*
Chapter Eight: *An Untimely Reappearance* *64*
Chapter Nine: *Disappeared* *69*
Chapter Ten: *Foul Fowl Feathers* *77*
Chapter Eleven: *Nine Lives* *84*
Chapter Twelve: *Into the Void* *89*
Chapter Thirteen: *Too Late* *95*
Chapter Fourteen: *Saving a Squire* *102*
Chapter Fifteen: *Spies and Lies* *109*
Chapter Sixteen: *Feeding Fishy* *112*
Chapter Seventeen: *To Forget* *116*
Chapter Eighteen: *Trapped* *121*
Chapter Nineteen: *Final Chance* *128*
Chapter Twenty: *Bad Dreams* *132*
Chapter Twenty-One: *We Can Be Heroes* *139*
A Sneak Peek! *147*
Cipher: Chapter One *149*
Learn With *The Cadwaladr* Series *161*
Parents, Get FIVE Free Comprehension Exercises *163*
Reviews, please! *165*
Errata and Information *165*

PREFACE

I wrote *Trap*, the first of *The Cadwaladr Chronicles*, prequels to *The Cadwaladr Quests,* after receiving so many requests from parents asking for books more suited to years two, three and four.

Some readers of the original *The Cadwaladr Quests* are in year three, but I don't recommend that for most children as the narrative is more suited to readers from late year four and above, including, of course, year six.

Although the prequels are aimed at younger readers, the narrative and vocabulary are as challenging as in *The Cadwaladr Quests* but they are age-appropriate.

Many of the words included and defined in this book come from the practice materials I covered and amassed with my two children when working towards the 11+ exams and SATs in primary school. We worked with both GL and CEM materials.

Of course, no published aids can guarantee that their material will appear on any exam paper, and neither can I. However, considering *The Cadwaladr Chronicles: Trap* contains over 1,600 word definitions and hundreds of corresponding synonyms and antonyms (in a fun story for girls and boys), what does any parent or young reader have to lose?

I hope you enjoy Callwen's gripping adventure in the first book of *The Cadwaladr Chronicles*, but moreover, I hope it helps you and your children with any challenging vocabulary exams they are facing.

HOW TO USE THIS BOOK

This story has been specially written to help young readers prepare for their 11+, SATs and independent schools' entrance exams. It includes difficult vocabulary embedded in a fun narrative that provides context for the new words and makes them easier to learn and understand.

On every page, key words are in bold, and each has a correlated footnote with a concise definition. The words are defined using the context in which they appear in the text, and definitions are as child-friendly as possible. Chosen key words are defined only once, usually when they first appear in the story, unless they appear again in a different context.

Synonyms and antonyms, where applicable, are also provided.

This book does not aim to replace a dictionary or purport to be one, but dictionaries have been used to check the accuracy of each definition.

PS: There are a few Welsh words in the story. To learn how to pronounce them, please visit slager.co.uk/welsh-words.

TOP READING TIPS

- Children, you may find it beneficial to read this book for the first time with an adult, but you and your parents can decide.
- The definitions are included for convenience and to guide the learning, not as a definitive 'must learn' list.
- Chosen key words are defined only once, usually when they first appear in the story, unless they appear again in a different context.
- To make learning difficult words easier, try to associate the words with the relevant scene in the book and to picture their meanings.
- Chapter lengths vary, so do not necessarily aim to finish a chapter in each sitting.
- Some pages have more definitions than others to fit in with the storytelling.
- Read the book as often as is needed, and continue to use its vast resource of definitions, synonyms and antonyms to reinforce learning.
- The best way to learn new words is to read as widely and with as much variety as possible. Every book is a world of adventure waiting for you to turn to the first page. I hope my book helps in this journey of discovery and learning.

KEY TO ABBREVIATIONS OF WORD TYPE

(v) verb

(n) noun

(adj) adjective

(adv) adverb

(prep) preposition

(con) conjunction

(int) interjection

(s) synonym

(ant) antonym

PARENTS, GET FIVE FREE COMPREHENSION EXERCISES

Parents, to receive your free comprehensions (with answers) based on *The Cadwaladr Chronicles: Book 1 – Trap,* please leave a review for *Trap* on Amazon and email a screenshot to:

freebies@slager.co.uk.

I will add you to my mailing list[1] and send you the comprehensions by email.

1 You can unsubscribe from the mailing list at any time. Further details will be emailed to you as soon as you are added.

INTRODUCTION TO THE KEY CHARACTERS, ITEMS AND LOCATIONS

Callwen (Cad) Cadwaladr. Adopted daughter of Prince Llywelyn and his wife, Siân.

The Knights Hawk. A magical order of hand-picked knights.

The Gwalch Gem bracelet. A magical combination of Welsh gold and emerald cut into the shape of a hawk.

Instinct. Powers bestowed by the bracelet which must be earned in order to become a Knight Hawk.

Cadwaladr Castle. Prince Llywelyn's residence.

Catrin Castle. Prince Dewi's residence. Cad's current home.

Prince Llywelyn. Knight Hawk. Ruler of Wales. Adoptive father to Cad and father of her baby brother, Prince John.

Princess Siân Cadwaladr. Wife of Prince Llywelyn. Mother to baby Prince John. Cad's adoptive mother.

Prince Dewi. Prince Llywelyn's younger brother.

Prince John. Baby son of Llywelyn and Siân. Cad's brother.

Gelert. Prince Llywelyn's faithful hound.

Dylan Rogers. Cad's friend and fellow page.

Rhys Price. Cad's friend and fellow page.

May. A hawk.

Bryn Davis. An older squire.

Jack Jones. Bryn's trainee.

Sir Robert Evans. Llywelyn's associate. A Knight Hawk.

Sir Owain Glyn. Llywelyn's second-in-command. A Knight Hawk.

Anwen Cadwaladr. Llywelyn's sister. Cad's aunt.

Peggy (Hari). Prince Dewi's former henchman.

Goodwife Hughes. A servant in Anwen Cadwaladr's employ.

Hugh Hughes. Goodwife Hughes's son.

Fishy. A dog.

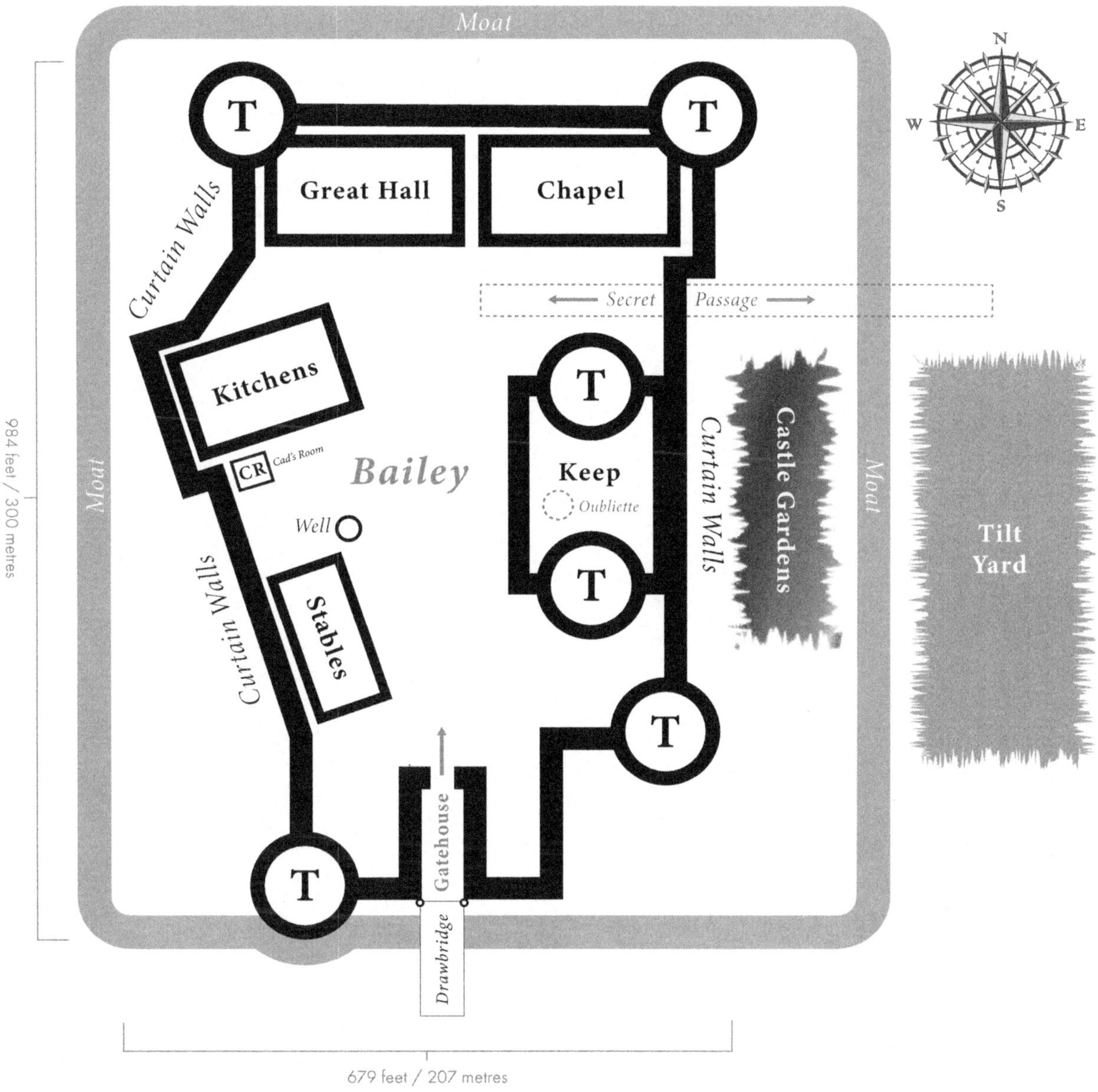

Map of Catrin Castle

TWELFTH-CENTURY WALES

CHAPTER ONE

The Pages

Cad **scowled**[1] at her enemy, raising her sword high in the air.

'**Surrender**[2], **traitor**[3], or taste my blade,' she cried, **lunging**[4] at the man with swift strokes – the stuffing was now spilling out through the **gashes**[5] in his **makeshift**[6] **garments**[7].

With the **nonchalance**[8] of a cat, she stepped back, then like a striking panther, and with a final **flourish**[9], she lunged again, **spearing**[10] her target perfectly. As quick as a blink, it was all over, and she **yanked**[11] out the stick **lodged**[12] in his **midriff**[13].

'That's you finished,' she said, stepping away from the straw man.

---

1 **scowl** *(v)* frown in an angry way. *(s)* glare, glower, grimace. *(ant)* smile.
2 **surrender** *(v)* stop resisting an enemy or opponent. *(s)* submit, capitulate, yield. *(ant)* fight, win.
3 **traitor** *(n)* someone who betrays (double-crosser). *(s)* conspirator, turncoat, collaborator. *(ant)* loyalist.
4 **lunge** *(v)* thrust forward. *(s)* pounce, rush, leap, spring, jump.
5 **gash** *(n)* a deep and long cut or wound. *(s)* slash, incision, laceration.
6 **makeshift** *(adj)* acting as a temporary or make-do measure. *(s)* pretend, improvised. *(ant)* permanent.
7 **garment** *(n)* an item of clothing. *(s)* clothes, outfit, attire, dress.
8 **nonchalance** *(n)* the state of being nonchalant (unemotional). *(s)* calmness, indifference. *(ant)* concern, anxiety.
9 **flourish** *(n)* a bold or extravagant gesture or action. *(s)* display, wave, brandish.
10 **spear** *(v)* strike with a pointed (sharp) object. *(s)* spike, stab, poke.
11 **yank** *(v)* pull with a sudden, hard movement. *(s)* tug, jerk, wrench. *(ant)* push, shove.
12 **lodge** *(v)* firmly wedge, embed or stick in a place. *(s)* fix, plant, jam. *(ant)* dislodge.
13 **midriff** *(n)* the front area between the chest and the waist. *(s)* middle, belly, midsection.

Triumphant[1], she turned to her friends who were practising with her in the castle's **tilt yard**[2], a beaming smile lighting up her face.

'Rhys, it's your turn to stuff him and sew up his **doublet**[3] before the next battle.'

With a wave, Cad **gestured**[4] to the straw dummy, nodding at her friend, who flashed a toothless grin, his **vivid**[5] copper curls glinting in the morning sun.

Eager[6] to continue their training, Cad turned to her other friend, Dylan.

'Your fight next,' she said, her chin **jutting**[7], her **tone**[8] that of a born leader.

'Yes, Sire Bossy Boots of Catrin Castle,' Dylan **mocked**[9] in a light-hearted response. 'However, your tone displeases me,' he added, his **expression**[10] now that of an enemy.

In preparation for his attack, Dylan squared his shoulders, spread his feet apart and faced Cad. For further effect, he scowled, curling his lip. Then he **tilted**[11] his head, raised his weapon and, in a deep, **lofty**[12] voice, said, 'Prepare, knight, for I will run you through with my sword.'

As quick as a fox and as **agile**[13] as a cat, he sprang, lunging at Cad, and with the skill of a **fully fledged**[14] knight, not a twelve-year-old page, he **brandished**[15] his stick for battle.

All three friends scattered in delight, hooting and shooing away **stray**[16] chickens before

---

1 **triumphant** *(adj)* showing great jubilation (joy) after a victory. *(s)* elated, delighted. *(ant)* defeated.

2 **tilt yard** *(n)* a place or courtyard where jousts took place, sometimes enclosed.

3 **doublet** *(n)* a short, close-fitting jacket, commonly worn by men in the Middle Ages.

4 **gesture** *(v)* make a movement to convey a feeling or intention of something. *(s)* indicate, signal.

5 **vivid** *(adj)* (of a colour) intensely deep or bright. *(s)* vibrant, radiant, rich. *(ant)* dull, muted.

6 **eager** *(adj)* wanting to do or have something keenly. *(s)* impatient, enthusiastic. *(ant)* unenthusiastic.

7 **jut** *(v)* protrude (stick out from). *(s)* poke out, project. *(ant)* indent, depress, recede.

8 **tone** *(n)* the sound of one's voice. *(s)* pitch, timbre, intonation.

9 **mock** *(v)* tease or make fun of. *(s)* ridicule, joke, taunt. *(ant)* praise, compliment.

10 **expression** *(n)* a look that conveys (shows) a certain emotion. *(s)* face, appearance, air.

11 **tilt** *(v)* move into a sloping position. *(s)* incline, cock. *(ant)* level.

12 **lofty** *(adj)* haughty and aloof. *(s)* disdainful, superior, arrogant. *(ant)* humble.

13 **agile** *(adj)* able to move easily and quickly. *(s)* nimble, spry, swift. *(ant)* sluggish, stiff.

14 **fully fledged** *(adj)* developed or established completely. *(s)* mature, grown. *(ant)* fledgling, immature.

15 **brandish** *(v)* wave as a threat or in excitement. *(s)* shake, wield, display. *(ant)* conceal.

16 **stray** *(adj)* not in the usual place or with the right group. *(s)* scattered.

preparing for their next **faux**[1]-fight. The three **pageboys**[2], too young for real **combat**[3], fought **mock**[4] battles for now. Soon they would progress to real **lances**[5] and horses in Catrin Castle's tilt yard in preparation to become **squires**[6] when they turned fifteen. But until then, they needed to repair their dummy's doublet and re-stuff him, ready for the next **bout**[7].

Cad **regarded**[8] Dylan and Rhys as they **bustled**[9] about, preparing the dummy. She **cherished**[10] her friends, and her **prestigious**[11] knight's training. **Grateful**[12] for her **privilege**[13], she **glanced**[14] across at the **magnificent**[15] castle, which was commanded by Prince Dewi, the brother of her father, Prince Llywelyn.

As always, struck by Catrin's **stature**[16], Cad **peered**[17] up at the castle's towering grey-stone **curtain wall**[18] in admiration. The purpose-built tilt yard, **constructed**[19] for training and **jousting**[20] **tournaments**[21], lay to the castle's east yet was separated by a wide and deep **moat**[22]. Never tiring

---

1 **faux** *(adj)* not genuine. *(s)* fake, pretend, imitation. *(ant)* authentic, genuine.

2 **pageboy** *(n)* a boy in training for a knighthood, ranking one level below a squire in a knight's personal service.

3 **combat** *(n)* fighting. *(s)* battle, conflict, warfare. *(ant)* peace.

4 **mock** *(adj)* not real. *(s)* imitation, simulated. *(ant)* real.

5 **lance** *(n)* a long wooden weapon with a pointed steel tip, used in medieval jousting and battle.

6 **squire** *(n)* a young nobleman serving a knight in exchange for training to be a knight himself.

7 **bout** *(n)* a contest of strength. *(s)* match, encounter, fight, clash.

8 **regard** *(v)* look at steadily. *(s)* eye, watch, contemplate. *(ant)* disregard, ignore.

9 **bustle** *(v)* move in a quick or busy manner. *(s)* hasten, hurry, fuss, scamper. *(ant)* amble.

10 **cherish** *(v)* hold dear and protect. *(s)* treasure, adore, appreciate, value. *(ant)* neglect.

11 **prestigious** *(adj)* having a good reputation. *(s)* impressive, esteemed, distinguished. *(ant)* ordinary, modest.

12 **grateful** *(adj)* feeling or showing appreciation for something. *(s)* thankful, glad, appreciative. *(ant)* ungrateful.

13 **privilege** *(n)* a special right. *(s)* benefit, entitlement, advantage. *(ant)* burden.

14 **glance** *(v)* take a hurried look. *(s)* glimpse, peep, peek. *(ant)* stare, peer.

15 **magnificent** *(adj)* spectacular, impressive and awesome. *(s)* superb, superlative. *(ant)* unimpressive.

16 **stature** *(n)* size, build and standing. *(s)* height, position, prestige, distinction. *(ant)* lowliness.

17 **peer** *(v)* look with concentration. *(s)* stare, gaze, gape. *(ant)* glance.

18 **curtain wall** *(n)* a fortified wall surrounding a medieval castle, often linking towers together.

19 **construct** *(v)* make or build. *(s)* assemble. *(ant)* deconstruct.

20 **joust** *(n)* a medieval contest in which two opponents fought on horseback using lances. *(s)* tourney, tilt.

21 **tournament** *(n)* a series of contests with multiple contestants. *(s)* competition, series, event.

22 **moat** *(n)* a defensive, water-filled trench surrounding a castle or town.

of the view, Cad **marvelled**[1] at the **magnificence**[2] of Catrin, built on a **broad**[3] **plateau**[4] **atop**[5] mountains as if **spawned**[6] from the rocks that supported her **foundations**[7].

Ever thankful, Cad turned back to the yard, putting thoughts of Catrin's **majesty**[8] aside because **falconry**[9] practice now **beckoned**[10]. She narrowed her eyes, **squinting**[11] up against the blazing sun, and, bringing two fingers from each hand to her mouth, whistled. Within seconds, a grey-brown bird swooped from above. As light as a leaf on the wind, it landed on Cad's shoulder, its sharp **talons**[12] gripping her **tunic**[13] for **purchase**[14].

'I **dread**[15] the **consequences**[16] if the master **falconer**[17] catches you with that hawk,' Dylan warned Cad, with a nod at the bird perched next to her ear.

'He won't find her. May is far too **wily**[18],' Cad snapped with **confidence**[19]. Even so, her protective hand stroked May's head as she spoke.

Cad studied her hawk, **ruffling**[20] the bird's **proud**[21] white chest, the **mottled**[22] feathers so

---

1 **marvel** *(v)* be filled with amazement and wonder. *(s)* gape, stare. *(ant)* deride, disregard.
2 **magnificence** *(n)* being magnificent (impressive). *(s)* greatness, splendour, majesty. *(ant)* insignificance.
3 **broad** *(adj)* physically wide. *(s)* big, large. *(ant)* narrow.
4 **plateau** *(n)* a level area of high ground. *(s)* upland, table, highland. *(ant)* mountain.
5 **atop** *(prep)* on the top of. *(s)* upon.
6 **spawn** *(v)* produce or generate from something.
7 **foundation** *(n)* an underground, weight-bearing part of a building. *(s)* base, footing, substructure.
8 **majesty** *(n)* impressive scale, beauty and stateliness. *(s)* splendour, grandeur. *(ant)* insignificance, lowliness.
9 **falconry** *(n)* the sport of hunting with specific birds of prey such as hawks, eagles and falcons.
10 **beckon** *(v)* appear inviting or attractive. *(s)* call, tempt, attract. *(ant)* repel, deter.
11 **squint** *(v)* look with one's eyes screwed up or partly closed. *(s)* peer, peek, glance.
12 **talon** *(n)* a sharp claw, particularly one belonging to a bird of prey. *(s)* nail, fingernail.
13 **tunic** *(n)* a loose garment, often sleeveless and worn with a belt. *(s)* surcoat, robe.
14 **purchase** *(n)* a firm contact or grip. *(s)* hold, toehold. *(ant)* release.
15 **dread** *(v)* anticipate with apprehension. *(s)* fear *(ant)* look forward to.
16 **consequence** *(n)* a result or effect. *(s)* outcome, upshot, repercussion. *(ant)* cause.
17 **falconer** *(n)* someone who keeps, train or hunts with falcons or other birds of prey.
18 **wily** *(adj)* clever and sharp, sometimes deceitfully so. *(s)* shrewd, astute, crafty, cunning. *(ant)* guileless.
19 **confidence** *(n)* a feeling of self-assurance and belief in oneself. *(s)* certainty. *(ant)* uncertainty.
20 **ruffle** *(v)* mess up something or someone's hair. *(s)* tousle, dishevel. *(ant)* smooth, straighten.
21 **proud** *(adj)* splendid and impressive. *(s)* dignified, noble, striking. *(ant)* unimpressive.
22 **mottled** *(adj)* marked with spots or smears of colour. *(s)* speckled, streaked, flecked. *(ant)* monochrome.

distinct[1]. Pale grey-brown **horizontal**[2] bars split the softness into **intricate**[3], **angular**[4] patterns.

'Such beauty,' Cad **muttered**[5], marvelling at May's **plumage**[6], the **subtle**[7] shades providing the perfect **camouflage**[8] for this agile **bird of prey**[9].

May, **slight**[10] for a female **goshawk**[11], tilted her **pert**[12] head towards Cad's voice; the bird's **keen**[13] eyes long since blinded by the cruel falconers. May was once a sought-after goshawk, but her sharp eyes, sewn closed by a clumsy **apprentice**[14], had become **infected**[15] and **pus**[16]-filled, and had been **callously**[17] **gouged**[18] out. **Thus**[19], May **lacked**[20] hunting skills, and because of her **scant**[21] survival chances, the falconers had **abandoned**[22] her. Cad had rescued May, hiding her from the men who would kill her if she were discovered at Catrin Castle.

'Rhys Price, you **utter**[23] nothing of May either,' Dylan warned his younger friend with a finger wag. 'Your lips can be loose once they finally part to speak,' he added, frowning at the slightly built boy.

---

1 **distinct** *(adj)* recognisably different from something else of a similar type. *(s)* marked, noticeable. *(ant)* indistinct.
2 **horizontal** *(adj)* level with the plane of the horizon. *(s)* parallel, level, even. *(ant)* vertical.
3 **intricate** *(adj)* detailed and complicated. *(s)* complex, elaborate. *(ant)* plain, simple.
4 **angular** *(adj)* having sharp corners. *(s)* pointed. *(ant)* rounded.
5 **mutter** *(v)* say something that is difficult to hear. *(s)* murmur, mumble, whisper. *(ant)* shout.
6 **plumage** *(n)* a bird's feathers. *(s)* tuft.
7 **subtle** *(adj)* delicate or difficult to describe. *(s)* indistinct, imperceptible. *(ant)* obvious.
8 **camouflage** *(n)* a disguise. *(s)* concealment, veil.
9 **bird of prey** *(n)* a bird that hunts and feeds on other animal flesh. *(s)* raptor.
10 **slight** *(adj)* small in build. *(s)* slim, slender, delicate. *(ant)* sturdy, big.
11 **goshawk** *(n)* a large white-grey hawk with cream coloured underwings. *(s)* raptor.
12 **pert** *(adj)* (of a body part) small and well shaped. *(s)* neat, perky, animated. *(ant)* limp, lifeless.
13 **keen** *(adj)* sharp and intense. *(s)* astute, deep, bright, responsive. *(ant)* dull.
14 **apprentice** *(n)* a person learning from a skilled person. *(s)* trainee, novice, pupil. *(ant)* veteran, master.
15 **infected** *(adj)* affected by an organism that causes disease. *(s)* rotten, ailing, afflicted. *(ant)* healthy.
16 **pus** *(n)* a thick yellowy-green liquid produced in infected tissue. *(s)* secretion.
17 **callously** *(adv)* in a callous (cruel) manner. *(s)* ruthlessly, mercilessly. *(ant)* kindly.
18 **gouge** *(v)* make a hole. *(s)* scoop, dig, claw. *(ant)* fill.
19 **thus** *(adv)* as a result of this. *(s)* so, consequently, therefore, hence, ergo.
20 **lack** *(v)* to be without. *(s)* be in need of, want. *(ant)* possess, have.
21 **scant** *(adj)* barely sufficient or adequate. *(s)* meagre, negligible, limited, scarce. *(ant)* extensive. .
22 **abandon** *(v)* leave alone or behind. *(s)* discard, forsake, ditch, dump. *(ant)* keep.
23 **utter** *(v)* speak *(s)* say, voice.

Rhys, the youngest of the three, **cast**[1] a half-smile Dylan's way and kicked at the dirt and straw with the toe of his boot.

'Why be so cruel?' Cad said, her voice **grave**[2]. 'Do these creatures not suffer fear and pain as we do? My father forbids such **savage**[3] practice at his castle. Why does he allow his brother's cruelty here? When I am a Knight Hawk, I will speak with him and halt these **brutal**[4] ways.'

'Regardless, *you* will suffer their **wrath**[5] if they catch you with May and that pup you're hiding in the **dungeons**[6],' Dylan warned. 'Beware, Cad; certain pages and squires **strive**[7] for your downfall—' Dylan **abruptly**[8] stopped, his brows lifting as he bobbed his head towards two distant figures entering the sandy yard.

Cad glanced towards the approaching boys, clicked her tongue, and, as swiftly as she'd appeared, May **soared**[9] away before the nearing boys saw her. Cad stilled, **steeling**[10] herself for the oncoming **altercation**[11], because when Bryn Davis approached, as always, trouble would follow.

A **purposeful**[12] silence fell amongst the three friends as the two older boys neared.

'At knights' play again, *children*. Fighting like girls,' Bryn Davis **sniped**[13], **jabbing**[14] a finger in the air towards the three friends in turn, his tone underlining his words. 'You'll never make squires,' he **scoffed**[15], his hands now on his hips.

Cad felt the **potent**[16] spice of anger stirring in her stomach as she bared her teeth in an

---

1 **cast** *(v)* direct one's expression at someone or something *(s)* throw, shoot, send.

2 **grave** *(adj)* serious or solemn. *(s)* sombre, sober, thoughtful. *(ant)* cheerful, upbeat.

3 **savage** *(adj)* aggressively hostile. *(s)* brutal, vicious, cruel. *(ant)* gentle, mild.

4 **brutal** *(adj)* cruel or unpleasant. *(s)* vicious, harsh, callous, ruthless. *(ant)* gentle, humane.

5 **wrath** *(n)* anger. *(s)* fury, rage, outrage, vexation. *(ant)* happiness.

6 **dungeon** *(n)* a cell or room where prisoners are held. *(s)* prison, jail, oubliette, donjon.

7 **strive** *(v)* make huge efforts to acquire or accomplish something. *(s)* endeavour, try. *(ant)* shirk, quit.

8 **abruptly** *(adv)* in an abrupt (unexpected and sudden) way. *(s)* hastily, quickly. *(ant)* gradually.

9 **soar** *(v)* climb or fly rapidly above usual levels. *(s)* ascend, escalate, rise. *(ant)* decline, descend, plummet.

10 **steel** *(v)* mentally prepare for something difficult. *(s)* strengthen, fortify, brace. *(ant)* weaken.

11 **altercation** *(n)* an audible (can be heard) argument. *(s)* quarrel, disagreement. *(ant)* agreement.

12 **purposeful** *(adj)* done with intention. *(s)* deliberate, calculated. *(ant)* unintentional, accidental.

13 **snipe** *(v)* make a sly or petty verbal attack. *(s)* scoff, taunt, ridicule, jeer, dig. *(ant)* praise, applaud.

14 **jab** *(v)* poke roughly or quickly. *(s)* prod, stab, push, point.

15 **scoff** *(v)* speak in a mocking or derisive way. *(s)* ridicule, deride, sneer. *(ant)* praise, respect.

16 **potent** *(adj)* having great influence, strength or power. *(s)* strong, formidable. *(ant)* weak.

undiluted[1] smile of **malice**[2], the words she **itched**[3] to say **dissolving**[4] on her tongue.

Bryn was the older of the two boys, his **underling**[5] page and trainee, Jack Jones, **meek**[6] and trailing behind him. 'Perhaps you can be *ladies'* maids instead,' he added, shoving their straw man to the ground. Then with a savage kick, Bryn **severed**[7] the dummy's head from its shoulders.

Without hesitation, Cad lunged at the **strapping**[8] boy, but Dylan yanked her shoulder and hissed, 'Cad, he's not worth it. He's **goading**[9] you. Ignore his **bait**[10].'

'Bryn Davis, you're nothing but a **maggot**[11],' Cad spat, ignoring Dylan's advice. 'And a squire you may be, but you'll never make knight, *never*!'

Bryn curled his lip, snarling like a dog, his face twisted, but surprisingly he said nothing.

'Strip away your fancy clothes, **coiffed**[12] hair and squire's **status**[13], then what's left is the **chivalry**[14] of a rat.'

Now it was Bryn's turn to lunge, but Dylan's **stout**[15] figure, swiftly inserted between Bryn and Cad, proved a worthy barrier.

'Bryn, what is it you want from us?' Dylan's soft tone immediately **soothed**[16] the **tension**[17]. 'I am certain it is not our company you seek,' he added with a hint of **sarcasm**[18].

Bryn stood tall, puffed out his chest and announced, 'The prince commands his pages and

---

1 **undiluted** *(adj)* not weakened. *(s)* strong, full strength. *(ant)* diluted, weak.
2 **malice** *(n)* the desire to hurt or harm someone. *(s)* spite, malevolence, badness. *(ant)* kindness.
3 **itch** *(v)* an overwhelming desire to do something. *(s)* yearn, hanker, crave.
4 **dissolve** *(v)* disappear. *(s)* vanish, evaporate, disperse. *(ant)* appear.
5 **underling** *(n)* someone of lower rank or status. *(s)* junior, inferior, subordinate. *(ant)* superior, boss.
6 **meek** *(adj)* easily imposed on. *(s)* submissive, quiet, timid, weak. *(ant)* assertive.
7 **sever** *(v)* cut off. *(s)* remove, separate, detach. *(ant)* unite, attach, combine, join.
8 **strapping** *(adj)* strong and often big (of a person). *(s)* sturdy, burly, brawny. *(ant)* puny, weedy.
9 **goad** *(v)* annoy or provoke into a reaction. *(s)* badger, prod, push. *(ant)* calm.
10 **bait** *(n)* something for luring (enticing). *(s)* snare, trap, lure.
11 **maggot** *(n)* a soft, legless larva of a fly, found in decaying matter. *(s)* grub.
12 **coif** *(v)* arrange or style a person's hair.
13 **status** *(n)* social or professional standing. *(s)* rank, position, class, grade, level.
14 **chivalry** *(n)* polite and courteous behaviour. *(s)* gallantry, consideration. *(ant)* rudeness.
15 **stout** *(adj)* heavily built. *(s)* strong, solid, sturdy, robust. *(ant)* thin, slight.
16 **soothe** *(v)* gently calm or quieten. *(s)* pacify, mollify. *(ant)* aggravate, exacerbate.
17 **tension** *(n)* stress or unrest. *(s)* strain, agitation, unease. *(ant)* calmness.
18 **sarcasm** *(n)* the use of irony (the opposite) to mock or convey dislike. *(s)* derision, scorn, disdain. *(ant)* flattery.

squires to gather at once in the great hall. So **hasten**[1], that is, if you value your **reputations**[2], *children*.' As he said 'children', he **glared**[3] at Cad, his tone **oozing**[4] **contempt**[5].

Cad lunged again but met only Dylan's broad chest.

'We will leave once we clear your mess,' Dylan said, gesturing to the straw **strewn**[6] across the ground. Young Rhys was already gathering stray pieces, his head **bowed**[7] low to avoid Bryn, who **terrorised**[8] him whenever the **opportunity**[9] arose.

'**Wantwit**[10],' Cad muttered, picking up straw, as Bryn and his silent **sidekick**[11], Jack, marched off.

When they'd gone, Cad looked up and caught Dylan's death stare. Now **abashed**[12] by her actions, her face softened.

'Cad, contain your **rage**[13] around Davis. He **suspects**[14] something is different about you. If he learns the truth, I doubt even Prince Llywelyn could help you, as he would appear foolish to have **sanctioned**[15] your training here.'

'I know. Dylan, you are right. My **temper**[16] **governs**[17] me to my **detriment**[18],' Cad said, brushing off Dylan's advice and bending to scoop up handfuls of straw instead.

---

1 **hasten** *(v)* move quickly. *(s)* hurry, dash, race, run, hare. *(ant)* dawdle.

2 **reputation** *(n)* the general opinion held about something or someone. *(s)* stature, repute, status.

3 **glare** *(v)* stare angrily or fiercely. *(s)* scowl, glower, frown. *(ant)* grin, smile.

4 **ooze** *(v)* give a strong impression of. *(s)* exude, display, drip, exhibit, demonstrate.

5 **contempt** *(n)* the feeling that someone or something is worthless. *(s)* disdain, dislike, scorn. *(ant)* admiration.

6 **strew** *(v)* scatter or spread things untidily (past participle: strewn). *(s)* throw, cast, toss, litter. *(ant)* gather, assemble.

7 **bow** *(v)* bend the upper part of the body or head to greet, or to show respect or shame. *(s)* nod, bob.

8 **terrorise** *(v)* create and maintain a state of fear *(s)* scare, torment, persecute, bully.

9 **opportunity** *(n)* the chance to be able to do or achieve something. *(s)* prospect, occasion.

10 **wantwit** *(n)* a person in need of wit. *(s)* fool, halfwit, dolt, clod, ninny. *(ant)* genius.

11 **sidekick** *(n)* slang for a person's assistant or companion. *(s)* crony, associate, accomplice.

12 **abashed** *(adj)* embarrassed, ashamed or disconcerted. *(s)* deflated, mortified. *(ant)* undaunted.

13 **rage** *(n)* extreme anger. *(s)* wrath, fury, indignation, outrage. *(ant)* calmness.

14 **suspect** *(v)* believe in the existence or truth of something without proof. *(s)* assume, think, suppose. *(ant)* know.

15 **sanction** *(v)* approve or permit. *(s)* allow, authorise, endorse, consent. *(ant)* veto, disapprove.

16 **temper** *(n)* someone's level of calmness or anger. *(s)* temperament, nature, personality.

17 **govern** *(v)* to control (one's behaviour or conduct). *(s)* rule, steer, guide. *(ant)* neglect, yield.

18 **detriment** *(n)* a cause of damage or harm. *(s)* loss, disadvantage. *(ant)* benefit.

But Dylan continued, adding, 'Bryn wonders why we have separate **quarters**[1] to the other pages. He doesn't fall for the reason of 'age separation' Llywelyn gives. Even though Prince Dewi and Llywelyn are brothers, you know Llywelyn could not openly sanction a girl for knight's training. The **nobles**[2] would **veto**[3] it, and you would become a ladies' maid, as that **weasel**[4], Bryn Davis, wants.'

Deep in thought, Cad **pursed**[5] her lips, then half-smiled – her **level-headed**[6] friend was right. She must practise **prudence**[7] and **curb**[8] her **unruly**[9] tongue because it too often **unfurled**[10] to trip her.

'Even I struggle to call you Cad. I forget sometimes,' Dylan continued. 'And praise be to God that young Rhys here **barely**[11] talks. You **witness**[12] his **naivety**[13], and one day I fear he will slip. It is difficult to cast aside the lifelong **habits**[14] of **addressing**[15] you as a girl.'

Cad stared at Dylan, **weighing**[16] his words of **caution**[17], but hoping he'd soon finish his 'don't forget you are a girl' **sermon**[18]; she'd heard it many times before and knew there was probably more to come.

'You have clung to the **notion**[19] of being a knight since you were seven years old. Before then,

---

1 **quarters** *(n)* accommodation. *(s)* chambers, rooms, apartment.

2 **noble** *(n)* a person of high birth or rank. *(s)* aristocrat, peer, patrician. *(ant)* peasant.

3 **veto** *(v)* impose a veto (ban) against. *(s)* reject, overrule, quash. *(ant)* approve, allow.

4 **weasel** *(n)* a deceitful person, (or a small animal). *(s)* rogue, scoundrel, wretch. *(ant)* altruist.

5 **purse** *(v)* contract or pucker (the lips) to express a feeling. *(s)* pout, tighten.

6 **level-headed** *(adj)* sensible and calm. *(s)* wise, prudent, mature. *(ant)* excitable, hot-headed.

7 **prudence** *(n)* wisdom or cautiousness. *(s)* judgement, shrewdness, sense. *(ant)* folly, carelessness.

8 **curb** *(v)* keep in check. *(s)* control, restrain, suppress, silence. *(ant)* release, increase.

9 **unruly** *(adj)* disruptive and uncontrollable. *(s)* unrestrained, wilful. *(ant)* disciplined, well behaved.

10 **unfurl** *(v)* unroll or roll out. *(s)* open out, unfold. *(ant)* furl, fold up.

11 **barely** *(adv)* hardly, almost not. *(s)* rarely, scarcely. *(ant)* often.

12 **witness** *(v)* see something happen. *(s)* observe, perceive, notice. *(ant)* ignore, overlook.

13 **naivety** *(n)* lack of wisdom, experience or judgment. *(s)* innocence, simplicity, gullibility. *(ant)* wisdom, sophistication.

14 **habit** *(n)* a regular practice and sometimes one that is hard to stop. *(s)* custom, routine, tendency.

15 **address** *(v)* name someone. *(s)* label, identify, call.

16 **weigh** *(v)* assess the importance of something. *(s)* contemplate, consider. *(ant)* ignore.

17 **caution** *(n)* care. *(s)* vigilance, wariness. *(ant)* recklessness.

18 **sermon** *(n)* a long, boring piece of advice. *(s)* lecture, speech, monologue.

19 **notion** *(n)* an idea or something imagined. *(s)* thought, concept, desire.

you were Callwen, Prince Llywelyn's **adopted**[1] daughter, and my childhood friend, and now you are Cad, a pageboy in Prince Dewi's castle. It is easy to trip up over this secret, Cad.'

Cad regarded Dylan, whose eyes shone with **genuine**[2] **concern**[3]. Still, she refused to **submit**[4] to his warnings. **Determined**[5] by nature, Cad would become a knight in Llywelyn's **elite**[6] order, the Knights Hawk. Hand-chosen knights to whom Llywelyn had **granted**[7] the magical powers of the Gwalch Gem bracelet. Cad would earn these powers of *Instinct* **bestowed**[8] by the **mystical**[9] bracelet that Llywelyn had **sacrificed**[10] much of his adult life to creating. And although Cad knew Dylan spoke the truth, she was determined to make her father proud.

'We will **address**[11] that problem if it arises,' Cad eventually said, **reassuring**[12] Dylan with a wink. But inside, she worried, not for herself, but for the people who shared in her secret.

Cad was no longer seven, and **masquerading**[13] as a boy would become more **challenging**[14] every day. Fortunately for Cad, her build was **stocky**[15] and strong, and her face, being neither pretty nor ugly, **bore**[16] a bone structure that **betrayed**[17] no **gender**[18].

'Hello. Anyone there?' Dylan chuckled, rapping on Cad's head as though it were a door.

---

1 **adopt** *(v)* legally take another person's child to raise as one's own.

2 **genuine** *(adj)* real, truthful or sincere. *(s)* honest, candid. *(ant)* insincere, false.

3 **concern** *(n)* worry. *(s)* anxiety, apprehension. *(ant)* indifference, calm.

4 **submit** *(v)* give in to. *(s)* yield, capitulate. *(ant)* defy, resist.

5 **determined** *(adj)* having or displaying resolve. *(s)* resolute, firm, unwavering. *(ant)* irresolute.

6 **elite** *(adj)* a chosen individual or group that is superior in ability. *(s)* best, pick, elect. *(ant)* worst, dregs.

7 **grant** *(v)* allow or give. *(s)* award, assign, bestow. *(ant)* deny.

8 **bestow** *(v)* offer or give an honour, gift or right. *(s)* grant, present. *(ant)* withdraw.

9 **mystical** *(adj)* inspiring a sense of fascination not obvious to the senses or intelligence. *(s)* magical. *(ant)* earthly.

10 **sacrifice** *(v)* give up something for the sake of others. *(s)* surrender, forgo, forfeit. *(ant)* keep.

11 **address** *(v)* deal with a problem. *(s)* tackle, confront. *(ant)* ignore.

12 **reassure** *(v)* do or say something to remove someone's fears or doubts. *(s)* comfort, hearten. *(ant)* unnerve.

13 **masquerade** *(v)* make a false and deceptive show of pretence. *(s)* act, pose, behave.

14 **challenging** *(adj)* demanding or testing one's abilities. *(s)* taxing, difficult, tough, arduous. *(ant)* easy.

15 **stocky** *(adj)* broad and heavily built. *(s)* stout, chunky, burly, hefty. *(ant)* slight, slender.

16 **bear** *(v)* have or display a visible mark or feature (past tense: bore). *(s)* convey, deliver, present.

17 **betray** *(v)* expose (show) information. *(s)* reveal, disclose. *(ant)* conceal, hide.

18 **gender** *(n)* characteristics pertaining to the two sexes; social and cultural identities beyond these established categories.

'Sorry. I was miles away.' Cad laughed, and then said, 'Dylan, don't **fret**[1] about the future. I trust you and, of course, young Rhys here,' she finished, ruffling Rhys's copper curls. Cad grinned at Rhys's **flushing**[2] cheeks, then switching the sore subject, said, 'Rhys, you grab the dummy's head. We'll carry his body.'

Cad gestured to the straw man on the floor. 'There's no time to stitch him up. We'll do that later.'

And with that, Cad **stooped**[3] to gather up the headless dummy and said, 'Come, friends. Let us make haste to Dewi's great hall to see what it is of such **vital**[4] **import**[5] that awaits us there.'

---

1 **fret** *(v)* be anxious. *(s)* worry, fuss, agonise, anguish.

2 **flush** *(v)* become red. *(s)* blush. *(ant)* pale.

3 **stoop** *(v)* bend one's head or body forward and downwards into a hunch. *(s)* crouch, slouch. *(ant)* straighten.

4 **vital** *(adj)* completely necessary. *(s)* essential, key, crucial. *(ant)* unimportant, secondary.

5 **import** *(n)* importance. *(s)* significance, magnitude, note. *(ant)* insignificance.

CHAPTER TWO

Slingshot

When Cad entered the packed great hall, its hushed **atmosphere**[1] alarmed her. Although **crammed**[2] to its **majestic**[3] oak **rafters**[4], the flames flickering in its grand stone fireplace seemed **deafening**[5]. **Unnerved**[6], Cad glanced at Dylan, whose confused face mirrored hers. Why was her father, Prince Llywelyn, addressing Dewi's hall? This was **unprecedented**[7]. Dewi was in **residence**[8], for they had seen him earlier leaving the tilt yard **via**[9] the tunnel beneath the castle's moat and gardens.

An unwelcome ball of **anxiety**[10] bounced into Cad's chest. Her father's angular face wore a

---

1 **atmosphere** *(n)* the tone, mood or ambience. *(s)* feeling, air, mood, aspect.

2 **cram** *(v)* completely fill to the point of overflowing. *(s)* pack, jam, fill, stuff, ram. *(ant)* empty.

3 **majestic** *(adj)* showing or having magnificent beauty or size. *(s)* awesome, splendid. *(ant)* pathetic, pitiful.

4 **rafter** *(n)* a beam which makes up part of the internal framework of a roof.

5 **deafening** *(adj)* a noise so loud one cannot hear anything else. *(s)* thunderous, booming. *(ant)* quiet.

6 **unnerved** *(adj)* made to lose confidence or courage. *(s)* alarmed, worried. *(ant)* encouraged.

7 **unprecedented** *(adj)* never known or done before. *(s)* unparalleled, extraordinary. *(ant)* common.

8 **residence** *(n)* living in a particular place. *(s)* residency, occupancy.

9 **via** *(prep)* through. *(s)* by.

10 **anxiety** *(n)* a worried and nervous feeling. *(s)* apprehension, unease, disquiet. *(ant)* calmness, reassurance.

harrowed[1] expression **hitherto**[2] unseen by Cad, and although **clad**[3] in **partial**[4] armour, his broad shoulders **slumped**[5] as if bearing the weight of the world.

'Pages and squires. **Ensure**[6] your knight's **armour**[7] is ready and pack supplies for a **quest**[8]. We leave today.' Prince Llywelyn gave his surprise orders from the **dais**[9] at the front of the hall, his face **dour**[10]. As his words settled, the air in the room slowly thickened with dread.

Cad **shuddered**[11] as a wave of fear rippled through her. She cast Dylan a **baffled**[12] glance and with her wide green eyes full of unanswered questions whispered, 'What quest?'

But Dylan simply shrugged, shaking his head as Llywelyn instructed the Knights Hawk who would **accompany**[13] him.

Cad's mind whirled, her thoughts trapped behind a frown. Why such sudden plans? Where was her uncle, Dewi? Catrin was his castle to command; he should be here. Cad sensed **doom**[14] as Dylan's elbow poked her ribs, **rousing**[15] her from her **reverie**[16]. She noticed Rhys had joined them, his copper curls bobbing as he **fidgeted**[17] beside Dylan. Rhys's friendly face seemed clouded by an odd look, his eyes heavy and unsure. Cad's stomach swirled.

Dylan, now with an **anguished**[18] expression darkening his face too, stooped to whisper in Cad's ear, his voice sounding thin. 'Rhys says Dewi has fled the castle with your mother. He's left

---

1 **harrow** *(v)* cause upset or distress to. *(s)* trouble, torment, pain. *(ant)* comfort, calm.

2 **hitherto** *(adv)* until this point. *(s)* previously, thus far. *(ant)* henceforth.

3 **clad** *(adj)* clothed or dressed. *(s)* attired, wearing, cloaked. *(ant)* unclothed, undressed.

4 **partial** *(adj)* part of something. *(s)* incomplete, fragmentary. *(ant)* complete, full.

5 **slump** *(v)* fall, sit or lean heavily. *(s)* sag, slouch, collapse. *(ant)* lift, straighten.

6 **ensure** *(v)* make certain. *(s)* guarantee, check, confirm, insure. *(ant)* deny.

7 **armour** *(n)* the metal plates formerly worn to protect the body in battle. *(s)* covering, shield.

8 **quest** *(n)* a long or difficult search for something. *(s)* mission, expedition, journey.

9 **dais** *(n)* a low platform for a throne or lectern. *(s)* stage, rostrum, stand, podium.

10 **dour** *(adj)* unfriendly, gloomy or miserable. *(s)* sour, stern, severe, grim. *(ant)* kindly, cheerful.

11 **shudder** *(v)* tremble unwittingly *(s)* shiver, shake, quiver, convulse.

12 **baffled** *(adj)* totally confused. *(s)* bewildered, perplexed, confounded. *(ant)* enlightened.

13 **accompany** *(v)* go with someone. *(s)* chaperone, attend, escort. *(ant)* abandon, desert.

14 **doom** *(n)* a terrible situation or thing. *(s)* ruin, destruction.

15 **rouse** *(v)* bring out of inactivity. *(s)* stimulate, prompt, wake. *(ant)* calm.

16 **reverie** *(n)* a state of being lost in thought. *(s)* daydream, musing, contemplation. *(ant)* concentration.

17 **fidget** *(v)* make small, nervous or impatient movements. *(s)* fret, fiddle, twiddle. *(ant)* sit still.

18 **anguished** *(adj)* suffering or expressing anguish (pain, distress). *(s)* agonised, woeful. *(ant)* happy.

with Siân. And …' Dylan paused to look at Cad, his eyes full of **sorrow**[1].

'Go on!' Cad **urged**[2], **panic**[3] rising in waves and **clutching**[4] her throat. For what could be worse than what he'd just told her?

'And … and … Gelert is dead.'

'What?' Cad spat her words too loudly, her face sharpening with shock. Stunned, she struggled to **fathom**[5] his words. What Dylan had said was unimaginable, Llywelyn's wife had fled with his brother, and Gelert, his **faithful**[6] dog, was dead. But when? And why?

Without thinking, Cad reached across Dylan, grabbing Rhys by the shoulder and yanking him close to her face. Her legs weakened as her heart **boxed**[7] at her ribs.

'Rhys, who told you this **tale**[8]?'

The shy boy **paled**[9], **trembling**[10] as he retold the **rumours**[11] that raced through the castle like a field on fire.

'Quiet!' boomed a voice from one of Llywelyn's towering knights.

Rhys **cowered**[12] as Cad leaned in and said, 'Whisper. Now continue.'

As Llywelyn instructed the crowd, clad in armour and his magnificent sword at his side, Cad heard not a word he said. **Bewildered**[13] and absorbed by Rhys's **account**[14], Cad's heart ached as she wished for her friend to be wrong.

---

1 **sorrow** *(n)* a feeling of grief or sadness. *(s)* anguish, agony, distress. *(ant)* joy, cheer.

2 **urge** *(v)* try to persuade someone. *(s)* encourage, press. *(ant)* deter, discourage.

3 **panic** *(n)* uncontrollable anxiety or fear. *(s)* fright, dread, alarm. *(ant)* calm, self-control.

4 **clutch** *(v)* grab or grasp something tightly. *(s)* hold, grip, seize. *(ant)* release, let go.

5 **fathom** *(v)* comprehend after much thought. *(s)* understand, grasp, perceive. *(ant)* misunderstand.

6 **faithful** *(adj)* remaining loyal, steadfast, constant and true. *(s)* dedicated, dependable, reliable. *(ant)* disloyal.

7 **box** *(v)* punch an opponent with one's fist. *(s)* thump, fight.

8 **tale** *(n)* a true or fictitious story. *(s)* account, anecdote, gossip, hearsay.

9 **pale** *(v)* lose colour in one's face from fear or shock. *(s)* blanch, blench, whiten. *(ant)* flush.

10 **tremble** *(v)* shake involuntarily (automatically) from fear or excitement. *(s)* quake, quiver. *(ant)* still.

11 **rumour** *(n)* a circulating story of little or doubtful truth. *(s)* gossip, tale, tittle-tattle. *(ant)* fact.

12 **cower** *(v)* crouch or squat in fear. *(s)* shrink, recoil, flinch, cringe. *(ant)* stand tall.

13 **bewildered** *(adj)* perplexed or confused. *(s)* baffled, mystified, confounded. *(ant)* enlightened.

14 **account** *(n)* a description or recounting of something. *(s)* story, explanation, portrayal.

In castle courts, **malicious**[1] **gossip**[2] was **commonplace**[3], yet one **glimpse**[4] at Llywelyn's anguished face gave Cad the truth. Cad's **adoptive**[5] mother, Siân, had fled with Llywelyn's brother. But even worse, they had stolen the Gwalch Gem bracelet. Cad knew that in the wrong hands, the bracelet's power could prove disastrous.

A horrid feeling gripped Cad's body as the **grim**[6] **realisation**[7] hit her. Then, as the icy grip of fear **subsided**[8], into its place poured the hot burn of **despair**[9]. She stared at her father, hearing the sadness as his strained voice drifted into her ears. He tried to hide the anguish, but the lines on his face lay heavy like he'd been trying to face an awful problem. He did not fool his daughter for a moment.

'All pages will remain at Catrin. Some squires may one day accompany me and the Knights Hawk to **retrieve**[10] the bracelet, but for now, you too will remain here.'

It struck Cad that Llywelyn had not said his brother's name. Was that to keep Dewi's **treachery**[11] secret, or was the pain too **raw**[12]? Cad felt sure it was the **latter**[13]. Llywelyn was an **honourable**[14] man. Cad had not **foreseen**[15] this **appalling**[16] **betrayal**[17], and neither, **apparently**[18], had he.

---

1 **malicious** *(adj)* having malice, intending harm. *(s)* malevolent, spiteful, mean, cruel. *(ant)* kind.
2 **gossip** *(n)* casual talk or rumour that has not been confirmed as true. *(s)* tattle, tales, hearsay. *(ant)* facts.
3 **commonplace** *(adj)* usual. *(s)* normal, routine, conventional. *(ant)* abnormal, unconventional.
4 **glimpse** *(n)* a partial or momentary view. *(s)* peep, peek, glance. *(ant)* stare.
5 **adoptive** *(adj)* (of a person) related by adoption (legally raising someone else's child).
6 **grim** *(adj)* serious or bleak. *(s)* horrid, miserable, dismal. *(ant)* pleasant, amiable.
7 **realisation** *(n)* the act of becoming aware that something is a fact. *(s)* understanding, awareness. *(ant)* ignorance.
8 **subside** *(v)* become less severe or intense. *(s)* diminish, ease, abate. *(ant)* increase.
9 **despair** *(n)* the loss of all hope. *(s)* hopelessness, desperation. *(ant)* hope, joy.
10 **retrieve** *(v)* bring or get something back. *(s)* reclaim, recover, rescue. *(ant)* lose, forfeit.
11 **treachery** *(n)* a breach of trust. *(s)* betrayal, deceit, disloyalty, dishonesty. *(ant)* loyalty, honesty.
12 **raw** *(adj)* very sensitive. *(s)* intense, painful, acute. *(ant)* numb.
13 **latter** *(n)* the second mentioned of two people or things. *(s)* last. *(ant)* former.
14 **honourable** *(adj)* morally correct. *(s)* honest, respectable, virtuous. *(ant)* dishonourable, dishonest.
15 **foresee** *(v)* be aware of something beforehand (past participle: foreseen). *(s)* anticipate, predict, envision.
16 **appalling** *(adj)* very bad. *(s)* horrible, awful, shocking, ghastly. *(ant)* pleasant.
17 **betrayal** *(n)* the action of being gravely disloyal (untrue) to someone. *(s)* deception, treachery. *(ant)* loyalty.
18 **apparently** *(adv)* as far as one knows or can see. *(s)* supposedly, seemingly, evidently. *(ant)* implausibly.

Once poor Rhys, the **innocent**[1] **harbinger**[2], had finished his tale, Cad gently nudged him away and **inched**[3] closer to Dylan.

'I must **seek**[4] my father's **audience**[5] before he leaves,' she whispered in Dylan's ear, her thoughts whirling like leaves in a **gale**[6].

Dylan gave her a **sympathetic**[7] look, but said nothing. Together, they **gazed**[8] at the dais where Llywelyn continued, his voice grave, his expression grim.

'In my **absence**[9], I leave my trusted Knight Hawk, Sir Robert Evans, to command my brother's castle.'

Cad **detected**[10] a **hitch**[11] in Llywelyn's voice as he said the word 'brother'. Her heart tore in two. Her father looked broken.

'I bestow all control to my trusted **associate**[12].' Llywelyn removed his huge hand from Sir Robert's shoulder, who bowed his head in respect.

Cad watched as Robert Evans stood in silence by Llywelyn's side. **Intrigued**[13], she wondered how this almost **dainty**[14] man had become one of Llywelyn's Knights Hawk. He was most unlike any other. Perhaps that was his **appeal**[15]. **Despite**[16] her doubts, Evans *was* Llywelyn's trusted **adviser**[17], and she must respect him for that.

---

1 **innocent** *(adj)* not guilty. *(s)* blameless, guiltless. *(ant)* guilty.

2 **harbinger** *(n)* a person who brings news of something. *(s)* herald, announcer.

3 **inch** *(v)* move along carefully and slowly. *(s)* budge, edge, shuffle. *(ant)* rush, leap.

4 **seek** *(v)* try to find. *(s)* look for, hunt for, search for, pursue. *(ant)* lose.

5 **audience** *(n)* an interview with an important person. *(s)* contact, reception, consideration.

6 **gale** *(n)* a strong wind. *(s)* windstorm, storm, tempest. *(ant)* breeze.

7 **sympathetic** *(adj)* showing or feeling sympathy (pity). *(s)* consoling, compassionate. *(ant)* unsympathetic, indifferent.

8 **gaze** *(v)* look steadily. *(s)* stare, gape, peer. *(ant)* glimpse.

9 **absence** *(n)* the state of not being at an occasion or a place. *(s)* absenteeism. *(ant)* presence.

10 **detect** *(v)* discern the presence of something. *(s)* notice, sense, perceive. *(ant)* miss, overlook.

11 **hitch** *(n)* an instability in the voice. *(s)* catch, stammer, stutter, tremor, wobble.

12 **associate** *(n)* a business partner or companion. *(s)* colleague, ally, comrade, supporter.

13 **intrigue** *(v)* arouse curiosity or interest. *(s)* fascinate. *(ant)* bore, disenchant.

14 **dainty** *(adj)* small and pretty. *(s)* delicate, prim, prissy. *(ant)* rough, large, course.

15 **appeal** *(n)* the quality of being interesting or attractive. *(s)* allure, magnetism, pull.

16 **despite** *(prep)* in spite of, regardless of. *(s)* even with. *(ant)* because of.

17 **adviser** *(n)* someone who gives advice in a specific field. *(s)* consultant, confidant, aide.

'Pages, squires, return to your **duties**[1]. Prepare for your knights' departures,' Llywelyn ordered. Then, with his head held high and followed by his **courtiers**[2], the noble prince left the hall in silence.

'Don't cry, girls,' Bryn Davis sniped as he **filed**[3] past the three friends. 'You can **scour**[4] and **polish**[5] the kitchens while we squires do manly work because nobody remains here to train you. Boohoo,' he **sneered**[6], using his fists to rub away fake tears.

Cad's face **tensed**[7], and her eye twitched. Dylan noticed and shook his head. 'Not worth it,' he mouthed. But when Bryn blew Cad a **sly**[8] little kiss, the way to an audience with Llywelyn, without raising **suspicion**[9] from his court, popped straight into her head.

'Davis,' she **bellowed**[10] at the squire's back, white-hot anger rising from her **gut**[11].

As Bryn turned, Cad, as quick as a wink, already whirling the cord around her head, let go, and her pre-loaded **sling**[12] released its **projectile**[13]. A flat stone sailed with pinpoint **accuracy**[14] straight at Bryn. It found his nose with a crunching sound, bounced onto the head of another squire, and landed with a crack on the floor.

Davis **wailed**[15], his face **incredulous**[16] as he pinched his nose to **stem**[17] the rush of **scarlet**[18]

---

1 **duty** *(n)* an action or task one must do as part of one's job. *(s)* chore, responsibility, obligation.
2 **courtier** *(n)* a person who attends a royal court. *(s)* aristocrat, noble, peer, attendant.
3 **file** *(v)* walk behind one another in a line (single file). *(s)* march, troop, parade. *(ant)* crowd.
4 **scour** *(v)* clean something by rubbing hard. *(s)* scrub, wash, cleanse, abrade.
5 **polish** *(v)* make something shiny by rubbing it. *(s)* buff, gloss, shine. *(ant)* dull.
6 **sneer** *(v)* speak or smile in a nasty manner. *(s)* smirk, snigger, snicker. *(ant)* chirp.
7 **tense** *(v)* become rigid, usually from anxiety. *(s)* tighten, stiffen, harden. *(ant)* relax.
8 **sly** *(adj)* (of an action) intended for one or few, not all. *(s)* furtive, surreptitious, secret. *(ant)* open.
9 **suspicion** *(n)* a state of doubt or distrust. *(s)* mistrust, wariness, uncertainty. *(ant)* certainty.
10 **bellow** *(v)* shout loudly and deeply. *(s)* holler, bark, roar, cry, yell. *(ant)* whisper.
11 **gut** *(n)* the stomach. *(s)* belly, abdomen, tummy.
12 **sling** *(n)* a simple weapon in the shape of a loop, used to throw stones, etc. *(s)* catapult, slingshot.
13 **projectile** *(n)* a missile (object) that is forcibly fired from something.
14 **accuracy** *(n)* correctness or precision. *(s)* certainty, exactitude. *(ant)* inaccuracy.
15 **wail** *(v)* make a prolonged, high-pitched sound. *(s)* howl, cry, yowl. *(ant)* laugh, giggle.
16 **incredulous** *(adj)* not able to believe. *(s)* unbelieving, disbelieving. *(ant)* believing.
17 **stem** *(v)* restrict or stop the flow of something. *(s)* halt, check, staunch, curb. *(ant)* increase.
18 **scarlet** *(n)* a bright red colour. *(s)* crimson, vermillion.

blood now **seeping**[1] into his hand. He spread his fingers, his eyes wide with shock. Then, like a cat on a mouse, Bryn sprang at Cad, his bloodied hands bashing into her chest. Like a rag doll, she flew backwards and dropped down on her rear with an **almighty**[2] thud.

'Ouch!' Cad cried as her tail bone met the floor with a crack. Then, in a blink, Davis **straddled**[3] her chest and pulled back his fisted hand ready to thump her.

'*Halt!*' Llywelyn's voice boomed. Everyone froze. Even the dogs stilled.

Silence **smothered**[4] the hall, and all heads turned towards Cad, who stared up at Bryn's **looming**[5] fist.

Bryn's eyes, bead bright, glared at Cad. Their stares drew each other like magnets. Heat filled her lungs. What would Llywelyn do now? What *could* he do now? She'd **committed**[6] a **rash**[7] act of stupidity and was a **lowly**[8] page in the eyes of the **folks**[9] gathered. He must punish her. Cad glanced at her father. Llywelyn's expression set fear in her heart, yet her face wore a look that she prayed he would recognise. A look that said, 'Please, Father, I need to speak with you, now.'

'Squire!' Llywelyn barked, pointing at Davis. 'Go! Clean your nose. You!' The prince nodded to another.

'Sire?' replied the **colossal**[10] knight standing beside Llywelyn.

'Take the page and lock him away.' Llywelyn did not look at Cad once.

Cad's heart fell, **contracting**[11] with shame[12]. Her **reckless**[13] **outburst**[14] had put her father in an impossible position. He could not reveal that Cad was his disguised daughter, never. Cad had

---

1 **seep** *(v)* slowly leak through. *(s)* ooze, bleed, trickle, permeate. *(ant)* pour.

2 **almighty** *(adj)* great or enormous. *(s)* massive, tremendous, mighty. *(ant)* weak, insignificant, feeble.

3 **straddle** *(v)* spread the legs wide apart (either side of something). *(s)* span.

4 **smother** *(v)* suppress an action or feeling. *(s)* stifle, strangle, gag, suppress.

5 **looming** *(adj)* about to happen. *(s)* approaching, threatening, impending. *(ant)* remote.

6 **commit** *(v)* carry out. *(s)* perpetrate, perform, execute. *(ant)* abstain, fail.

7 **rash** *(adj)* acting without consideration of the outcome. *(s)* hasty, reckless, impulsive. *(ant)* careful, prudent.

8 **lowly** *(adj)* low in importance or rank. *(s)* humble, ordinary, simple, common. *(ant)* noble.

9 **folk** *(n)* people. *(s)* persons, individuals.

10 **colossal** *(adj)* exceptionally large or great. *(s)* massive, enormous, huge. *(ant)* tiny.

11 **contract** *(v)* become tighter, shorter or smaller. *(s)* shrink, wither. *(ant)* expand, grow.

12 **shame** *(n)* a feeling of distress and humiliation caused by one's own wrongdoing. *(s)* embarrassment. *(ant)* pride.

13 **reckless** *(adj)* heedless of danger or the consequences of an action. *(s)* irresponsible, wild, rash. *(ant)* cautious.

14 **outburst** *(n)* an abrupt release of emotion. *(s)* eruption, outpouring, explosion.

failed him. Now they would lock her away, unable to say goodbye to her father before he left on his quest.

I'm such a reckless fool, she thought, **lamenting**[1] her actions, her eyes **filmy**[2] with **unshed**[3] tears.

As the colossal knight **hauled**[4] Cad to her feet, her face now the colour of **dough**[5], Bryn Davis snuck her a **smug**[6] look of contempt.

You will regret that, she **vowed**[7], but with an expression as **blank**[8] as a full moon.

Dylan, seemingly **paralysed**[9] by Cad's **unspeakable**[10] behaviour, **gawked**[11] at her, a baffled expression **crumpling**[12] his face.

'I'm sorry,' she mouthed to her friends as the knight's huge hand grasped her shoulder, pushing her towards the exit. She saw Rhys's tears **hovering**[13], **threatening**[14] to surface. Shame **scorched**[15] her cheeks. He would feel lost without her, but Cad knew Dylan would support him.

Cad's gaze dropped to her feet as Llywelyn's voice boomed, 'To the tower.'

Her friends watched in horror as the knight shoved her from the great hall, her head hanging low in **abject**[16] **humiliation**[17].

---

1 **lament** *(v)* feel or express disappointment or regret. *(s)* deplore, rue. *(ant)* celebrate.

2 **filmy** *(adj)* covered with a thin layer of something. *(s)* blurry, hazy. *(ant)* clear.

3 **unshed** *(adj)* (of tears) there but not yet falling onto the cheeks.

4 **haul** *(v)* drag or pull with force or effort. *(s)* heave, yank. *(ant)* push, shove.

5 **dough** *(n)* an often pale mixture of flour and liquid for baking into pastry or bread.

6 **smug** *(adj)* having an overly high opinion of oneself. *(s)* self-satisfied, superior. *(ant)* humble, modest.

7 **vow** *(v)* make a solemn (serious) promise. *(s)* swear, guarantee, assure.

8 **blank** *(adj)* figuratively showing a lack of understanding or reaction. *(s)* vacant, deadpan. *(ant)* expressive.

9 **paralysed** *(adj)* partly or wholly incapable of movement. *(s)* disabled, incapacitated. *(ant)* mobilised.

10 **unspeakable** *(adj)* too bad to express in words. *(s)* terrible, appalling, dreadful. *(ant)* commendable.

11 **gawk** *(v)* stare stupidly. *(s)* gape, gaze, gawp. *(ant)* ignore.

12 **crumple** *(v)* become creased or lined. *(s)* rumple, wrinkle, crinkle. *(ant)* iron.

13 **hover** *(v)* linger close by. *(s)* remain, stay. *(ant)* leave.

14 **threaten** *(v)* seem likely to produce an unpleasant result. *(s)* promise.

15 **scorch** *(v)* burn the surface of something. *(s)* sear.

16 **abject** *(adj)* something bad experienced to the maximum degree. *(s)* complete, absolute, extreme. *(ant)* minimal.

17 **humiliation** *(n)* the feeling of being humiliated (embarrassed). *(s)* shame, disgrace. *(ant)* pride, honour, dignity.

CHAPTER THREE

The Tower

Imprisoned, Cad **grimaced**[1] at the tower's **stark**[2] walls and **bare**[3] stone floor. It was a tired and unhappy room made worse by its **forlorn**[4] smell of despair and **desolation**[5]. The dungeon's single arrow slit **afforded**[6] but a scant **sliver**[7] of light, yet it seemed to point out everything she'd rather forget. Catrin's twin towers, the castle's most **secure**[8] places, held prisoners and **concealed**[9] the crown's gold and jewels too. No jewels in this cell, though.

Cad **crouched**[10] in a corner, **fondling**[11] the **hem**[12] of her tunic and **contemplating**[13] her

---

1 **grimace** *(v)* make an ugly, twisted expression on one's face. *(s)* scowl, frown. *(ant)* smile.
2 **stark** *(adj)* bare. *(s)* dreary, gloomy, sombre. *(ant)* ornate.
3 **bare** *(adj)* without adornment. *(s)* plain, basic, simple. *(ant)* comfortable.
4 **forlorn** *(adj)* sad and abandoned or lonely. *(s)* pitiful, dejected, despondent, hopeless, pathetic. *(ant)* cheerful.
5 **desolation** *(n)* great unhappiness or loneliness. *(s)* misery, despair, woe. *(ant)* gladness.
6 **afford** *(v)* provide an opportunity. *(s)* offer, give, present. *(ant)* remove.
7 **sliver** *(n)* a small, thin, narrow piece. *(s)* fragment, shard, bit. *(ant)* whole.
8 **secure** *(adj)* sure to stay safe. *(s)* guarded, strong, protected. *(ant)* insecure, vulnerable.
9 **conceal** *(v)* hide or disguise. *(s)* screen, secrete, obscure. *(ant)* reveal.
10 **crouch** *(v)* to lower the body by bending one's knees. *(s)* squat, huddle. *(ant)* stand.
11 **fondle** *(v)* stroke or touch. *(s)* pull, finger, twiddle, knead.
12 **hem** *(n)* the edges of clothing which has been turned under and sewn into place. *(s)* edge, border.
13 **contemplate** *(v)* think about. *(s)* ponder, consider, deliberate. *(ant)* disregard.

confinement[1]. At least Dewi's **gaolers**[2] had not **shackled**[3] her – yet.

Crestfallen[4], Cad thought of Llywelyn. **Guilt**[5] sat like a stone on her heart. Her father was no **tyrant**[6], but a kind nobleman who ensured that Dewi treated all apprentices with respect. He fed them well, providing the best combat training of any castle. Llywelyn's **kingdom**[7] **boasted**[8] the finest knights, the **envy**[9] of many nobles, even before the Gwalch Gem and Welsh gold's **spectacular**[10] **coupling**[11].

Before Cad came to Cadwaladr Castle, Llywelyn had **toiled**[12] for many years to find the Welsh gold rumoured to have **extraordinary**[13] powers if **combined**[14] with the Gwalch Gem. The jewel, a stunning emerald cut into the shape of a hawk, had been in Llywelyn's **possession**[15] for **generations**[16]. Not one to **abuse**[17] power, Llywelyn never misused the bracelet. Cad doubted that Dewi would be so noble.

With a stab to her heart, Cad **pondered**[18] Siân. What madness possessed the kind princess who had treated Cad as her own, even after the birth of her own child, John? How could Siân **abscond**[19] with her husband's brother and leave her son motherless? Cad's **current**[20] life melted away before

---

1 **confinement** *(n)* imprisonment. *(s)* captivity, custody, internment. *(ant)* freedom.

2 **gaoler** *(n)* a person who locks prisoners in jail. *(s)* keeper, captor, turnkey. *(ant)* liberator.

3 **shackle** *(v)* chain together with shackles (restraints). *(s)* tether, manacle, bind. *(ant)* free.

4 **crestfallen** *(adj)* sad, disappointed, low in confidence. *(s)* downcast, despondent *(ant)* upbeat.

5 **guilt** *(n)* a bad feeling about one's wrongdoing. *(s)* regret, remorse, shame. *(ant)* innocence.

6 **tyrant** *(n)* a cruel and oppressive ruler. *(s)* dictator, bully, tormentor, persecutor.

7 **kingdom** *(n)* a place ruled by a monarch (king or queen). *(s)* realm, dominion. *(ant)* republic.

8 **boast** *(v)* possess a feature to be proud of. *(s)* have, enjoy.

9 **envy** *(n)* an unpleasant feeling of wanting what other people have. *(s)* jealousy, desire. *(ant)* generosity.

10 **spectacular** *(adj)* impressive. *(s)* amazing, staggering, dramatic. *(ant)* dull.

11 **coupling** *(n)* the pairing of two things. *(s)* combination, merging. *(ant)* separation.

12 **toil** *(v)* work incessantly (non-stop) or extremely hard. *(s)* labour, slog, strive. *(ant)* laze, relax.

13 **extraordinary** *(adj)* remarkable or extremely unusual. *(s)* exceptional, phenomenal. *(ant)* normal.

14 **combine** *(v)* merge or join, unite for a common purpose. *(s)* unify, mix. *(ant)* separate.

15 **possession** *(n)* the state of owning or having something. *(s)* ownership, keeping.

16 **generations** *(n)* a period of time encompassing many steps in a line of descent. *(s)* ages, years, aeons.

17 **abuse** *(v)* use something for bad purposes. *(s)* misuse, exploit, mishandle.

18 **ponder** *(v)* think carefully about. *(s)* consider, contemplate, deliberate. *(ant)* disregard.

19 **abscond** *(v)* leave in rushed secret. *(s)* flee, run away, make off. *(ant)* remain, stay.

20 **current** *(adj)* in the present. *(s)* ongoing. *(ant)* past.

her eyes. The family unit that had saved Cad as a baby and raised her as their own had vanished.

Now with her father leaving, and down to her foolish actions, Cad was a prisoner. Would she ever see Llywelyn again, who might well **perish**[1] on this quest? Because of her **impulsive**[2] behaviour, Cad may never get the chance to prove her worth to him. Never before had she felt such **overwhelming**[3] **hopelessness**[4] and desolation. Everything was landing in **tatters**[5] around her feet.

As she contemplated her **folly**[6], a fat rat appeared, its whiskers twitching, its tail wiggling. It **scuttled**[7] by her, disappearing via a narrow **cranny**[8] in the wall. **Accustomed**[9] to rats, Cad didn't **flinch**[10], but the dungeon's walls closed in like rain clouds in a storm. She shivered. At least this dungeon wasn't beneath the castle, unlike other cells rumoured to **exist**[11]. That thought chilled Cad's blood. To be **confined**[12] underground was the worst thing imaginable to her. Cad had no memories of the well from which Llywelyn had rescued her as a baby, but the scars still cut deep.

Recent rumours **abounded**[13] that Dewi had **installed**[14] such dungeons in Catrin's **bowels**[15]. **Repulsed**[16] by the thought, Cad had **baulked**[17] at **verifying**[18] **idle**[19] gossip, which she knew to be,

---

1 **perish** *(v)* die, especially suddenly. *(s)* depart, pass away. *(ant)* live, survive.

2 **impulsive** *(adj)* done without thinking about beforehand. *(s)* rash, reckless, hasty. *(ant)* cautious.

3 **overwhelming** *(adj)* having a strong emotional effect. *(s)* profound, overpowering. *(ant)* underwhelming.

4 **hopelessness** *(n)* a state or feeling of unhappiness. *(s)* distress, desperation, anguish. *(ant)* hope.

5 **tatters** *(n)* shreds of some sort. *(s)* bits, pieces.

6 **folly** *(n)* a foolish idea or act. *(s)* idiocy, silliness, stupidity. *(ant)* wisdom.

7 **scuttle** *(v)* run or scamper hurriedly or furtively (secretly). *(s)* dart, bustle, scurry. *(ant)* saunter.

8 **cranny** *(n)* a little, narrow space or opening. *(s)* gap, niche, crevice, crack. *(ant)* closure.

9 **accustomed** *(adj)* used to something. *(s)* adapted, acclimatised. *(ant)* unaccustomed.

10 **flinch** *(v)* shy away from instinctively. *(s)* move, twitch, recoil, wince. *(ant)* stand firm.

11 **exist** *(v)* be. *(s)* be present.

12 **confine** *(v)* keep within certain limits. *(s)* enclose, trap, imprison. *(s)* release.

13 **abound** *(v)* exist in large amounts or numbers. *(s)* flourish, thrive, proliferate. *(ant)* lack.

14 **install** *(v)* place, ready for use. *(s)* fit, put, situate. *(ant)* remove.

15 **bowels** *(n)* the depths, the deepest part. *(s)* core, recesses, interior. *(ant)* peak, summit.

16 **repulse** *(v)* cause to feel intense distaste, displeasure or disgust. *(s)* repel, sicken. *(ant)* attract.

17 **baulk** *(v)* hesitate or be unwilling. *(s)* recoil, resist. *(ant)* proceed.

18 **verify** *(v)* make sure something is true. *(s)* prove, confirm. *(ant)* refute.

19 **idle** *(adj)* pointless. *(s)* trivial, frivolous, trifling. *(ant)* meaningful, serious.

more often than not, envy in disguise. And besides, Llywelyn **deplored**[1] such cruelty, and surely would have forbidden his brother to do so.

Appalled[2] by just imagining these things, Cad shuddered, picturing such a place. Determined to be brave, she pulled her tunic closer and rubbed her arms, the **friction**[3] it produced barely warming her.

When a **jarring**[4] clanging noise **startled**[5] her, **disorientated**[6], Cad realised she must have dozed off because she lay curled up on the cold floor. Expecting a gaoler, she stumbled to her feet. Instead, bewildered at what she saw, Cad gasped. No **turnkey**[7] entered her cell; it was the great Knight Hawk, Owain Glyn, her father's second-in-command, who stood before her.

Owain raised a finger to his lips in a 'shush', glanced back over his shoulder, and nodded. The **hulking**[8] figure of Prince Llywelyn strode into the dungeon, his face **wrung**[9] with **woe**[10]. As Owain closed the door, locking it with an **ominous**[11] clang, Cad **gushed**[12], 'I'm so sorry, Papa,' and flung her arms around the colossal man's midriff.

'There is little time, Callwen,' said Llywelyn, gently **prising**[13] his **ward**[14] away. 'Why did you sling a shot at Bryn Davis, and especially his face? You could have killed him.'

'I'm so sorry, Papa,' Cad replied, but she knew that if she'd wanted to kill him, she could have. That was never her **intention**[15].

'Well, we cannot unring this bell, Callwen. You left me no choice but to imprison you. I must

---

1 **deplore** *(v)* express or feel strong dislike. *(s)* hate, despise. *(ant)* admire.

2 **appalled** *(adj)* greatly dismayed or shocked. *(s)* horrified, outraged. *(ant)* charmed.

3 **friction** *(n)* resistance when two surfaces rub together. *(s)* chafing, rubbing, abrasion.

4 **jar** *(v)* shock or disturb slightly. *(s)* shake, jolt, rattle. *(ant)* appease, please.

5 **startle** *(v)* cause to feel sudden alarm or shock. *(s)* scare, frighten, surprise. *(ant)* calm, ease.

6 **disorientated** *(adj)* confused. *(s)* confounded, thrown. *(ant)* clear, lucid.

7 **turnkey** *(n)* a person who locks prisoners in jail. *(s)* keeper, captor, gaoler. *(ant)* liberator.

8 **hulking** *(adj)* (of a person) large and heavy. *(s)* colossal, massive, imposing. *(ant)* dainty.

9 **wring** *(v)* cause distress or pain to (past tense: wrung). *(s)* wound, rack. *(ant)* please.

10 **woe** *(n)* great distress, misery or sorrow. *(s)* anguish, despair, gloom. *(ant)* happiness, joy.

11 **ominous** *(adj)* indicating imminent misfortune. *(s)* threatening, warning. *(ant)* favourable.

12 **gush** *(v)* speak quickly and enthusiastically. *(s)* enthuse, effuse, babble. *(ant)* drawl.

13 **prise** *(v)* use force to move. *(s)* push, pry.

14 **ward** *(n)* a young person under the care of a guardian. *(s)* dependent, charge. *(ant)* guardian.

15 **intention** *(n)* purpose or plan. *(s)* aim, objective, goal, desire.

maintain appearances, or I will lose my men's respect. You are to stay here for several days, but I will ensure your comfort.'

Hanging her head, Cad knew Llywelyn had no choice but this course of action. Still, at least her **ploy**[1] had worked. She was before her father now, and with little time left, she must **glean**[2] all she could from him.

'Are the rumours true? Has mother fled with uncle Dewi?' Cad's voice cracked, her eyes misting as she coughed to hide the break in her words.

Llywelyn looked away, then replied, 'Yes, Callwen. It is true.'

Cad swallowed over the **enormous**[3] lump lodged in her throat. 'And Gelert, our hound … And the Gwalch Gem bracelet, are they … are they … gone?'

The noble prince hesitated, his eyes **brimming**[4] with sorrow. Eventually, he faced her with the slightest of nods.

Cad turned away, dashing the tears off her cheeks.

'It helps to cry,' said Llywelyn. 'You suffer great shock and loss.'

'Knights don't cry,' Cad said, a cloak of despair hanging around her.

'But they do.' Llywelyn laid his hand on Cad's shoulder. 'Pain is a part of life. And remember, I have not knighted you yet, young Callwen.'

'What happened to Gelert, Father?' Cad asked, gathering her thoughts as she realised time was **trickling**[5] away.

Llywelyn swallowed hard, then began. 'I was hunting. **Unbeknownst**[6] to me, Gelert remained guarding Prince John's **crib**[7], along with his mother and Dewi, who was visiting Cadwaladr Castle. When I returned …'

Cad waited, her heart tearing as she pretended not to notice the tears **welling**[8] in Llywelyn's eyes.

---

1 **ploy** *(n)* a cunning (clever, shrewd) plan or action. *(s)* manoeuvre, strategy, tactic.

2 **glean** *(v)* get information from a source. *(s)* obtain, draw, extract, gather.

3 **enormous** *(adj)* extremely large in size, extent or quantity. *(s)* big, huge. *(ant)* tiny, small.

4 **brim** *(v)* to be full to the top of. *(s)* overflow, spill, flood.

5 **trickle** *(v)* come, go, appear or pass by gradually or slowly. *(s)* flow, seep. *(ant)* gush.

6 **unbeknownst** *(adj)* without knowing something. *(s)* unknown, unrealised. *(ant)* known.

7 **crib** *(n)* a baby's bed. *(s)* cot, cradle.

8 **well** *(v)* to rise or pool. *(s)* accumulate. *(ant)* drain.

Surely there are simpler pains than this, thought Cad sharing her father's agony, *those that are easier to* **endure**[1].

'When I returned, I found Gelert, his jaws and body bloodstained. John was gone, his overturned crib a tangle of torn sheets and blood. The Gwalch Gem bracelet, which he had worn for both their safekeeping, was gone too ...'

Again, the prince turned away, but Cad saw his **Adam's apple**[2] bob at his throat.

She waited a while, then said, 'Father?'

'In my **fury**[3], I **unsheathed**[4] my sword and **slew**[5] Gelert.' Llywelyn **suppressed**[6] a **choke**[7].

Unchecked[8] tears **drenched**[9] Cad's cheeks. To see her father so broken was **unbearable**[10].

'As Gelert lay dying, I heard a baby's cry. I **delved**[11] beneath the crib, and there, entangled in the bloodstained sheets, lay Prince John, unharmed. Beside John lay the body of a **gigantic**[12] wolf. At once, I realised my **blunder**[13].'

Llywelyn paused again, but Cad dared not speak **lest**[14] the great prince cry; his eyes were **dewy**[15] with tears.

'I **cradled**[16] Gelert's head as he died, Callwen; his gaze **implored**[17] me to help, but I could not

---

1 **endure** *(v)* suffer pain or difficulty patiently. *(s)* bear, tolerate, withstand. *(ant)* succumb.

2 **Adam's apple** *(n)* the prominent cartilage that wraps around the front of the voice box in the throat.

3 **fury** *(n)* wild anger. *(s)* rage, wrath, outrage, frenzy. *(ant)* calmness.

4 **unsheathe** *(v)* pull a weapon from its covering (sheath). *(s)* remove, draw. *(ant)* replace, sheathe.

5 **slay** *(v)* kill in a violent and brutal way (past tense: slew). *(s)* murder, butcher, slaughter.

6 **suppress** *(v)* force something to stop or end. *(s)* repress, quell, quash. *(ant)* encourage.

7 **choke** *(n)* a sound made when a person is having difficulty breathing normally. *(s)* gasp.

8 **unchecked** *(adj)* not restrained or controlled. *(s)* unimpeded, unhindered. *(ant)* checked.

9 **drench** *(v)* wet thoroughly. *(s)* soak, saturate, flood. *(ant)* dry.

10 **unbearable** *(adj)* difficult or impossible to endure (suffer). *(s)* intolerable. *(ant)* bearable.

11 **delve** *(v)* reach inside something and search. *(s)* rummage, dig, root. *(ant)* withdraw.

12 **gigantic** *(adj)* great in extent or size. *(s)* enormous, huge. *(ant)* tiny.

13 **blunder** *(n)* a careless or foolish mistake. *(s)* fault, error. *(ant)* correctness.

14 **lest** *(con)* with the intention of preventing or to avoid the risk of. *(s)* in case, for fear that.

15 **dewy** *(adj)* wet. *(s)* damp, moist. *(ant)* dry.

16 **cradle** *(v)* hold gently and protectively. *(s)* support, embrace. *(ant)* drop, abandon.

17 **implore** *(v)* plead or beg desperately. *(s)* beseech. *(ant)* offer.

save him. I will never **forgive**[1] myself. I was rash, hot-headed, **heedless**[2].'

As Llywelyn's fist thumped the stone wall with a **hideous**[3] crunch, Cad flinched, her face crumpling.

'I fear they **duped**[4] me. My wife and brother **hoodwinked**[5] me.' He turned away, head in hands.

Cad rushed at him, flinging her arms around his waist. 'I am here for you, Papa. I will never leave you. I will become a Knight Hawk. I will make you smile again.'

Llywelyn looked down at her, the great man's blue-green eyes meeting hers. He stepped back from his daughter, his face **wrought**[6] with **torment**[7].

'I believe Dewi and Siân **lured**[8] the wolf into the bedchamber to **distract**[9] Gelert whilst they stole the bracelet. One, or both, took it from Prince John's thigh where I had **tethered**[10] it, for only they knew how. Both knew Gelert would protect John and the bracelet with his life. This my **loyal**[11] friend did, and I killed him for it.' A **heart-rending**[12] sob escaped Llywelyn's throat.

Hopelessness **consumed**[13] Cad, who knew the cry was not for Gelert alone. Llywelyn's wife and brother had chosen power and greed over family, and Llywelyn must find them before they **wreaked**[14] **havoc**[15] in his **realm**[16].

'Father, what do you plan?'

---

1 **forgive** *(v)* grant pardon to someone. *(s)* excuse, exonerate. *(ant)* blame.

2 **heedless** *(adj)* showing a reckless lack of attention or care. *(s)* rash, foolhardy. *(ant)* heedful, careful.

3 **hideous** *(adj)* extremely unpleasant. *(s)* gruesome, appalling, ghastly. *(ant)* attractive.

4 **dupe** *(v)* deceive and trick. *(s)* fool, hoodwink, mislead, cheat.

5 **hoodwink** *(v)* trick or deceive. *(s)* fool, dupe, mislead, cheat.

6 **wrought** *(adj)* (archaic past and past participle of 'work') shaped or formed. *(s)* cast, sculpted.

7 **torment** *(n)* extreme mental or physical suffering. *(s)* pain, anguish, distress, trauma. *(ant)* pleasure.

8 **lure** *(v)* tempt to do something, often by offering a reward. *(s)* entice, persuade. *(ant)* dissuade.

9 **distract** *(v)* deflect attention from something or someone. *(s)* divert, sidetrack. *(ant)* focus.

10 **tether** *(v)* tie something up to restrict movement, fix securely. *(s)* fasten, bind. *(ant)* untie, release.

11 **loyal** *(adj)* remaining consistent and true. *(s)* trusty, reliable, dependable, faithful. *(ant)* disloyal.

12 **heart-rending** *(adj)* causing great upset or sadness. *(s)* distressing, heartbreaking. *(ant)* comforting.

13 **consume** *(v)* strongly affect or overwhelm with a feeling. *(s)* dominate, overpower. *(ant)* abandon.

14 **wreak** *(v)* cause. *(s)* create, inflict, unleash, bestow.

15 **havoc** *(n)* destruction. *(s)* damage, devastation, catastrophe. *(ant)* peace.

16 **realm** *(n)* an area of responsibility or rule. *(s)* kingdom, domain, monarchy.

'He ... They cannot be far away,' said Llywelyn. 'Even if they are on the **fleetest**[1] of horses, I believe they are still in my kingdom. But once they **harness**[2] the gem's force, there is no telling what either might do.'

'What do you mean?' Cad asked as an icy fear rinsed through her chest.

'When I found the Welsh gold and **coupled**[3] it with the Gwalch Gem, I used it to bestow **longevity**[4] and magical **wisdom**[5], which you know as Instinct. What I did not understand was the bracelet's **potential**[6].' Llywelyn's eyes **bored**[7] deep into hers as if deciding whether to reveal more secrets.

Cad stared back with an **encouraging**[8] look. 'What do you mean, Papa?' she repeated.

'**Albeit**[9] **somewhat**[10] **crudely**[11], Sir Robert and I have realised the Gwalch Gem bracelet has far more potent abilities.'

Cad blinked and shook her head, his meaning passing her by.

'With the Gwalch Gem bracelet, your mother and uncle may be able to grant the same longevity and Instinct to people of their choosing and for **ill-conceived**[12] means, that is a given. But **furthermore**[13], and much worse, if they are **competent**[14], they may be able to **manipulate**[15] time.'

'Papa, what in heaven do you mean by "manipulate time"?'

'Evans and I have been experimenting with the bracelet, and like your ring, it has many

---

1 **fleet** *(adj)* fast. *(s)* quick, speedy, swift, rapid. *(ant)* slow, lumbering.

2 **harness** *(v)* control a resource. *(s)* use, exploit, utilise. *(ant)* underuse.

3 **couple** *(v)* combine or link together with something else. *(s)* pair, join, match. *(ant)* separate.

4 **longevity** *(n)* long life. *(s)* durability, endurance, lastingness. *(ant)* impermanence, death.

5 **wisdom** *(n)* the quality of having experience or good judgement. *(s)* intelligence, insight. *(ant)* foolishness.

6 **potential** *(n)* unrealised qualities that may appear in the future. *(s)* possibilities, prospects, power.

7 **bore** *(v)* drill a hole into (often used figuratively as it is here). *(s)* stare, penetrate.

8 **encourage** *(v)* persuade or support. *(s)* urge, spur. *(ant)* dissuade, discourage.

9 **albeit** *(con)* although. *(s)* though, even though, while.

10 **somewhat** *(adv)* a little but not a lot. *(s)* a bit, rather, quite. *(ant)* extremely.

11 **crudely** *(adv)* in a rudimentary (basic) or makeshift way. *(s)* simply, roughly. *(ant)* formally.

12 **ill-conceived** *(adj)* not well thought through or planned. *(s)* irresponsible, senseless. *(ant)* sensible.

13 **furthermore** *(adv)* in addition. *(s)* moreover, also, further.

14 **competent** *(adj)* capable, able and efficient (good at something). *(s)* proficient, adept. *(ant)* incompetent.

15 **manipulate** *(v)* alter, control or influence. *(s)* direct, affect, change.

attributes[1], but we found we could move through time and space. We must retrieve it before they realise this.'

With her mind swaying like a wildly swinging **pendulum**[2], Cad asked, 'What do you think they **intend**[3] with the bracelet?'

'That, Callwen, is a question I cannot answer, but one I fear greatly. And now I must prepare to leave with my fellow Knights Hawk. Peace could be slipping away from us in all directions. And beware, Callwen. We have traitors **in our midst**[4]. They do not operate alone.'

'Father, where will you begin?'

'Close to home, I believe,' Llywelyn replied. 'I believe them to be close to home.'

A sudden rattling of a key, then the lock turning, pulled Cad's attention to the door. Owain, his head bowed, stepped in. 'Sire, we must leave. If your court hears of this visit, they will wonder why you spend time with an unruly page.'

'Yes, Owain. I will hasten.'

'Sire,' replied Owain with a deep bow as he backed out of the cell.

Llywelyn took Cad by the shoulder and **ushered**[5] her to the furthest corner from the door. 'Presently, perhaps I might not trust even my greatest Knight Hawk,' he whispered. 'Callwen. The ring your stepmother gave to you. You know it is **fashioned**[6] from the original Gwalch Gem?'

'Yes,' Cad replied.

'Have you … Have you experimented with it before?' he asked.

Cad hesitated, her face flushing a deep pink. 'Yes,' she muttered.

'Then use it wisely, sparingly, for we do not know its true character now that your uncle Dewi controls its main power **source**[7], the bracelet.'

As his words settled, an emptiness **gnawed**[8] at Cad's stomach.

'Before I leave, I have something for you. It was your mother's … It was Siân's.'

---

1 **attribute** *(n)* a feature or quality seen as a characteristic. *(s)* trait, aspect, quirk.

2 **pendulum** *(n)* a swinging weight that regulates the mechanism of a clock.

3 **intend** *(v)* to have in mind to do with something or someone. *(s)* plan, expect, propose.

4 **in our midst** (phrase) among us. *(s)* with us, around us, in our group.

5 **usher** *(v)* show, escort or guide someone somewhere. *(s)* accompany, shepherd, lead. *(ant)* follow.

6 **fashion** *(v)* make into a specific form. *(s)* create, construct, fabricate. *(ant)* destroy.

7 **source** *(n)* from where something originates. *(s)* creator, root, cause.

8 **gnaw** *(v)* cause constant concern. *(s)* nag, eat at. *(ant)* soothe, placate.

Cad stepped back in surprise. She hadn't expected this.

Llywelyn handed Cad a thin leather **sheath**[1]. It was about the length of her hand, and it was light.

'Open it,' he urged.

Somewhat **reluctant**[2] to take anything more from Siân, Cad lifted the flap to reveal a **miniature**[3] emerald hawk attached to the end of a gold hairpin. She **inhaled**[4] deeply, taken aback by its beauty: its **exquisitely**[5] cut glistening angles, their **precision**[6] **breathtaking**[7]. She fixed her wide green eyes onto Llywelyn's. 'It's beautiful,' she said, amazed, then **blurted**[8] **anxiously**[9], 'What if I lose it?'

'Well, you are unable to wear it in your hair whilst masquerading as a boy, so keep it safe. Have you lost Siân's ring yet, Callwen?' he asked with a slight **irony**[10] to his voice.

Cad shook her head.

'Then keep this pin safely on your person, **accessible**[11]. You may find uses for it.'

'Is it … like the ring, magic?'

'It was, but we no longer know—'

'Sire,' interrupted Owain from beyond the door, 'we must hasten, lest Dewi and Siân **flee**[12] your realm.'

'Callwen, beware my brother's courtiers,' Llywelyn added with urgency. The greatest plots hide behind the most ordinary of masks. 'Although my Instinctive knight, Sir Robert, now commands this castle, traitors still abound. Remain **vigilant**[13]. Evans will now guard Prince

---

1 **sheath** *(n)* a cover for a blade. *(s)* case, sleeve.

2 **reluctant** *(adj)* unwilling or hesitant. *(s)* opposed, grudging, resistant. *(s)* eager, willing.

3 **miniature** *(adj)* small compared to others. *(s)* tiny, diminutive. *(ant)* giant.

4 **inhale** *(v)* breathe in. *(s)* suck in, gasp. *(ant)* exhale, breathe out.

5 **exquisitely** *(adv)* in an exquisite (perfect and beautiful) way. *(s)* flawlessly, elegantly. *(ant)* crudely.

6 **precision** *(n)* an instance of exactness or preciseness. *(s)* accuracy. *(ant)* inaccuracy.

7 **breathtaking** *(adj)* so astonishing as to take one's breath away. *(s)* spectacular, impressive. *(ant)* unimpressive.

8 **blurt** *(v)* say something suddenly and without consideration. *(s)* announce, exclaim, cry.

9 **anxiously** *(adv)* in an anxious (worried) manner. *(s)* apprehensively, nervously. *(ant)* calmly.

10 **irony** *(n)* something that signifies the opposite meaning. *(s)* sarcasm, dryness. *(ant)* sincerity.

11 **accessible** *(adj)* able to be reached. *(s)* handy, available. *(ant)* inaccessible.

12 **flee** *(v)* run away. *(s)* depart, abscond, leave. *(ant)* linger, remain.

13 **vigilant** *(adj)* watching carefully for problems or danger. *(s)* watchful, observant, attentive. *(ant)* inattentive.

John, who I brought here with me. In my absence, Cadwaladr Castle is unsafe.'

Cad threw her arms around him again, clinging like ivy to a wall. 'I will help guard baby John.'

'You cannot!' Llywelyn barked, causing her to jump away from him. 'His **presence**[1] here must be secret. I do not want his mother or uncle returning to **kidnap**[2] him,' he added in a softer voice, clearly realising he had **distressed**[3] Cad.

Cad gazed into her father's eyes. The sorrow and anger there, both raw, **wrenched**[4] her heart in two. Feeling a sob begin to build in her throat, Cad **begged**[5] through the now-open door, 'Owain, please look after Father. I cannot **bear**[6] to lose him.' She'd lost both her birth parents to battle. She could not endure that loss a second time.

'I will, young Callwen. You have my word,' Owain replied with a **shallow**[7] bow.

She was sure Llywelyn could trust Owain Glyn. Owain had known Cad since Llywelyn had rescued her from the well, for he had been there by his side when he'd hauled her from its depths.

As Llywelyn moved to leave, his eyes moist, he said, 'You will remain in the tower for one week. If you behave well, then Evans can shorten your **sentence**[8]. That is the best I can offer, lest I lose the respect of my court.'

Her face grave, Cad nodded. She could cope with that: she would have to.

'Of course, Father,' she replied, abashed. 'I am sorry I put you in such a dreadful position, but I could not let you leave without saying goodbye.'

'Callwen, I would not have left without a **farewell**[9]. You must trust me and **temper**[10] that hot head of yours. **Henceforth**[11], think before you act, for it will land you in trouble again.'

---

1 **presence** *(n)* the state of being present or occurring. *(s)* existence, residence. *(ant)* absence.

2 **kidnap** *(v)* abduct (take someone) and hold them captive against their will. *(s)* seize, snatch. *(ant)* release, free.

3 **distress** *(v)* cause upset or pain. *(s)* worry, perturb. *(ant)* calm, soothe.

4 **wrench** *(v)* twist or pull suddenly. *(s)* yank, wrest, tug, heave.

5 **beg** *(v)* ask honestly. *(s)* beseech, implore, plead, request. *(ant)* offer.

6 **bear** *(v)* tolerate. *(s)* stand, abide. *(ant)* reject, avoid.

7 **shallow** *(adj)* not deep. *(s)* slight, cursory.

8 **sentence** *(n)* the punishment given for a person found guilty of a crime. *(s)* time, stint. *(ant)* freedom, liberty.

9 **farewell** *(n)* a parting wish for well-being. *(s)* goodbye, send-off, adieu. *(ant)* hello, greeting.

10 **temper** *(v)* weaken the influence of something. *(s)* moderate, soften, assuage. *(ant)* strengthen.

11 **henceforth** *(adv)* from this or that time forward. *(s)* hereafter.

'Yes, Father,' whispered Cad, her voice sounding **hollow**[1], 'I will.'

But as the giant oak door clanged shut behind the knights, and the key turned in its great lock, Cad's mind raced **headlong**[2], hurrying to **hatch**[3] its **fledgling**[4] plan, her eyes blazing with the flame of an idea.

---

1 **hollow** *(adj)* without meaning or truth. *(s)* insincere, false, untrue. *(ant)* sincere.

2 **headlong** *(adv)* with reckless haste. *(s)* recklessly, rashly. *(ant)* slowly.

3 **hatch** *(v)* make up. *(s)* devise, concoct, invent.

4 **fledgling** *(adj)* underdeveloped (still in process). *(s)* emergent, budding. *(ant)* expert.

CHAPTER FOUR

Peggy

Alone in the miserable dungeon, Cad twirled her mother's stunning hairpin between her thumb and **forefinger**[1]. The emerald hawk **pirouetted**[2] in the **sole**[3] **shard**[4] of sunlight which streaked in through the arrow slit above her.

Even though the sun shone on Catrin, Cad shivered. Locked up, and with nothing to do but wait, her hand **wandered**[5] to the invisible hem she'd sewn into her tunic. Living as a lady in Llywelyn's household had **sealed**[6] Cad's needlework skills. No one would ever find the items buried within the folds of her garments. And to guard her gender, she ensured her garments and underclothes were worn in **numerous**[7] layers. If she was to hide her **femininity**[8], she could not risk a tear revealing anything **untoward**[9].

---

1 **forefinger** *(n)* the first finger (the one next to the thumb). *(s)* pointer, index finger.

2 **pirouette** *(v)* perform a pirouette. *(s)* twirl, spin, rotate, turn, circle.

3 **sole** *(adj)* one and only. *(s)* solitary, single, individual. *(ant)* numerous, many.

4 **shard** *(n)* a small piece of something, creating sharp edges or fragments. *(s)* sliver, fragment, spike.

5 **wander** *(v)* move in an aimless or leisurely way. *(s)* drift, stray.

6 **seal** *(v)* establish or conclude something in a definite way. *(s)* prove, clinch, complete.

7 **numerous** *(adj)* many. *(s)* plentiful, abundant, copious. *(ant)* few, one.

8 **femininity** *(n)* attributes seen as characteristics of women. *(s)* womanliness. *(ant)* masculinity.

9 **untoward** *(adj)* unanticipated, inappropriate or inconvenient. *(s)* troublesome, problematic. *(ant)* pleasant.

Several[1] **scrapes**[2] in the tilt yard with Bryn and his **cronies**[3] had resulted in torn clothes. These **scuffles**[4] were commonplace amongst the pages and squires. **Nonetheless**[5], too much was **at stake**[6] for Cad, who was unsure whether Bryn, who **frequently**[7] **referred**[8] to the three friends as 'girls', suspected her secret, or if his comments were simply **snide**[9] sniping.

Either way, if discovered, she would become a ladies' maid and leave Llywelyn in a dreadful position of **embarrassment**[10].

Lost in thought, an unexpected jangling of keys startled Cad into the present, the threads of her thoughts vanishing. Her hands **fumbled**[11] as she buried the emerald pin within the folds of her tunic. Tense, she watched as the door creaked open.

'Aunt Anwen,' she shrieked, rising and almost dropping the hairpin as she flung her arms around Llywelyn's sister.

'Now, now Callwen bach,' chuckled Anwen, peeling Cad's arms away. 'To my relief, my brother **insisted**[12] we move you to the tower's "better" rooms. That is if one can use "better" to describe a prison. What on earth have you done, Callwen?'

Cad stepped away from her aunt, and with a grave voice said, 'Aunt Anwen, in this castle, you must refer to me as Cad. There are folks here who suspect our secret.'

'Why is it you insist on being a knight? You'll turn our heads white.' Anwen gave a hearty chuckle and ruffled Cad's pageboy haircut.

'I won't change my mind, Aunt. You know that.'

---

1 **several** *(adj)* more than two but not a vast quantity of. *(s)* some, various. *(ant)* many.

2 **scrape** *(n)* a difficult situation. *(s)* scuffle, scrap, problem.

3 **crony** *(n)* a companion or close friend. *(s)* associate, comrade, colleague, mate.

4 **scuffle** *(n)* a short fight. *(s)* tussle, rumpus, disturbance, scrap.

5 **nonetheless** *(adv)* but. *(s)* in spite of, still, regardless.

6 **at stake** (phrase) at risk. *(s)* being risked.

7 **frequently** *(adv)* often. *(s)* regularly, habitually. *(ant)* infrequently.

8 **refer** *(v)* name or allude to (suggest). *(s)* imply, call.

9 **snide** *(adj)* slyly mocking. *(s)* scornful, spiteful. *(ant)* complimentary.

10 **embarrassment** *(n)* a feeling of shame or awkwardness. *(s)* disgrace, humiliation. *(ant)* esteem.

11 **fumble** *(v)* move the hands about clumsily. *(s)* scrabble, search, root, dig, rummage.

12 **insist** *(v)* demand forcefully without allowing refusal. *(s)* command, require. *(ant)* give up.

'I do. Well, what **capers**[1] have you committed this time?' Anwen's eyes narrowed, her expression **stern**[2].

'I bloodied a squire's nose. But he deserved it.'

'Well then! You leave Llywelyn no choice but to imprison you. Rules exist for a reason. He must appear as **harsh**[3] with you as any other **wayward**[4] boy. Come, follow me. We are moving you to the **dignitaries'**[5] quarters. Unfortunately, still here in the tower, but far more comfortable.'

With an **immense**[6] wave of relief and ensuring the hairpin in her tunic remained **in situ**[7], Cad followed Anwen up to the top of the tower. After climbing several flights, they reached the dungeon where Dewi held **political**[8] prisoners until he solved their problems in one way or another. Anwen turned the key and unlocked the door.

Heaven above! Cad thought.

A fire flickered in a **grate**[9], a bed lay beneath an arrow slit, and absolute luxury leaned against one wall: a desk, **parchment**[10], **quill**[11] and ink.

A smile slid across Cad's face, the **rigid**[12] block of tension between her shoulders lifting at the sight of the cell.

'You can practise writing. Be wise with your time here. **Ample**[13] light enters until nightfall when the turnkey will fetch candles until bedtime. She will provide food, and your bed linen is clean.'

---

1 **caper** *(n)* a silly or foolish activity. *(s)* mischief, shenanigan, antic.

2 **stern** *(adj)* serious and strict. *(s)* severe, firm, formidable, dour. *(ant)* cheerful, lenient.

3 **harsh** *(adj)* hard. *(s)* severe, strict, punitive, stern. *(ant)* gentle, kind.

4 **wayward** *(adj)* difficult to control. *(s)* unruly, disobedient, wilful, defiant. *(ant)* obedient, compliant.

5 **dignitary** *(n)* an important person because of rank. *(s)* VIP, notable. *(ant)* nonentity.

6 **immense** *(adj)* large in scale or degree. *(s)* great, enormous, huge. *(ant)* tiny, small.

7 **in situ** *(adv)* in the appropriate place or position. *(s)* in place.

8 **political** *(adj)* relating to the ruling authority, government or affairs of a country or area. *(s)* ideological, enemy.

9 **grate** *(n)* a metal frame used for holding fuel, such as coal or wood, in a fireplace.

10 **parchment** *(n)* prepared animal skin with a papery appearance used in ancient writing. *(s)* vellum, scroll.

11 **quill** *(n)* a pen made from the main wing or tail feathers of a large bird.

12 **rigid** *(adj)* stiff and unmoving. *(s)* fixed, set. *(ant)* floppy, flexible.

13 **ample** *(adj)* enough or more than enough. *(s)* abundant, generous. *(ant)* insufficient, meagre.

'Don't cry!' **exclaimed**[1] Cad, noticing tears and hugging her aunt. 'This is **luxurious**[2]. I am so grateful.'

'I cannot bear to see you here,' Anwen sniffled.

'It's my stupid fault. I will be fine. I promise to study.' Cad **gesticulated**[3] to **punctuate**[4] her sentences.

'I cannot visit daily, or the courtiers will become suspicious, but I have ensured you have a kind turnkey: Goodwife Hughes. If possible, I will come again. Hopefully, with news of Llywelyn. I will pray he has recovered the bracelet.'

A sharp pain stabbed Cad's chest. She, too, prayed for his safe return, but she doubted prayer would help him.

'I will look forward to seeing you soon, Aunt.'

Anwen ruffled Cad's hair, kissing her cheek. 'You must temper that temper of yours,' she said with a chuckle.

'Yes, Aunt,' said Cad, grinning at the **pun**[5]. 'I will try.'

As the door clanged shut and the key turned, relief **surged**[6] through Cad. It could have been so much worse. This cell was warm and clean; she could write. Cad not only intended to be a noble knight on the battlefield, but a **scholar**[7]. Where Bryn Davis was so able in the tilt yard, Cad **outshone**[8] him in studies.

As soon as Anwen was gone, Cad took the chair from the desk, dragged it beneath the arrow slit, and climbed up to it. With a half-decent view of the tilt yard, Cad saw boys practising their battle skills. With most knights accompanying Llywelyn on the quest, many pages were left to train themselves. Sir Robert, the Knight Hawk now in charge, would take no nonsense from underlings.

---

1 **exclaim** *(v)* cry out suddenly. *(s)* blurt, proclaim, declare. *(ant)* whisper, mutter.

2 **luxurious** *(adj)* extremely comfortable and often expensive. *(s)* opulent, extravagant. *(ant)* meagre.

3 **gesticulate** *(v)* use gestures (movements) to communicate. *(s)* wave, signal, motion, indicate.

4 **punctuate** *(v)* interrupt. *(s)* break up.

5 **pun** *(n)* a joke using words with double meaning. *(s)* wordplay.

6 **surge** *(v)* increase suddenly and with more power. *(s)* rise, gush, course. *(ant)* decline, ebb.

7 **scholar** *(n)* a highly educated person. *(s)* intellectual, academic.

8 **outshine** *(v)* be better than someone else at something (past tense: outshone). *(s)* surpass, outclass. *(ant)* fall short.

A slight man, Sir Robert's **air**[1] **perturbed**[2] Cad, and it forced most pages to fall into line. Cad knew he had helped fashion the Gwalch Gem bracelet and several other jewellery pieces, including the ring from Siân which she hid in her tunic's hem. She wondered if he had made the hairpin she now twirled in her fingers again, watching it **glint**[3] in the sunlight which streamed in through the slit. She also wondered whether Evans knew Cad possessed both magical pieces.

Cad moved the chair a little to the right, but the view to the yard proved disappointing, so she jumped down. Dylan wasn't in the tilt yard, **ergo**[4] he would be unaware of Llywelyn's visit and Cad's current comfort. Dylan was older than she, and had been **initially**[5] sent to Llywelyn's Cadwaladr Castle for knight's training before following Cad to Catrin. Unlike her, Dylan was **descended from**[6] nobles. As a child, when watching Dylan and the other pages train, Cad had **yearned**[7] to be a knight.

Llywelyn, not being a **typical**[8] master, ensured his pages' work be split between cleaning and repairing armour, serving at mealtimes and running **errands**[9]. Also, he **guaranteed**[10] education, ensuring the teaching of reading, writing and music. Pages in the Cadwaladr households cherished their good **fortune**[11]. Moving to Dewi's household had been the only way Cad could masquerade as a boy, and Dylan had insisted he join her. Of course, Dewi and his closest advisers knew her real **identity**[12], but they were few. **Thus far**[13], Cad had maintained her secret. But with Dewi now an enemy and Llywelyn **pursuing**[14] him, the future might not

---

1 **air** *(n)* a portrayal, quality, manner or impression. *(s)* appearance, aura, tone.

2 **perturb** *(v)* make uneasy or anxious. *(s)* worry, concern. *(ant)* reassure, calm.

3 **glint** *(v)* give out a small gleam or flash of light. *(s)* glimmer, shine, shimmer, sparkle. *(ant)* dull.

4 **ergo** *(adv)* for that reason. *(s)* therefore, hence, consequently, as a result, thus.

5 **initially** *(adv)* at first. *(s)* to begin with, in the first place. *(ant)* afterwards.

6 **descend from** (phrase) originate from someone or something in the past. *(s)* come from, hail from.

7 **yearn** *(v)* really want something. *(s)* long, ache, crave, desire. *(ant)* reject.

8 **typical** *(adj)* characteristic of something. *(s)* regular, normal, standard. *(ant)* atypical.

9 **errand** *(n)* a short journey undertaken to do a job of work. *(s)* chore, task.

10 **guarantee** *(v)* provide a formal assurance. *(s)* secure, promise. *(ant)* undermine.

11 **fortune** *(n)* the chance or luck which affects something or someone. *(s)* circumstance, outcome.

12 **identity** *(n)* the characteristics determining what someone or something is. *(s)* identification, existence.

13 **thus far** *(adv)* up to now. *(s)* hitherto, to this point, so far.

14 **pursue** *(v)* chase or follow. *(s)* hunt, track, search, seek. *(ant)* guide, lead.

be so rosy. From now on, prudence would be **paramount**[1].

Cad was about to sit at her desk, when clunky keys rattled in the lock again. Instead of sitting, she spun and hid her hairpin in her tunic. As the door creaked open, she turned towards it, smiling, expecting to see **Goodwife**[2] Hughes. At once, the smile slid from Cad's face, and the gaoler standing opposite her noticed.

'Food,' grunted the man, **baring**[3] grey stumps for teeth.

Lost for words, Cad glanced at him, then down at the plate he **proffered**[4]; bread and cheese.

Why is Peggy here? she thought, sharp anxiety tying her stomach in knots.

'I heard you broke a squire's nose.' The man spat the words through his grey-black pegs, then cackled like a crow. 'Bit of a noddle-head, aren't you?' he added, his voice loaded with menace. Then too slowly, his hungry eyes travelled around the room before landing back on Cad.

Will he take my writing materials? she worried, but quickly wiping the **evidence**[5] from her face.

Cad gathered herself, **desperate**[6] to **retaliate**[7] with a **quip**[8], but thought better of it.

'Thank you,' she mumbled through a fake smile, eyeing the **fare**[9] with hidden **disdain**[10].

Where is Goodwife Hughes? she wondered, but dared not ask.

To ruffle this gaoler's feathers would be unwise. Peggy, **dubbed**[11] so, because of his **decayed**[12] teeth, was the most **notorious**[13] of Dewi's **henchmen**[14] and not to be **underestimated**[15]. Why

---

1 **paramount** *(adj)* more important than all else. *(s)* predominant, uppermost. *(ant)* secondary, inferior.
2 **goodwife** *(n)* the female head of a household; a term often used in the Middle Ages.
3 **bare** *(v)* reveal and expose something to view. *(s)* uncover, unveil, display. *(ant)* cover, hide.
4 **proffer** *(v)* put forward or hold out to someone. *(s)* offer, give, present. *(ant)* withdraw.
5 **evidence** *(n)* facts or information presented to support the truth. *(s)* proof, confirmation.
6 **desperate** *(adj)* having great desire or need. *(s)* longing, craving, itching. *(ant)* indifferent.
7 **retaliate** *(v)* react to or fight back. *(s)* respond, retort, counter. *(ant)* excuse.
8 **quip** *(n)* a witty (humorous) remark. *(s)* witticism, retort, jibe.
9 **fare** *(n)* a selection of foods of a certain type. *(s)* foodstuffs, grub, eats.
10 **disdain** *(n)* the feeling that something is unworthy of respect. *(s)* contempt, derision, scorn. *(ant)* admiration.
11 **dub** *(v)* give a nickname to. *(s)* call, label, name, term, tag.
12 **decay** *(v)* decompose or rot. *(s)* spoil, degrade. *(ant)* thrive, improve.
13 **notorious** *(adj)* well known for something bad. *(s)* infamous, noted, renowned. *(ant)* unknown.
14 **henchman** *(n)* a follower prepared to engage in criminality. *(s)* supporter, underling, minion. *(ant)* leader.
15 **underestimate** *(v)* regard someone as less capable than they really are. *(s)* undervalue, misjudge. *(ant)* overestimate.

was he here? Who had sanctioned this **flouting**[1] of Llywelyn's orders?

'I'll be back, but no candles tonight,' he barked, **spittle**[2] spraying **forth**[3].

Disgusted[4], but **feigning**[5] good-natured patience, Cad gave a **gracious**[6] nod, then with a **surreptitious**[7] move, she **sidled**[8] towards her desk. Again, she forced a smile, standing before its **expanse**[9], hoping Peggy wouldn't spot her parchment and quill and **confiscate**[10] them.

Fortunately for Cad, he seemed **indifferent**[11] and as Peggy **shambled**[12] from the cell grunting like a pig, dragging his right leg behind him, Cad **exhaled**[13], watching his **gammy**[14] leg round the door. Rumour was, he'd kicked a **docile**[15] hound one too many times, and the old mutt had finally retaliated, helping himself to a chunk of Peggy's **calf**[16]. Peggy had limped ever since.

Once he'd gone, Cad squinted up at the arrow slit and, **gauging**[17] the light, **reckoned**[18] it was getting late. She **penned**[19] a note in her neatest hand and tore it from the parchment. With her ear **cocked**[20], listening for further footsteps, Cad dragged the chair back to the arrow slit, climbed on it, and whistled. With one **trill**[21], and in no time, May, the blind hawk, was through the narrow gap, clutching her master's shoulder.

---

1 **flout** *(v)* openly ignore. *(s)* disregard, defy, violate. *(ant)* observe, obey.

2 **spittle** *(n)* saliva, especially when spraying from the mouth. *(s)* spit, slobber, slaver.

3 **forth** *(adv)* forward in direction (or time). *(s)* onwards, ahead, headlong. *(ant)* back.

4 **disgusted** *(adj)* expressing or feeling extreme disapproval or revulsion. *(s)* sickened, repulsed, revolted. *(ant)* delighted.

5 **feign** *(v)* simulate or pretend. *(s)* affect, fake, bluff.

6 **gracious** *(adj)* kind, especially to those less fortunate. *(s)* courteous, polite, pleasant. *(ant)* ungracious, impolite.

7 **surreptitious** *(adj)* kept secret. *(s)* clandestine, stealthy, sneaky, furtive. *(ant)* open, blatant.

8 **sidle** *(v)* walk in a furtive (secretive) manner. *(s)* slink, edge. *(ant)* stride.

9 **expanse** *(n)* a stretch or wide area of something. *(s)* span, breadth, width, reach. *(ant)* enclosure.

10 **confiscate** *(v)* take ownership with authority. *(s)* seize, commandeer. *(ant)* return.

11 **indifferent** *(adj)* not bothered by something. *(s)* unperturbed, unconcerned. *(ant)* concerned, bothered.

12 **shamble** *(v)* move slowly with an awkward gait. *(s)* shuffle, dodder, lumber. *(ant)* bound.

13 **exhale** *(v)* breathe out. *(s)* expire, respire. *(ant)* inhale, breathe in.

14 **gammy** *(adj)* unable to work properly. *(s)* damaged, wounded. *(ant)* fit, able.

15 **docile** *(adj)* accepting of control or instruction. *(s)* passive, obedient, pliant. *(ant)* wilful, disobedient.

16 **calf** *(n)* the fleshy part at the back of a person's leg below the knee (plural: calves).

17 **gauge** *(v)* measure or estimate the amount of. *(s)* judge, assess, evaluate.

18 **reckon** *(v)* work something out. *(s)* calculate, appraise.

19 **pen** *(v)* write. *(s)* compose, draft.

20 **cock** *(v)* tilt in a particular direction. *(s)* angle, tip, incline.

21 **trill** *(n)* a quavering sound. *(s)* whistle, twitter, warble.

'I'm sorry I only have dry bread for you now,' Cad whispered to May, feeding her crumbs from her palm and **manoeuvring**[1] her sharp claws to a more comfortable position.

When May had finished the bread, Cad placed her on the desk and, with **deft**[2] twists, untied the leather **jess**[3] from May's **skinny**[4] leg. Then she wound the parchment around it, **securing**[5] it back in place.

'May,' Cad said, making sure the hawk was listening, her pert head cocked towards Cad's. 'Master Dylan. Dylan,' she repeated, taking May onto her hand and climbing back onto the chair beneath the arrow slit. 'Master Dylan, now,' Cad ordered, guiding May through the gap and watching her soar away.

May, familiar with Dylan, trusted him. After all, both Cad and Dylan were May's **saviours**[6]. Without a doubt, Cad knew that when next Dylan **ventured**[7] outdoors alone, May would swoop and deliver her note. Whether that be today or tomorrow remained to be seen, but Cad knew May would continue to search until she found Dylan, for that was what she was trained to do. Cad must have patience, not her finest attribute, but she forced her mind to calm and think.

Ever **wary**[8] of her uncle Dewi, who was so popular among the court ladies, Cad had often wondered why he remained unmarried. **Handsome**[9], noble and a prince, it was unheard of to be single at his age, but now she realised that he cared only for himself. Even though he had frequently visited Siân when Llywelyn was away or hunting, Cad was sure it was all a **ruse**[10] to steal the gem. She was certain his only **motive**[11] was greed and power.

It pained Cad to think Siân had left not only Llywelyn, but her baby, Prince John, and of course Callwen herself. Had they lured the wolf into John's bedchamber to dupe Llywelyn into

---

1 **manoeuvre** *(v)* guide or move carefully. *(s)* direct, steer.

2 **deft** *(adj)* neatly skilful and quick. *(s)* dexterous, adept, able, capable, adroit. *(ant)* clumsy, lumbering.

3 **jess** *(n)* a leather strap fixed round the leg of a hawk to which a leash can be attached to restrain flight.

4 **skinny** *(adj)* thin. *(s)* scrawny, bony, scraggy. *(ant)* fat, fleshy, meaty.

5 **secure** *(v)* fix, attach or fasten firmly. *(s)* position, tighten, bind, tie. *(ant)* unfasten, release.

6 **saviour** *(n)* someone who saves someone else from peril or hardship. *(s)* rescuer, champion. *(ant)* condemner.

7 **venture** *(v)* begin a journey or undertaking. *(s)* proceed, go, move, wander.

8 **wary** *(adj)* cautious about a problem or danger. *(s)* watchful, heedful, careful. *(ant)* unwary.

9 **handsome** *(adj)* good-looking. *(s)* attractive, fetching, striking, appealing. *(ant)* ugly, unattractive, plain.

10 **ruse** *(n)* an action intended to deceive (trick) someone. *(s)* deception, ploy. *(ant)* truth.

11 **motive** *(n)* an incentive for acting or behaving in a certain way. *(s)* motivation, basis, reason. *(ant)* deterrent.

believing Gelert had killed his son? If that was true, Dewi was not working alone, especially at Llywelyn's Cadwaladr Castle. He must **employ**[1] spies in both castles. If Cad could not join her father on his quest, she would **sleuth**[2] to uncover the traitors in their midst.

With May gone, Cad settled on her bed and regarded her powerful jewels. To ensure their safety, she **secreted**[3] the hairpin in her tunic, and her ring in its hem. Not overly tired, she curled up and pulled the blanket towards her chin, closing her eyes. If her plan was to succeed, she must get some sleep now, for she knew that the night stretching out before her may prove to be a complete unknown.

---

1 **employ** *(v)* give work to and pay. *(s)* retain, engage, use, hire, place. *(ant)* dismiss, sack, fire.

2 **sleuth** *(v)* track, search or investigate in secret. *(s)* detect, spy, snoop, stalk. *(ant)* overlook.

3 **secrete** *(v)* hide. *(s)* conceal, stash, stow. *(ant)* display, reveal.

CHAPTER FIVE

The Ring

Woken by another clattering of keys and clanging of doors, Cad shot out of bed, ready to face the **ghastly**[1] gaoler, Peggy. But she was **taken aback**[2] by who she saw; Cad's eyes widened, her face **expanding**[3] with delight. 'Goodwife Hughes,' she cried, surprised and **elated**[4]. 'How my heart soars to see you.'

Goodwife Hughes stood before her, bearing a **divine**[5]-smelling supper. Cad beamed as the woman lay a **platter**[6] of **roasted**[7] chicken on the desk, and lit two **tallow**[8] candles, placing them into holders.

---

1 **ghastly** *(adj)* extremely unpleasant. *(s)* grim, frightful, hideous. *(ant)* pleasant.

2 **take aback** *(v)* surprise or shock. *(s)* confuse, startle, astonish, throw off. *(ant)* reassure.

3 **expand** *(v)* make or become larger or wider. *(s)* broaden. *(ant)* shrink, contract.

4 **elated** *(adj)* incredibly happy. *(s)* exhilarated, thrilled, excited. *(ant)* depressed, disheartened.

5 **divine** *(adj)* incredibly pleasing. *(s)* delightful, heavenly, exquisite. *(ant)* unsatisfactory.

6 **platter** *(n)* a large flat plate for serving food. *(s)* trencher, tray.

7 **roast** *(v)* cook something by prolonged exposure to high temperature in an oven or over a fire.

8 **tallow** *(n)* animal fat (formerly) used in making candles and soap.

'I apologise for my late arrival. **Alas**[1], I was otherwise **engaged**[2] when sent for, and the journey from Cadwaladr Castle was more **arduous**[3] than expected,' said Mrs Hughes, bustling about Cad's room.

Cad had already bitten into a chicken leg, and her mouth was stuffed full.

'Now I am here; I will **tend**[4] to your comfort the best I can.'

'Thank you, Goodwife Hughes,' Cad said after swallowing the **tender**[5] chicken. 'I am **ravenous**[6]. I have eaten nothing since breakfast,' she added, **devouring**[7] the **succulent**[8] meat, its juices trickling down her chin.

'I will bring washing water for you tomorrow.' Goodwife Hughes eyed Cad with a wrinkled nose and a sniff. 'Ahh! I see you have writing materials.' The goodwife's right eyebrow had arched.

'I am fortunate,' Cad said, feigning nonchalance, for Mrs Hughes may wonder why a lowly page **languished**[9] in such luxurious confinement. Cad, fully aware that Goodwife Hughes would be in Anwen's employ, guessed her aunt had paid for the lady's **discretion**[10].

'You have drinking water and blankets. Out **yonder**[11], I suspect a frosty night falls.'

Goodwife Hughes looked towards the arrow slit as she cleared away Cad's empty platter. 'I will visit later to **extinguish**[12] your candles. Sir Robert's orders, I'm afraid.'

Disappointed, but hiding it, Cad said, 'Thank you.' Then she flopped onto the bed, her stomach **bulging**[13]. 'I may sleep right now. I am so stuffed.' Cad chuckled, **sprawling**[14]

---

1 **alas** *(int)* used to express pity, regret, grief, disappointment or concern.

2 **engaged** *(adj)* busy. *(s)* employed, committed, occupied. *(ant)* available.

3 **arduous** *(adj)* difficult and tiring. *(s)* taxing, laborious, toilsome. *(ant)* easy.

4 **tend** *(v)* look after, care for. *(s)* attend to. *(ant)* neglect.

5 **tender** *(adj)* (of food) not tough, and easy to chew. *(ant)* soft, succulent, juicy. *(ant)* leathery, tough.

6 **ravenous** *(adj)* very hungry. *(s)* famished, starving. *(ant)* full, sated, satiated.

7 **devour** *(v)* eat quickly. *(s)* consume, gobble, scoff, wolf. *(ant)* reject, abstain from.

8 **succulent** *(adj)* moist and tasty. *(s)* juicy, delicious, mouth-watering. *(ant)* dry, unappetising.

9 **languish** *(v)* be forced to remain in a situation. *(s)* suffer. *(ant)* thrive.

10 **discretion** *(n)* the attribute of avoiding offence or revealing secrets. *(s)* caution, diplomacy, tact. *(ant)* indiscretion.

11 **yonder** *(adv)* over there. *(s)* in the distance.

12 **extinguish** *(v)* put out something burning. *(s)* smother, snuff out, douse, blow out. *(ant)* light.

13 **bulge** *(v)* to swell or extend an otherwise flat surface. *(s)* protrude, balloon, expand. *(ant)* contract.

14 **sprawl** *(v)* fall, sit or lie with one's arms and legs spread awkwardly. *(s)* stretch, flop, loll.

backwards, her **limbs**[1] **splayed**[2] in a star shape.

'Well, you have an **abundance**[3] of *time*, young sire,' replied Goodwife Hughes. 'And I have no *time* for that squire, Bryn Davis,' she added with a **self-congratulatory**[4] grin at her quip.

Cad smiled back but said nothing: it was time the goodwife left.

'I will see you later,' said Goodwife Hughes, her hands full as she sailed from the cell, her **kirtle**[5] swooshing behind her.

The door clanged shut, and Cad closed her eyes. May, the hawk, hadn't yet appeared with word from Dylan, and Cad now doubted she would this evening. Dylan was probably indoors until dawn, when he would rise for the day's **chores**[6] and training.

Cad crossed her fingers that May might deliver the note soon. It reminded Dylan to feed and water her hidden puppy, Fishy, who would otherwise perish in the **keep's**[7] depths. Cad would not let that happen. She'd named her pup Fishy because when someone had tossed her into the moat, as Cad suspected they had, they hadn't **bargained**[8] on her ability to swim like a fish. Cad had found Fishy **scrabbling**[9] up the bank, **nigh on**[10] **exhausted**[11] and close to **submission**[12].

Assuming[13] the pup's mother had perished, Cad and Dylan hand-raised Fishy, squeezing goat's milk and **minuscule**[14] **scraps**[15] of **pilfered**[16] meat into her mouth. If Cad didn't hear from Dylan soon, she would ask Goodwife Hughes to feed Fishy, and hope the woman might agree.

---

1 **limb** *(n)* an arm, leg or wing. *(s)* appendage, offshoot.

2 **splay** *(v)* spread or thrust apart. *(s)* spread out, extend, stretch, span. *(ant)* huddle.

3 **abundance** *(n)* a large quantity of something. *(s)* plenty, bounty. *(ant)* lack, deficiency.

4 **self-congratulatory** *(adj)* overly proud of one's achievements or qualities. *(s)* smug, arrogant. *(ant)* self-deprecating.

5 **kirtle** *(n)* a woman's outer petticoat or gown. *(s)* surcoat, skirt.

6 **chore** *(n)* a task, often a household one. *(s)* job, work, errand, duty, drudgery.

7 **keep** *(n)* the strongest (sometimes highest) tower of a castle. *(s)* donjon, stronghold, fort, dungeon.

8 **bargain** *(v)* expect. *(s)* anticipate, imagine, envisage, foresee, predict.

9 **scrabble** *(v)* scratch around trying to hold something. *(s)* grope, scramble.

10 **nigh on** *(adv)* almost. *(s)* nearly, about, just about, more or less.

11 **exhausted** *(adj)* extremely tired. *(s)* drained, shattered, debilitated. *(ant)* refreshed, energised.

12 **submission** *(n)* the action of acceptance or yielding (surrender). *(s)* capitulation, resignation. *(ant)* rebellion.

13 **assume** *(v)* presume to be the case without any proof of it. *(s)* suppose, conclude, believe. *(ant)* prove.

14 **minuscule** *(adj)* incredibly small. *(s)* tiny, minute, diminutive. *(ant)* gigantic, vast.

15 **scrap** *(n)* a small piece of something, especially one that is left over. *(s)* morsel, bit.

16 **pilfer** *(v)* steal. *(s)* rob, thieve, snatch, purloin. *(ant)* give.

As Cad contemplated her prison sentence, something **akin**[1] to **remorse**[2] pulled at her chest, yet she no longer regretted slinging a stone at Bryn.

What a shot. Black eyes, she thought with **glee**[3]. Bryn had blacked hers before, so she'd long since owed him one. She pondered the **hapless**[4] page, Jack Jones, who trained with Bryn. Did Jack admire Bryn, or were his days a **misery**[5], having to follow him around to do his **spiteful**[6] **bidding**[7]?

After a short while, when Cad was sure Goodwife Hughes had left the tower, she delved into the folds of her tunic to retrieve the slim leather sheath. With care, she removed the hairpin, whose exquisite emerald hawk winked at her in the flickering candlelight. Sitting up, Cad reached for the bulge in the tunic's hem. Cad sewed secret **compartments**[8] into every garment she owned – places to hide food, messages, valuables and even weapons. By the time Cad had left Cadwaladr Castle to be a page, she had **acquired**[9] the skills needed to **embroider**[10] a wedding **gown**[11].

Using her sharp fingernails, Cad unpicked the hem's almost invisible stitches. Her steady hand removed the ring made of Welsh gold and emerald, gifted by Siân when Cad had left Cadwaladr Castle. As if alive, the hawk glittered.

As Cad held Siân's ring, studying the emerald hawk twinkling in its centre filled her with both sadness and anger. A strange mix which **ignited**[12] a fury she must **quash**[13] for her plan to **prevail**[14]. Why had her loving mother betrayed her and Llywelyn, and with such cruelty? And to **forsake**[15] her only son – a baby.

---

1 **akin** *(adj)* similar in character. *(s)* related, close, comparable. *(ant)* unlike, dissimilar.

2 **remorse** *(n)* guilt or regret. *(s)* shame, repentance, ruefulness. *(ant)* remorselessness.

3 **glee** *(n)* extreme delight, often from one's good fortune or another's misfortune. *(s)* pleasure, amusement. *(ant)* gloom.

4 **hapless** *(adj)* unfortunate. *(s)* unlucky, wretched. *(ant)* fortunate, fortuitous.

5 **misery** *(n)* distress or discomfort. *(s)* unhappiness, suffering, anguish. *(ant)* cheer, happiness, joy.

6 **spiteful** *(adj)* mean and nasty. *(s)* malicious, cruel, vindictive, snide. *(ant)* kind, benevolent.

7 **bidding** *(n)* the asking or ordering of someone to do something. *(s)* request, command, behest.

8 **compartment** *(n)* a separate section of something. *(s)* part, pocket, pouch.

9 **acquire** *(v)* develop or learn. *(s)* achieve, gain, earn. *(ant)* lose.

10 **embroider** *(v)* sew decoratively with thread. *(s)* stitch, decorate, adorn, embellish.

11 **gown** *(n)* a long, formal dress. *(s)* robe.

12 **ignite** *(v)* arouse. *(s)* trigger, spark, kindle, stir up, agitate. *(ant)* dampen.

13 **quash** *(v)* put an end to. *(s)* suppress, quell, curb, defeat, conquer. *(ant)* allow.

14 **prevail** *(v)* succeed or win. *(s)* triumph. *(ant)* fail, lose.

15 **forsake** *(v)* leave. *(s)* abandon, desert, disown. *(ant)* stay with.

Cad, aware of new mothers' **melancholy**[1], understood relationships between families to be far more **complex**[2] than parents ever revealed, but this **deception**[3] was **abominable**[4]. Did Siân have a genuine motive, or had simple greed driven her? Cad prayed it was the **former**[5] and not the latter, and she vowed to discover the truth one day; no matter how long it might take, she must understand why her mother had abandoned her family.

Buried in thoughts, she stared at the jewellery, wondering if Sir Robert knew she possessed Siân's ring, and now the hairpin too. Evans knew Cad's secrets. That thought gave her pause, yet if Llywelyn allowed Evans to command Catrin Castle, he trusted Evans with his life, baby John's and hers too. Now was the wrong time to **consider**[6] Sir Robert's **character**[7]. She had to focus on the task at hand. With so many knights **absent**[8], Cad hoped Evans would not waste a man outside her door.

Almost ready to leave for her **foray**[9] into the castle, she slipped Siân's ring onto her right thumb, where it would not work, and marvelled at its intricate carving. How had the crown jewellers performed such complex **feats**[10] of magnificence? Even though Cad placed the ring on a **digit**[11] where she knew it was **dormant**[12], its **allure**[13] still **hypnotised**[14] her. Nonetheless, now the Gwalch Gem bracelet was under Dewi's power; she must test the ring to see if it still **functioned**[15]. It shimmered with life and power – it should work … For once it became dull, she knew it would not.

---

1 **melancholy** *(n)* sadness. *(s)* sorrow, woe, desolation, gloom. *(ant)* happiness.

2 **complex** *(adj)* difficult to understand. *(s)* complicated, involved, intricate. *(ant)* simple, clear.

3 **deception** *(n)* the action of deceiving. *(s)* deceit, cheating, dupery. *(ant)* honesty, fidelity.

4 **abominable** *(adj)* morally bad. *(s)* hateful, despicable, loathsome, detestable. *(ant)* admirable, good.

5 **former** *(n)* the first mentioned of two people or things. *(s)* previous, preceding. *(ant)* latter.

6 **consider** *(v)* think about before making a decision. *(s)* contemplate, examine, ponder.

7 **character** *(n)* a person's qualities and ways. *(s)* personality, temperament, nature, mentality.

8 **absent** *(adj)* not present. *(s)* out, missing, gone. *(ant)* present.

9 **foray** *(n)* a first venture. *(s)* sortie. *(ant)* retreat.

10 **feat** *(n)* a great achievement. *(s)* accomplishment, deed, effort. *(ant)* failure.

11 **digit** *(n)* one's finger, thumb or toe.

12 **dormant** *(adj)* temporarily inactive. *(s)* quiet, latent, idle, inert. *(ant)* active.

13 **allure** *(n)* a mysterious fascination or attraction. *(s)* magnetism, charm, appeal. *(ant)* repulsion.

14 **hypnotise** *(v)* completely capture the attention of someone. *(s)* fascinate, captivate, mesmerise. *(ant)* disenchant.

15 **function** *(v)* work in a specific way. *(s)* operate, perform. *(ant)* malfunction.

Cad carried the chair over to the arrow slit, climbed on, and peeped out. Nothing. All was quiet in the **bailey**[1] below the keep. She then approached the dungeon's door and, as silent as a shadow, listened for **eavesdroppers**[2] on the other side. She must be sure no eye peered through the hidden spyhole, one of which she knew existed throughout the castle, especially in the dungeons. No one must see the next step of her **transformation**[3]. For without these magical tools to help her, she might never discover the traitors **lurking**[4] in their midst. And even worse, what they planned next, for she was sure their **plotting**[5] would only **increase**[6] with Llywelyn gone to find the Gwalch Gem bracelet.

In **anticipation**[7] of the ring's magic, Cad's heart began to thump. She sat on her bed and secured the hairpin in her tunic lest something untoward occur and she drop it. Then she slipped the emerald ring off her right thumb and wiggled it onto her left. It fitted as though for Siân, and Cad must beware of it slipping off accidentally. She sucked in a breath, then with her right thumb pressed the hawk's centre, and in a blinding flash of emerald **incandescence**[8], her body **tingled**[9], bumps lifting on her skin. After a few moments passed, Cad tapped her thigh, feeling for the strange, yet still somehow strong **flimsiness**[10] she'd **encountered**[11] when testing it before. It was always **a tad**[12] sticky like a spider's web.

'Yes!' Cad cried in delight.

With ripples of excitement, she patted her other thigh, her arm and then her head, yet felt

---

1 **bailey** *(n)* a castle's inner courtyard, enclosed by an outer wall.

2 **eavesdropper** *(n)* someone who listens in on a private conversation without being seen or heard. *(s)* snoop, spy.

3 **transformation** *(n)* a noticeable change in form, nature or appearance. *(s)* alteration, metamorphosis. *(ant)* preservation.

4 **lurk** *(v)* be or remain hidden, hang about. *(s)* prowl, loiter, skulk. *(ant)* appear, materialise.

5 **plot** *(v)* devise a harmful or secret plan (often as a group). *(s)* conspire, connive, contrive, scheme.

6 **increase** *(v)* grow. *(s)* escalate, rise. *(ant)* decrease.

7 **anticipation** *(n)* the action of expecting something to happen. *(s)* expectation, hope.

8 **incandescence** *(n)* brightness due to high temperature. *(s)* brilliance, luminosity. *(ant)* dullness, darkness.

9 **tingle** *(v)* experience a prickling sensation. *(s)* prickle.

10 **flimsiness** *(n)* the state of being weak and easily damaged. *(s)* delicacy, fragility, frailty. *(ant)* sturdiness, robustness.

11 **encounter** *(v)* be faced with an experience. *(s)* find.

12 **a tad** *(adv)* by a small amount or extent. *(s)* a touch, somewhat, slightly. *(ant)* profoundly, considerably.

nothing but that slight **gauzy**[1] **sensation**[2] **yield**[3] a **fraction**[4] to the **pressure**[5]. Thanks to the hawk ring, her limbs were no longer there. Though, to be **complacent**[6] now would be foolhardy. With the bracelet gone and controlled by a **treacherous**[7] **foe**[8], how long this magic might work remained to be seen. Henceforth, caution would be king and queen. Now, to test the ring's strength. How long would it last without the Gwalch Gem close by to power it? Cad lay back on her bed, and with precision, she counted time in her head, and this she must continue until she became **visible**[9] once more.

---

1 **gauzy** *(adj)* transparent and thin, like gauze. *(s)* fine, sheer, transparent. *(ant)* coarse, thick.

2 **sensation** *(n)* a physical feeling or perception. *(s)* sense, impression, awareness.

3 **yield** *(v)* give way to pressure. *(s)* give, flex, bend. *(ant)* resist.

4 **fraction** *(n)* a small amount. *(s)* snippet, a tad, mite, smidge.

5 **pressure** *(n)* continuous physical force. *(s)* exertion, impact.

6 **complacent** *(adj)* showing too much pride and pleasure with one's achievements. *(s)* triumphant, gloating. *(ant)* humble.

7 **treacherous** *(adj)* presenting hidden or unforeseen dangers. *(s)* hazardous, precarious, perilous. *(ant)* safe.

8 **foe** *(n)* an enemy, nemesis or opponent. *(s)* antagonist, rival, opposition. *(ant)* friend, ally, comrade.

9 **visible** *(adj)* able to be seen. *(s)* noticeable, evident, perceptible, obvious. *(ant)* invisible, imperceptible.

CHAPTER SIX

Escape

The candle's flames flickered, shadows sliding across the cell's stone wall. Cad waited, visible once more, and her now dull and lifeless ring hidden away to refill with much-needed power from its **host**[1] until it shone, inviting its use once again. **Mercifully**[2], the invisibility ring had worked, and she had counted how long it had done so. To count **thus**[3] was her only way of knowing how long its energy might last, and with the bracelet distant, it was a **tenuous**[4] **calculation**[5] at best.

The moment Cad heard footsteps climbing the keep's stairs, she forced herself to relax and prepared to put on an act.

'Hello, Goodwife Hughes,' Cad said as the **vast**[6] **reinforced**[7] door creaked open.

'Good evening, Master Cad.'

---

1 **host** *(n)* something or someone on which a parasite (dependant) lives. *(s)* donor, contributor. *(ant)* parasite.

2 **mercifully** *(adv)* fortunately. *(s)* thankfully, luckily, happily. *(ant)* unfortunately.

3 **thus** *(adv)* in this way. *(s)* like this, like so.

4 **tenuous** *(adj)* (of a situation or concept) weak or slight. *(s)* vague, dubious, questionable. *(ant)* convincing.

5 **calculation** *(n)* assessment of possibilities, risks or effects. *(s)* estimate, reckoning.

6 **vast** *(adj)* large or immense. *(s)* enormous, colossal, huge, gigantic. *(ant)* small, insignificant.

7 **reinforce** *(v)* strengthen. *(s)* fortify, toughen. *(ant)* weaken.

Like a **plump**[1] **partridge**[2] **flushed**[3] from a hedge by a hound, Goodwife Hughes flew in, closing the door behind her.

Cad gave a half-smile and quickly said, 'I attempted to write verse, but it seems the dungeon imprisons my **muse**[4].' Before the goodwife had chance to speak, Cad added a frown, saying, 'Sadly, I've achieved very little.' Then still wearing her best acting chops, she gazed at the goodwife with her saddest face.

In reality, Cad's thoughts were far from poetry. During the goodwife's absence, she'd penned **hasty**[5] letters for her friends, and one for her father, in case she never saw him again. All were safely tucked away on her person along with her 'come and rescue me' notes.

'Come now,' fussed the stout lady, patting Cad's bed and **plumping**[6] up the feather-filled pillows. 'Sir Robert ordered I **snuff**[7] these candles for the night.'

'Mrs Hughes, how is your son?' Cad asked, a glint in her green eyes. The goodwife **doted**[8] on Hugh, so Cad softened her in preparation for her request. Although realising the **inopportune**[9] timing, Cad couldn't help wondering why Mrs Hughes had named her son Hugh. Hugh Hughes was such a mouthful.

'He's grand. Never better,' gushed Mrs Hughes.

Odd, had Cad heard a hitch in her voice?

'Hugh is an apprentice to Sir Robert. **Hence**[10] we lived at Cadwaladr Castle until this **tragedy**[11].' Goodwife Hughes sniffed, blew her nose and honked like a **strangled**[12] goose. 'Terrible business,' she added with a **dramatic**[13] flourish, before getting back around to her son.

---

1 **plump** *(adj)* having a rounded or full shape. *(s)* ample, well rounded. *(ant)* thin.

2 **partridge** *(n)* a medium-sized game bird found in Europe and Asia.

3 **flush** *(v)* force a bird or animal out from its cover.

4 **muse** *(n)* a person or thing that inspires a creative artist. *(s)* inspiration, stimulus.

5 **hasty** *(adj)* done in a hurry. *(s)* speedy, quick, brief, short. *(ant)* slow.

6 **plump** *(v)* shake and prod something to make rounder and fuller, such as a cushion or pillow.

7 **snuff** *(v)* put out a flame or candle. *(s)* extinguish, smother, douse. *(ant)* light, ignite.

8 **dote** *(v)* be uncritically fond of. *(s)* idolise, adore, worship, pamper. *(ant)* neglect, hate.

9 **inopportune** *(adj)* happening at an inconvenient time. *(s)* inapt, inappropriate. *(ant)* opportune, convenient.

10 **hence** *(adv)* for this reason. *(s)* therefore, consequently, thus, so.

11 **tragedy** *(n)* a terrible event. *(s)* disaster, calamity, catastrophe, misfortune. *(ant)* joy.

12 **strangled** *(adj)* sounding as if coming from a constricted throat. *(s)* choked, squeezed.

13 **dramatic** *(adj)* in a way which is intended to cause an effect. *(s)* theatrical, showy, affected, artificial. *(ant)* unaffected.

Cad's patience with this **drivel**[1] had already **waned**[2], but **beggars**[3] and choosers sprang to her mind, so she listened with a smile.

'Hugh assists Sir Robert with his **architectural**[4] plans and drawings. All too clever for me,' Mrs Hughes finished, her tone **drenched**[5] in **pride**[6].

'Sir Robert is indeed a fine architect. Hugh has such a **talent**[7]. How I wish I painted horses like he,' Cad said, flashing an **oily**[8] grin, a well-mannered look of deep interest on her face.

Goodwife Hughes's cheeks flushed with pleasure as she bobbed her head and **cooed**[9], 'Why thank you. Yes, he is, and he's **content**[10] with Sir Robert, too.'

'Hugh's **outstanding**[11] achievements are admirable. He deserves his appointment.' Cad poured on the honey, steeling herself to ask for the **favour**[12]. 'Goodwife Hughes, do you think you might look kindly upon me and allow me a candle a while longer, just one?' **Coy**[13], Cad tilted her head. 'If I promise to extinguish it soon?'

The goodwife snorted like a bull, lips tight as she peered at Cad. Cad's heart sank. Never mind, she must manage in the dark.

'Go ahead. Why not?' Goodwife Hughes **capitulated**[14], snorting again. '**Swear**[15], though, not too long. If Sir Robert gets wind of it, he'll boil,' she muttered, swooshing across the room like a ship in full sail.

'Thank you, Goodwife Hughes,' Cad cried. 'I promise,' she added, her fingers crossed, for she

---

1 **drivel** *(n)* nonsense. *(s)* claptrap, twaddle, balderdash, piffle. *(ant)* sense.

2 **wane** *(v)* become weaker. *(s)* decrease, lessen, decline, dwindle, diminish. *(ant)* grow, increase.

3 **beggar** *(n)* a person who lives by asking (begging) for food or money. *(s)* down-and-out.

4 **architectural** *(adj)* relating to the design and construction of buildings. *(s)* structural.

5 **drench** *(v)* flood with. *(s)* satiate, soak.

6 **pride** *(n)* a feeling of satisfaction. *(s)* pleasure, delight, joy. *(ant)* shame.

7 **talent** *(n)* a natural skill or ability. *(s)* gift, flair, aptitude, forte. *(ant)* inability.

8 **oily** *(adj)* (of a person) smooth and not genuine. *(s)* unctuous, fawning, fake. *(ant)* genuine, earnest.

9 **coo** *(v)* make soft murmuring sounds. *(s)* fuss, cluck, murmur.

10 **content** *(adj)* peaceful and happy. *(s)* fulfilled, pleased, *(ant)* dissatisfied.

11 **outstanding** *(adj)* exceptionally good. *(s)* distinguished, superlative, stupendous. *(ant)* abysmal, dire.

12 **favour** *(n)* an act of kindness. *(s)* goodwill, benevolence.

13 **coy** *(adj)* making a pretence of modesty or shyness. *(s)* bashful, evasive, reserved. *(ant)* brazen.

14 **capitulate** *(v)* stop resisting an opponent or demand. *(s)* surrender, yield, relent. *(ant)* resist.

15 **swear** *(v)* promise something is the case. *(s)* vow, agree, ensure, guarantee.

detested[1] **deceiving**[2] this kind lady and **loathed**[3] troubling her.

The goodwife's eyes narrowed, and with her hands **denting**[4] her **ample**[5] **hips**[6], she said, 'I will return after dawn with your breakfast. The candle's remaining wax will betray the time it burned. I am trusting you, Master Cad,' she finished with a **solemn**[7] nod and a **patronising**[8] finger wag.

'You can,' said Cad, meaning it. For she didn't plan to burn the candle for long.

Once Goodwife Hughes and her swishing skirts had left, Cad scribbled more notes to Dylan in their **invented**[9] **cipher**[10]. They'd **devised**[11] a kind of **gibberish**[12] speech code to cover her gender, and Llywelyn knew of it too. An **indecipherable**[13] language was vital for their **covert**[14] communication. It **infuriated**[15] Bryn Davis and his page, Jack Jones, who **accused**[16] them of talking nonsense. Cad and Dylan kept it from their knights, who **forbade**[17] such means of talk. The code had often saved Cad from the **prying**[18] eyes of Bryn and his boys. And it was the one thing that she and Dylan hid from Rhys, in case he tripped.

Once **satisfied**[19] with their content, Cad rolled up the notes and tucked them away in her secret hems. Without further **ado**[20], she placed Siân's emerald ring onto her left thumb, and

---

1 **detest** *(v)* dislike intensely. *(s)* abhor, despise, loathe, hate. *(ant)* love, adore.

2 **deceive** *(v)* give the wrong impression. *(s)* mislead, hoodwink, dupe, trick. *(ant)* be honest.

3 **loathe** *(v)* feel intense dislike or disgust for. *(s)* hate, despise, abhor, detest. *(ant)* adore, love.

4 **dent** *(v)* make a small hollow in a surface by a blow or pressure. *(s)* indent, depress.

5 **ample** *(adj)* large. *(s)* broad, extensive. *(ant)* small, meagre.

6 **hip** *(n)* the protruding pelvis bones of a human being.

7 **solemn** *(adj)* formal or genuine. *(s)* sincere, earnest, firm. *(ant)* insincere.

8 **patronise** *(v)* treat someone in an unhelpful or superior way. *(s)* belittle, deride.

9 **invent** *(v)* design or create something never made before. *(s)* devise, develop.

10 **cipher** *(n)* a disguised or secret way of writing something. *(s)* cryptograph, code, cryptogram.

11 **devise** *(v)* plan or invent. *(s)* conceive, formulate, create, develop. *(ant)* copy, replicate.

12 **gibberish** *(n)* nonsense speech. *(s)* blather, drivel, balderdash. *(ant)* sense.

13 **indecipherable** *(adj)* unable to be read or understood. *(s)* incomprehensible, unfathomable. *(ant)* understandable.

14 **covert** *(adj)* not openly displayed or acknowledged. *(s)* secret, concealed. *(ant)* obvious, overt.

15 **infuriate** *(v)* make or become very angry. *(s)* enrage, inflame, exasperate. *(ant)* soothe, calm.

16 **accuse** *(v)* blame someone for a wrong doing. *(s)* allege, charge. *(ant)* applaud, approve.

17 **forbid** *(v)* say no to (past tense: forbade). *(s)* ban, prohibit, veto, sanction. *(ant)* allow, sanction.

18 **prying** *(adj)* looking or enquiring too closely. *(s)* inquisitive, curious, probing. *(ant)* disinterested.

19 **satisfy** *(v)* meet someone's expectations, needs or desires. *(s)* please. *(ant)* dissatisfy.

20 **ado** *(n)* fuss. *(s)* trouble, bother, upset, delay. *(ant)* order, haste.

took the hairpin from its leather sheath.

Now ready to leave, Cad knelt by the door and placed the candle beside her. To make certain no one was listening in, she rested her ear against the lock and waited. Reassured that no one was lurking outside, Cad inserted the hairpin into the hole and wiggled it, taking pains to protect the emerald hawk end she held. A **remote**[1] chance existed that if the pin possessed magic, she might **lever**[2] the lock to the point of turning it.

In the **quivering**[3] candlelight, with her ear glued to the lock's sounds, she moved the pin to the left, then back to the centre. Tense, she manoeuvred it again, easing it to the right, feeling the **mechanism**[4] through the pin's **shaft**[5]. When she heard a satisfying click, her heart soared. She'd opened the lock.

Yes! she thought, ready to leave.

Though, when she tried to turn the pin further, it jammed, refusing to **revolve**[6]. A frown now **scored**[7] her brow, and no matter how much she wiggled the pin, up, down, left, right, the lock refused to turn. Exasperated, she removed the hairpin and slumped onto her **haunches**[8] against the wall of her prison cell.

As her hands sank into her face, Cad accepted she was captive. Despite her invisibility ring working, if she could not escape, she was stuck, unable to help her father and **dependent**[9] on May for **communication**[10] with Dylan and Rhys.

She stared at the ring glittering with life on her thumb, **futile**[11] and wasted here in this cell. The **lone**[12] candle flickered, the emerald end of the hairpin winking as if to **taunt**[13] her. With

---

1 **remote** *(adj)* possible or unlikely. *(s)* faint, slim, small. *(ant)* definite, likely, strong.

2 **lever** *(v)* move with concerted physical effort. *(s)* force, push, prise.

3 **quiver** *(v)* tremble or shake. *(s)* shiver, quaver, tremor. *(ant)* steady, still.

4 **mechanism** *(n)* a system of parts working together in a machine, tool or apparatus. *(s)* structure, workings.

5 **shaft** *(n)* the narrow part of something which forms the handle. *(s)* handle, hilt, stem.

6 **revolve** *(v)* move in circles. *(s)* rotate, spin, turn.

7 **score** *(v)* to make or cut lines into something. *(s)* mark, furrow, groove.

8 **haunches** *(n)* thighs and bottom together. *(s)* buttocks, hindquarters, rump, rear, backside.

9 **dependent** *(adj)* requiring the support of something or someone. *(s)* reliant, counting. *(ant)* independent.

10 **communication** *(n)* the exchange of information. *(s)* reporting, intelligence, knowledge.

11 **futile** *(adj)* useless and pointless. *(s)* ineffective, ineffectual, wasted. *(ant)* useful.

12 **lone** *(adj)* single. *(s)* individual, solitary, solo. *(ant)* myriad.

13 **taunt** *(v)* provoke or challenge someone. *(s)* mock, tease, goad. *(ant)* compliment.

tears hovering just below the surface, crestfallen, she grabbed the candle, stood and slid into her chair at the desk, placing the pin down before her. She dared not burn the candle too long lest Goodwife Hughes **scold**[1] her and forbid this **concession**[2] tomorrow. If stuck here for a week, **interminable**[3] nights loomed ahead, even if she slept well.

As Cad moved to **pluck**[4] the ring from her thumb, the hairpin's emerald hawk winked again. Sucked in by it, she picked it up, studying it, the candlelight catching its stunning angles. As she stared, she remembered Llywelyn's words when she'd asked him if it was magic. 'It was, but we no longer know—' is what he'd replied.

'I wonder?' Cad said, jumping to her feet and grabbing the candle again. **Buoyed**[5] with hope, she placed the candle on the floor by the door and regarded the **shimmering**[6] emerald. With a flick of her wrist, Cad turned the pin around, now holding it by its sharp tip. Using **minute**[7] precision, Cad inserted the hawk end into the lock, and as smooth as a knife through soft butter, the jewel turned, unlocking the dungeon's door with ease. As if made for that lock, it had worked like a key. Did she possess a magic key? Not wasting a second, her heart thumping, and taking great care to **preserve**[8] the hot, **transparent**[9] wax now **pooled**[10] around its **wick**[11], Cad returned the candle to the table.

Her heart found wings as she removed the sparkling ring from her right thumb, pushing it onto her left. Then, with her right thumb, she pressed the ring's hawk – hard. Suddenly, with a blinding emerald flash, Cad vanished. How long she might be invisible, again, was uncertain. Earlier, when testing, counting in her head, she'd gauged the timing. This **strategy**[12] should offer

---

1 **scold** *(v)* tell someone off angrily. *(s)* reprimand, admonish, chastise. *(ant)* praise.
2 **concession** *(n)* something given when asked for. *(s)* allowance, compromise, exception.
3 **interminable** *(adj)* endless or seemingly so. *(s)* unending, tedious, monotonous. *(ant)* ending.
4 **pluck** *(v)* take hold of and quickly remove from. *(s)* pull, tug, grasp, extract. *(ant)* insert.
5 **buoy** *(v)* make optimistic and confident. *(s)* encourage, boost, cheer, hearten. *(ant)* depress.
6 **shimmer** *(v)* shine. *(s)* twinkle, glisten, sparkle, glint. *(ant)* dull.
7 **minute** *(adj)* extremely small or exact. *(s)* meticulous, painstaking. *(ant)* rough, imprecise.
8 **preserve** *(v)* keep something in its original state. *(s)* protect, conserve. *(ant)* spoil, neglect.
9 **transparent** *(adj)* can be seen through. *(s)* see-through, clear, translucent. *(ant)* opaque, cloudy, dark.
10 **pool** *(v)* form a pool on a surface. *(s)* puddle. *(ant)* drain.
11 **wick** *(n)* a strip of material which runs through a candle, or such like, and is lit to produce a flame.
12 **strategy** *(n)* a plan to achieve an overall or long-term aim. *(s)* tactic, approach, method. *(ant)* disorder.

her ample time to **scope out**[1] the castle unseen, yet she must be vigilant, reminding herself that, although invisible, folk might hear and feel her. And dogs would certainly smell her.

With no time to waste, Cad clutched the candle and opened the door, cracking it just enough to slip through. Before closing it, she splashed hot wax into her palm, and with a **wince**[2], blew out the candle and placed it on the floor inside the cell. On high **alert**[3], she nudged the door to, closing it as quietly as its great **mass**[4] allowed. Before leaving, she tipped a **discreet**[5] blob of the transparent wax onto the door's handle, where it met the lock. A **breach**[6] of this seal would prove spies lurked in the shadows.

Once satisfied she was entirely invisible, armed with her hairpin in hand, Cad tiptoed down the tower's stone steps, the candles sparkling in their **sconces**[7] lighting the way before her.

---

1 **scope out** *(v)* investigate or assess something. *(s)* evaluate, check out, study.

2 **wince** *(n)* an instance of wincing (flinching) in reaction to pain or distress. *(s)* grimace. *(ant)* smile.

3 **alert** *(n)* a state of being watchful for danger. *(s)* vigilance, caution. *(ant)* carelessness.

4 **mass** *(n)* weight and size. *(s)* bulk, extent, dimension.

5 **discreet** *(adj)* intending to be unobtrusive. *(s)* subtle, inconspicuous. *(ant)* obtrusive.

6 **breach** *(n)* a break or gap in something, often made by an attacking enemy. *(s)* split, rupture. *(ant)* repair.

7 **sconce** *(n)* a fixture mounted onto a wall to hold a candle or an oil lamp.

CHAPTER SEVEN

Forbidden Friends

Invisibility did not **render**[1] Cad silent. Even though she tiptoed down the tower's stone stairway, to her ears, her steps rang like **pealing**[2] bells. Now faced with the reality of her foray, her invisible face worried itself into a pinch.

When she reached the bottom, good fortune prevailed: no guard **patrolled**[3] at the foot of the tower, and she quickly exited into the bailey. As it was the early hours of morning, and still so quiet, Cad quickly changed her plan. To avoid the sniffing dogs bedded down in the open bailey, she cut through the **adjoining**[4] chapel instead, doubting that folks would be praying yet.

Her body hummed with nerves as she **tentatively**[5] opened the chapel door, its hinges creaking as if waking from **slumber**[6]. **Innocent**[7] onlookers would have fled in horror at this strange sight, thinking the devil's work at play as the door swung open unaided. She must be careful not to open doors or move objects in people's view lest folks raise the alarm of **ungodly**[8] happenings in Catrin Castle.

---

1 **render** *(v)* cause to become. *(s)* make, leave.

2 **peal** *(v)* ring (of a bell or bells). *(s)* chime, clang, reverberate, ding.

3 **patrol** *(v)* keep watch over something by walking around it regularly. *(s)* inspect, protect.

4 **adjoining** *(adj)* next to or joined to (of a building or room). *(s)* neighbouring, abutting. *(ant)* separate.

5 **tentatively** *(adv)* in a hesitant way. *(s)* gingerly, cautiously. *(ant)* confidently.

6 **slumber** *(n)* sleep. *(s)* a rest, a nap.

7 **innocent** *(adj)* unknowing. *(s)* naive, gullible, ignorant. *(ant)* wise, knowledgeable.

8 **ungodly** *(adj)* without religion or morality. *(s)* unholy, immoral, godless. *(ant)* godly, holy, moral.

As she crept through the chapel, its rows of wooden **pews**[1] empty, its **lanterns**[2], dotted here and there, shimmered in sconces that **adorned**[3] the **effigy**[4]-clad walls.

*Why are chapels so **eerie**[5]?* she thought, starting at nothing but a shadow and almost losing her **footing**[6] as her heart leaped into her mouth.

At the end of the **aisle**[7] between the pews, an **array**[8] of candles flickered, their wax melting to form as blobs on the **ornate**[9] **altar**[10], no doubt lit as an offering for Llywelyn. With a heavy heart, Cad crossed the chapel and exited into the narrow stone passageway which hugged the great hall. All the while, she counted time in her head. She mustn't lose track lest the magic vanish without warning.

To help keep Cad's secret, Dewi had sanctioned separate quarters from all other pages. Thus, the three friends' bedchamber **nestled**[11] beyond the hall in a quiet corner on the opposite side of the kitchens. Dewi's, and many **senior**[12] knights' rooms, lay across the bailey on the keep's upper floors; all boasted comfortable **accommodation**[13] suitable for nobles. Cad may need to **peek**[14] up there in that tower before returning to hers. It was **adjacent**[15] to the prison cells and its high towers, **ironically**[16], protected both dignitaries and prisoners alike.

On her guard, Cad **padded**[17] along the **dim**[18] passageway beside the great hall, constantly

---

1 **pew** *(n)* a long wooden bench in churches for seating the congregation or choir.
2 **lantern** *(n)* a portable (moveable) lamp with a handle. *(s)* light.
3 **adorn** *(v)* make more attractive or beautiful. *(s)* decorate, embellish. *(ant)* strip.
4 **effigy** *(n)* a model or sculpture of a person. *(s)* statue, carving, figure, likeness.
5 **eerie** *(adj)* strange and scary. *(s)* spooky, creepy, weird, peculiar. *(ant)* familiar.
6 **footing** *(n)* a secure hold with one's feet. *(s)* grip, purchase, foothold.
7 **aisle** *(n)* a passageway between rows of seats. *(s)* walkway, gangway, gap.
8 **array** *(n)* a significant display or range of something. *(s)* arrangement, group. *(ant)* individual, one.
9 **ornate** *(adj)* decorative. *(s)* fancy, elaborate, adorned, decorated. *(ant)* dull, plain.
10 **altar** *(n)* a structure or table in churches used for the presentation of religious offerings.
11 **nestle** *(v)* be situated. *(s)* lie, settle, sit.
12 **senior** *(adj)* high in rank or status. *(s)* top, superior, high-ranking. *(ant)* junior.
13 **accommodation** *(n)* a place where a person can live or lodge (stay). *(s)* dwelling, living quarters, residence.
14 **peek** *(v)* take a quick or secretive look. *(s)* peep, glance, glimpse, gander. *(ant)* stare, gaze.
15 **adjacent** *(adj)* next to or adjoining. *(s)* beside, neighbouring, alongside. *(ant)* distant from.
16 **ironically** *(adv)* in a ironic (paradoxical, unexpected or coincidental) way. *(s)* paradoxically, coincidentally.
17 **pad** *(v)* walk making a soft, dull sound. *(s)* sneak, patter, shuffle. *(ant)* stomp, march, stride.
18 **dim** *(adj)* (of a light or colour) not bright or clear. *(s)* dull, dingy. *(ant)* bright, light, airy.

reminding herself she was invisible. As she crept along, wishing her boots were quieter, she **snagged**[1] her toe on a **protruding**[2] stone. Caught unaware, Cad tripped. Unable to stop, she flew headlong with **flailing**[3] arms and a sizeable **clatter**[4], just managing to **reduce**[5] the potential dive to an **ungainly**[6] stumble. All a **dither**[7], but relieved to be upright, she panted like a dog, clutching her hairpin lest she lose it. Her heart hammered so fast, blood swam through her ears, **pulsating**[8] to the **rhythm**[9] of raw fear.

Loath[10] to continue, but forcing herself on, Cad turned a corner, then froze, her face sharpening with surprise. Her **lurch**[11] had roused a sleepy guard, who, like a sack of **spuds**[12], leaned against the stone wall slumped on a stool, an empty **ewer**[13] at his feet. The man was clearly **napping**[14] on the job, a strong **fug**[15] of beer about him. Cad halted as his hulking **mastiff**[16] caught wind of her. The **massive**[17] hound, its lips pulled back and bearing **ferocious**[18] **canines**[19], flew at Cad, who, knowing she could never outrun it, stilled and **braced**[20] herself.

The **mighty**[21] dog's paws hit Cad's invisible chest, **exerting**[22] a power that forced the air from

---

1 **snag** *(v)* catch something on a protruding thing or object. *(s)* stub.
2 **protrude** *(v)* extend above or beyond a surface (stick out). *(s)* poke out, jut, project. *(ant)* withdraw.
3 **flail** *(v)* swing or wave wildly. *(s)* whirl, flap, lash.
4 **clatter** *(n)* a continuous rattling noise. *(s)* clank, bang, clunk.
5 **reduce** *(v)* make smaller or less. *(s)* decrease, lessen, minimise. *(ant)* increase.
6 **ungainly** *(adj)* clumsy. *(s)* awkward, graceless, inelegant, lumbering. *(ant)* elegant, graceful.
7 **dither** *(n)* a state of distress. *(s)* upset, disquiet, tizzy. *(ant)* composure.
8 **pulsate** *(v)* expand and contract regularly. *(s)* beat, throb, pulse, pound.
9 **rhythm** *(n)* a regular pattern of movement or sound. *(s)* beat, cadence, flow, pace.
10 **loath** *(adj)* unwilling or reluctant (not wanting to do something). *(s)* opposed, hesitant, averse. *(ant)* eager.
11 **lurch** *(n)* an uncontrolled movement. *(s)* stumble, stagger, sway.
12 **spud** *(n)* an informal word for potato.
13 **ewer** *(n)* a big jug with a wide opening, formerly used for carrying water. *(s)* urn, vessel.
14 **nap** *(v)* sleep briefly, especially during the day. *(s)* rest, snooze, doze, catnap.
15 **fug** *(n)* a stuffy atmosphere or air. *(s)* fustiness, staleness. *(ant)* freshness.
16 **mastiff** *(n)* a breed of large, strong dog, often used to guard places, things or people.
17 **massive** *(adj)* big and heavy or solid. *(s)* large, huge, enormous, great. *(ant)* small, tiny.
18 **ferocious** *(adj)* fierce. *(s)* vicious, aggressive, brutal, savage. *(ant)* gentle, mild.
19 **canine** *(n)* a pointed tooth found towards the front of the mouth, often enlarged in carnivores (meat eaters).
20 **brace** *(v)* prepare for something difficult or unpleasant. *(s)* steel, prime, fortify, ready. *(ant)* weaken.
21 **mighty** *(adj)* strong and powerful, especially due to size. *(s)* forceful, huge, almighty. *(ant)* weak.
22 **exert** *(v)* to put forth or into use. *(s)* apply, wield, exercise, utilise.

her lungs with a grunt. His colossal bodyweight **followed suit**[1], **propelling**[2] Cad backwards with such speed she soared, landing on her already sore rear with a **wallop**[3].

Fear **enveloped**[4] her body, and as her eyes screwed shut, she waited for the dog's jaws to snap. Whether she was invisible or not, he could kill her in an **instant**[5]. For what felt like an age, an invisible axe hacked at her chest as she waited for the dog's teeth to sink in. Then to her **utmost**[6] surprise, instead of savaging her, the gigantic dog's paws pinned down her chest, and **comically**[7], he **lapped**[8] her face with his **slobbery**[9] tongue which was as big as a slipper. This close up, Cad recognised the mastiff; a fair beast who wouldn't bite the hand that **plied**[10] him with scraps in the great hall.

'Brutus,' she whispered, weak with relief as he soaked her face with **drool**[11]. 'Off, boy,' she grunted under his enormous load, pushing him with all her might, to no **avail**[12]. So pleased to see the girl who fed him meat goodies under the table at dinner times, the dog didn't **budge**[13].

Now pinned beneath the **hefty**[14] hound as it licked her invisible face, Cad heard the guard splutter as he woke to the most **peculiar**[15] of sights. She turned her head, to see he'd paled to the colour of **whey**[16].

'Down, you daft mutt, down!' he grumbled, hauling his heft off the stool and yanking the poor mastiff by his **scruff**[17]. 'What you doin'? Sit! You darn near gave me a heart failure,' the

---

1 **follow suit** (phrase) do as someone or something else does. *(s)* come after, accompany. *(ant)* lead.

2 **propel** *(v)* drive or push into a specific direction. *(s)* move, thrust, shoot, force, launch. *(ant)* pull.

3 **wallop** *(n)* a heavy knock. *(s)* bang, crack, thwack, jolt, clout, battering.

4 **envelop** *(v)* surround completely. *(s)* encompass, engulf, smother.

5 **instant** *(n)* a short period of time. *(s)* a moment.

6 **utmost** *(adj)* most extreme. *(s)* greatest. *(ant)* least.

7 **comically** *(adv)* in a comical (funny or amusing) way. *(s)* hilariously. *(ant)* seriously, solemnly.

8 **lap** *(v)* lick repeatedly and especially noisily. *(s)* wash, slap, slosh.

9 **slobbery** *(adj)* unpleasantly wet. *(s)* dribbly, sopping, salivating. *(ant)* dry.

10 **ply** *(v)* to give consistently. *(s)* offer, proffer, hand. *(ant)* withhold.

11 **drool** *(n)* saliva dripping from the mouth. *(s)* spit, slobber, dribble, spittle.

12 **avail** *(n)* benefit or use. *(s)* advantage, reward. *(ant)* uselessness.

13 **budge** *(v)* move a small amount. *(s)* shift, stir, flinch.

14 **hefty** *(adj)* large. *(s)* sizeable, ample, substantial. *(ant)* little, paltry.

15 **peculiar** *(adj)* different from normal or usual. *(s)* bizarre, uncanny, queer, abnormal. *(ant)* normal.

16 **whey** *(n)* a pale yellow-beige liquid remaining after milk has been curdled and strained.

17 **scruff** *(n)* (of an animal or person) the back of the neck. *(s)* scrag, nape.

man muttered, flopping back onto his stool and letting out a fart. Then, with a look of cruel amusement, he gave the mastiff a sly toe to the ribs. To wake to see his **fierce**[1] dog up on his **hind**[2] legs licking the air must have been quite a shock to him, especially with beer filling his veins.

Cad, just about breathing again, rubbed her **throbbing**[3] backside and wobbled to her feet. It seemed that feeding the castle's dogs, who constantly begged under the dining tables, may have just saved her skin. Swiftly moving on and feeling **pity**[4] for the scolded dog, Cad headed for the kitchens, counting time in her head. Fingers crossed, she hoped the bakers weren't yet working. If they were not, she could slide through a service hatch and slip out that way and she might reach her bedchamber **undetected**[5].

Almost there, and thankful for no further **hitches**[6], Cad continued and turned the final corner to see the kitchen door.

Not another one, she thought, as she **jerked**[7] to a stop, her heart sinking.

Yet another guard sat **stationed**[8] there: Sir Robert's **vigilance**[9] more **apparent**[10] down here. Midnight food pilfering was commonplace at Catrin Castle, for there were many hungry pages and squires to feed, their bellies refusing to fill.

As Cad neared the guard, good fortune prevailed, for she saw he wasn't a knight but a **portly**[11] **servant**[12] with his equally stout **terrier**[13]. Even so, should she avoid the kitchens and risk the bailey instead? Folks couldn't see her, but the darned bailey dogs would smell her. No, she must cut through the kitchens to sneak into her bedchamber unseen.

---

1 **fierce** *(adj)* powerful and aggressive. *(s)* vicious, ferocious, savage. *(ant)* mild, tame.

2 **hind** *(adj)* back. *(s)* rear. *(ant)* fore, front.

3 **throb** *(v)* pulse steadily. *(s)* pulsate, ache.

4 **pity** *(n)* the feeling of sadness for the suffering of others. *(s)* compassion, regret, sorrow. *(ant)* indifference.

5 **undetected** *(adj)* not found or perceived. *(s)* unseen, unnoticed. *(ant)* detected, seen.

6 **hitch** *(n)* a temporary problem. *(s)* snag, hindrance, obstacle, glitch, setback.

7 **jerk** *(v)* move with a sudden, sharp movement. *(s)* jolt, lurch. *(ant)* glide, ease.

8 **station** *(v)* put in a place to watch or guard something or someone. *(v)* post, position, locate.

9 **vigilance** *(n)* the action of keeping watch for difficulty or danger. *(s)* attention, caution, wariness. *(ant)* inattentiveness.

10 **apparent** *(adj)* obvious, visible or understood. *(s)* evident, discernible, perceptible. *(ant)* unclear.

11 **portly** *(adj)* large, fat or overweight. *(s)* corpulent, chubby, tubby. *(ant)* slim, slender, skinny.

12 **servant** *(n)* someone who works for another person, often doing household tasks. *(s)* houseboy. *(ant)* master, mistress.

13 **terrier** *(n)* a small breed of dog typically used for controlling perceived verminous animals (pests).

Sweat prickled her body as she **scanned**[1] the scene again. The guard's head rested against the stone wall, and his mouth **drooped**[2] as **hog**[3]-like snores escaped his flapping lips. He had the look of a once well-built man **gone to seed**[4] and shouldn't pose a problem. But then her heart dropped again. His dog lay awake and alert, his broad terrier head resting on his front paws, his eyes fixed forward. Once he caught wind of Cad, he'd soon warn his master.

Thank goodness dogs were **slaves to**[5] food. Cad **stashed**[6] her hairpin and delved into her tunic's secret hem. Then, as swift as a **starling**[7], she **darted**[8] forward, and in one **adroit**[9] move, flung a piece of dried stinky cheese past the dog's nose, aiming as far away from the kitchen door as possible. Unable to **resist**[10], the stocky terrier leaped to its feet and **bounded**[11] after the tempting **morsel**[12]. The guard let out a giant snore, burped, but didn't wake. In a flash, Cad was through the kitchen door and gently closing it behind her.

She'd been right. The kitchen was still quiet, but the bakers would soon arrive. Passing the empty meat **spit**[13], which sat **idle**[14] above the great fireplace, which was big enough to roast a whole pig, Cad stooped and scooped up handfuls of pork scraps, shoving them into her pockets. Then, as quick as a **whippet**[15], she wriggled out through one of the service hatches. With ease, she landed in the passageway outside her chamber door, which, thankfully, was quiet as a grave.

Not wasting a moment, Cad opened her chamber door and crept inside, closing it behind her. She glanced over to the corner where the curved outline of Rhys slept. Holding her breath, Cad

---

1 **scan** *(v)* look carefully. *(s)* study, inspect. *(ant)* glance.

2 **droop** *(v)* hang down loosely. *(s)* sag, hang, drop.

3 **hog** *(n)* another word for a pig. *(s)* swine, grunter, porker.

4 **gone to seed** (idiom) to have become less healthy, attractive or efficient than someone or something once was.

5 **slave to** (phrase) to be controlled or overly influenced by something or someone.

6 **stash** *(v)* keep in a hidden place. *(s)* hide, conceal, stow, secrete. *(ant)* reveal, unpack.

7 **starling** *(n)* a type of songbird.

8 **dart** *(v)* run suddenly and quickly. *(s)* bolt, charge, bound. *(ant)* walk, dawdle, amble.

9 **adroit** *(adj)* skilful or clever. *(s)* able, competent, adept, accomplished, agile. *(ant)* clumsy, inept.

10 **resist** *(v)* hold back from doing something. *(s)* refuse, ignore. *(ant)* accept.

11 **bound** *(v)* walk or run with large strides. *(s)* bounce, jump, leap, spring.

12 **morsel** *(n)* a small piece or amount. *(s)* mouthful, bite, nibble, bit. *(ant)* chunk.

13 **spit** *(n)* a thin metal rod pushed through meat that one holds and turns while the meat roasts over a fire.

14 **idle** *(adj)* currently not working. *(s)* dormant, inactive, unoccupied. *(ant)* working.

15 **whippet** *(n)* a small slender dog, bred for racing.

padded into the room, hoping he wouldn't wake. For a moment, she watched, thankful he didn't **stir**[1], his breaths remaining steady and deep. Once certain he had not heard her, she tiptoed over to Dylan's bed.

I guess I must be thankful for small ***mercies***[2], she thought seeing her bed remained empty. No eager page had yet claimed it; they all knew this **proximity**[3] to the kitchens meant extra food from midnight raids.

'Dylan,' she whispered. Her friend didn't budge.

'Dylan,' she repeated with a gentle shake of his shoulder. He was such a **sound**[4] sleeper.

'Dylan,' she hissed in his ear, flicking his arm with envy: a pin hitting the floor could wake her.

Then, as if **singed**[5] by a flame, Dylan shot upright, his eyes like **saucers**[6], his mouth set to scream. **Armed**[7] with a pillow, Cad had **anticipated**[8] this and shoved it over his mouth.

His poor eyes, she thought. He looked as if he were about to be murdered.

'Dylan, it's me, Cad. Callwen,' she said as loudly as she could without waking Rhys. 'I am wearing the ring.' She poked him hard. 'Dylan, hear me,' she urged.

A few beats passed, then his body softened a little, recognition flooding his eyes. Cad spoke in their gibberish **pig Latin**[9], in case Rhys woke and heard her. She didn't want him **embroiled**[10] in her suspicions and woes.

'I thought I was about to be **slain**[11] in my bed,' Dylan said, shock **contorting**[12] his parchment-pale face.

'I'm sorry I scared you. I don't know how much time remains before I become visible,' she

---

1 **stir** *(v)* move slightly or wake up. *(s)* rouse, awake, budge. *(ant)* still.

2 **mercy** *(n)* an event that one can be grateful for. *(s)* godsend, blessing, favour. *(ant)* disadvantage.

3 **proximity** *(n)* nearness. *(s)* closeness, adjacency. *(ant)* remoteness, distance.

4 **sound** *(adj)* established and reliable. *(s)* dependable, solid. *(ant)* unreliable.

5 **singe** *(v)* burn something lightly. *(s)* scorch, char.

6 **saucer** *(n)* a shallow dish on which a cup is placed, but in the Middle Ages was used for serving sauces.

7 **armed** *(adj)* equipped with or carrying a weapon (usually a gun). *(s)* outfitted, supplied.

8 **anticipate** *(v)* expect. *(s)* predict, foresee, forecast, foretell. *(ant)* doubt.

9 **pig Latin** *(n)* a language game in which English words are reordered and understood by those privy to its attributes.

10 **embroil** *(v)* involve in a difficult situation. *(s)* enmesh, entangle. *(ant)* exclude.

11 **slay** *(v)* kill in a violent and brutal way (past participle: slain). *(s)* murder, butcher, slaughter.

12 **contort** *(v)* bend or twist out of normal shape. *(s)* distort, deform. *(ant)* straighten.

whispered. 'The ring's power is much **diminished**[1], as Llywelyn no longer controls the bracelet. We must act fast, lest they catch me out of my cell.'

'What can I do?' Dylan asked, catching up with the conversation.

'Everything Rhys said about Dewi and my mother is true. She has stolen the Gwalch Gem with him.'

Cad glanced over at the sleeping boy, who shared her **precious**[2] secret. 'Have Rhys help you whilst I'm confined. Dewi and Siân could not have snatched the bracelet from Prince John and lured in a wolf alone. They have **accomplices**[3] who still plot in this castle. We must find them.'

'But where do we begin?'

'I'm not sure. I guess Bryn Davis, Jack Jones and their band of **bandits**[4] are as good a place as any. Just remain extra vigilant. Keep your eyes and ears wide open for anything untoward.'

'I will, Cad. Of course.'

'With decent behaviour and a tad of luck, Sir Robert will release me early. I will visit you at night if I can. In the meantime, if you have news, send it via May. And keep this between us. Don't tell the little fellow over there.'

She gestured towards Rhys, forgetting Dylan couldn't see her.

'I don't want him to know about the invisibility ring or May's messages,' she added. 'I don't want to worry him more than need be.'

Dylan nodded, his eyes bright but fearful.

'Did May deliver my note to you?' Cad asked.

'Yes.' Dylan nodded like an eager puppy. 'To hear of the tower **horrified**[5] me and Rhys. I'm so relieved you're in the better dungeons and being looked after,' he added.

'Have you fed Fishy?' she asked, a serious look on her invisible face.

'Yes, she's **thriving**[6] – quite strong now,' said Dylan. 'And noisy. It will be hard to conceal her soon.'

---

1 **diminish** *(v)* become or make less. *(s)* reduce, decrease, lessen. *(ant)* increase.

2 **precious** *(adj)* of great value or importance. *(s)* extraordinary, special. *(ant)* unimportant.

3 **accomplice** *(n)* a person who helps another commit a crime. *(s)* co-conspirator, collaborator.

4 **bandit** *(n)* an outlaw belonging to a gang. *(s)* criminal, crook.

5 **horrify** *(v)* to fill someone with horror. *(s)* scare, alarm, panic. *(ant)* comfort.

6 **thrive** *(v)* do well. *(s)* flourish, grow, blossom. *(ant)* decline, deteriorate.

'Once able, I will find somewhere safe for her until she can **fend for herself**[1], for they'll forbid me to keep her,' Cad said. 'Now, I must leave. I am losing count of how long I have worn the ring.'

'Go, Cad. Hurry. Some will lock you away for **sorcery**[2] if they discover your ring. People who would steal it from you.'

Cad gave Dylan a tight hug, which she knew didn't feel quite like a normal **embrace**[3], but was almost as good.

'Dylan, open the door for me and peek out as I leave, lest someone sees it open unaided and dies of fright on the spot.'

At the door, and whispering farewell to Dylan, Cad knew little time remained before she reappeared. With no choice left, she must risk the dogs and take the short dash across the bailey and into the keep's towers. Sir Robert's quarters were high in the royal wing for safekeeping, ironically close to her dungeon. To make the **diversion**[4] to **investigate**[5] Sir Robert **posed**[6] a huge time **gamble**[7], but she must risk it while she could, and before it became too late to do so.

---

1 **fend for oneself** *(v)* look after oneself without help. *(s)* hold one's own, manage alone. *(ant)* be cared for.

2 **sorcery** *(n)* the use of magic. *(s)* witchcraft, conjuring, enchantment.

3 **embrace** *(n)* the act of holding in one's arms. *(s)* hug, squeeze, clinch. *(ant)* exclusion.

4 **diversion** *(n)* the action of turning away from one's course. *(s)* redirection, rerouting.

5 **investigate** *(v)* look into. *(s)* explore, inspect, consider, scrutinise, examine.

6 **pose** *(v)* present or be (a problem). *(s)* cause, constitute.

7 **gamble** *(n)* a risky action. *(s)* uncertainty, speculation, risk. *(ant)* safeguard.

CHAPTER EIGHT

An Untimely Reappearance

Now outside her room, and still invisible, Cad faced the bailey and stood tall, steeling herself for the sprint of a lifetime. She sucked in a deep breath and **bolted**[1], scattering the pork scraps pilfered from the kitchen to **divert**[2] the dogs, who pounced, gobbling them down with **gusto**[3]. Then, with wings on her heels, Cad sprinted to face the stone stairs which led to the upper floors' chambers.

I must work harder in the tilt yard, she thought, **ascending**[4] the keep's tower at speed, which proved **gruelling**[5] as she fought to **quell**[6] her noisy panting. When she reached her dungeon, she stopped to catch her breath, but this was a harsh reminder that time was slipping by, and she could reappear at any moment. The risks of being caught out of her cell were enormous, yet she pushed on. Finally, when she reached the uppermost level, forcing even breaths, she stopped again, her hands on her thighs, her head bent low. Once her breathing calmed, and with a glance in all directions, Cad crept from the stairs into the corridor leading to Dewi's quarters. In his absence, they now belonged to Sir Robert Evans.

---

1 **bolt** *(v)* move or run suddenly. *(s)* sprint, dash, dart, hurtle. *(ant)* linger.

2 **divert** *(v)* cause a change of course or direction. *(s)* distract, deter, redirect. *(ant)* focus.

3 **gusto** *(n)* enthusiasm and enjoyment in doing something. *(s)* relish, delight, pleasure. *(ant)* distaste.

4 **ascend** *(v)* go up or climb up. *(s)* mount, scale. *(ant)* descend, drop.

5 **gruelling** *(adj)* extremely demanding and tiring. *(s)* exhausting, arduous, strenuous. *(ant)* easy.

6 **quell** *(v)* suppress (put an end to) and silence. *(s)* subdue, quash, control. *(ant)* intensify.

Fortunately for Cad, the keep seemed quiet; everyone slept. She was almost there and her ring had held out thus far. Lady Luck was in Cad's corner. As she scuttled along the final section of passageway, candles winking at her from their sconces, her target in view, a door flew open just before her, almost striking her face. Startled, she stumbled sideways, tumbling and bashing her head on a metal sconce that held a flaming candle. The collision knocked the candle **askew**[1], its **scorching**[2] wax streaking across Cad's cheek, leaving **searing**[3] pain in its wake. Her hand flew to her mouth as she **mustered**[4] the **resolve**[5] to suppress a scream. But more pressing than that, the man now entering the passageway, Sir Robert Evans, witnessed the candle fly from its sconce unaided, **spewing**[6] its **molten**[7] wax into the air.

'Who goes there?' Evans barked, his face **ashen**[8]. 'Guard!' he yelled, stooping and scrabbling to gather up the parchments he'd dropped in shock. Cad **seized**[9] her chance, ducking through the open door and into the chambers as Evans fumbled with his papers on the floor.

Once inside, hoping nothing else would spike her wheel, Cad **scoured**[10] Evans's study area, bewildered by the array of parchments strewn over an enormous table. Sir Robert's quarters were not a restful place, but an area for planning, like a war room, the likes of which she'd never before seen at Catrin. In **desperation**[11], and worried her discovery was **imminent**[12], she **pored**[13] over the papers, trying to absorb their contents. Cad was neither **navigator**[14] nor **architect**[15], but

---

1 **askew** *(adj)* at an angle, out of the usual position, wrong. *(s)* awry, askance. *(ant)* straight.

2 **scorching** *(adj)* extreme heat. *(s)* burning, blistering, searing. *(ant)* cold.

3 **searing** *(adj)* intense. *(s)* agonising, severe, extreme. *(ant)* mild.

4 **muster** *(v)* summon up (a response, attitude or feeling). *(s)* gather, raise, call on. *(ant)* disperse.

5 **resolve** *(n)* firm determination. *(s)* steadfastness, willpower. *(ant)* indecision.

6 **spew** *(v)* expel or pour out rapidly. *(s)* eject, emit, spout, spill. *(ant)* trickle.

7 **molten** *(adj)* made liquid by heating. *(s)* flowing, soft, fluid, liquid. *(ant)* solidified.

8 **ashen** *(adj)* pale because of shock, fear or illness. *(s)* wan, pallid, sallow, ghostly, grey. *(ant)* rosy.

9 **seize** *(v)* take (an opportunity) quickly. *(s)* snatch, grab, grasp. *(ant)* relinquish.

10 **scour** *(v)* look or search thoroughly. *(s)* scrutinise, study, inspect. *(ant)* overlook.

11 **desperation** *(n)* a state of rashness or distress. *(s)* defiance, audacity, boldness. *(ant)* satisfaction.

12 **imminent** *(adj)* about to happen. *(s)* pending, forthcoming, likely, immediate. *(ant)* remote.

13 **pore** *(v)* be absorbed in reading or studying something. *(s)* examine, inspect, scrutinise.

14 **navigator** *(n)* someone who guides or steers something. *(s)* wayfinder, steersperson.

15 **architect** *(n)* someone who designs buildings and often supervises their construction. *(s)* designer, planner.

an **amateur**[1] could fathom these to be maps of some sort. Yet these charts were different, their markings **unique**[2] – **untranslatable**[3].

As time tore by, Cad prayed the ring's magic would last. To her **chagrin**[4], she found that to count in her head and **decipher**[5] the **symbols**[6] at the same time was too tricky. Indeed, it proved impossible, so the counting took second place to map reading. That's when the **scales fell**[7] from her eyes.

Tunnels! They're tunnels!

Before her lay **labyrinthine**[8] tunnels. A **network**[9] created by Sir Robert beneath the mountains of **Snowdonia**[10]. Cad so wished she could scoop up some of the smaller maps, but pieces of parchment floating unaided through the corridors would cause **chaos**[11].

Out in the corridor, the increasing **clamour**[12] from the gathering guards reminded Cad she must escape unseen, and right now. If she'd calculated correctly, not long remained of the ring's magic.

'The passage is empty, sire,' barked a **gruff**[13] voice from outside the room. 'It seems the candle's heat caused it to **warp**[14] and fall from its sconce.' The guard desperately tried to reassure Evans, whose face looked as cold as an icy sea.

'Fine. **Resume**[15] your posts,' Evans finally barked, sounding **flustered**[16].

---

1 **amateur** *(n)* a person who is inept or incompetent (not yet good at). *(s)* novice, beginner, apprentice. *(ant)* expert.

2 **unique** *(adj)* unlike anything else. *(s)* distinctive, individual. *(ant)* common.

3 **untranslatable** *(adj)* a word or phrase which cannot be made sense of in another language.

4 **chagrin** *(n)* annoyance or distress. *(s)* disappointment, exasperation, irritation. *(ant)* delight, joy.

5 **decipher** *(v)* succeed in understanding or identifying something. *(s)* decode, decrypt. *(ant)* cipher.

6 **symbol** *(n)* a mark or character that represents something. *(s)* sign, ideogram.

7 **scales fall** (from one's eyes) (phrase) one is no longer deceived.

8 **labyrinthine** *(adj)* like a labyrinth (network of tunnels). *(s)* maze-like, winding, meandering.

9 **network** *(n)* a complex system of something. *(s)* maze, structure, web.

10 **Snowdonia** *(n)* a mountainous region of north-west Wales.

11 **chaos** *(n)* total disorder and confusion. *(s)* mayhem, pandemonium. *(ant)* order, tranquillity.

12 **clamour** *(n)* a loud noise, especially from people yelling. *(s)* din, racket, tumult. *(ant)* quiet.

13 **gruff** *(adj)* rough and deep (voice), or abrupt in manner. *(s)* brusque, curt, stern. *(ant)* friendly.

14 **warp** *(v)* become or make bent or out of shape. *(s)* distort, buckle, misshape. *(ant)* straighten.

15 **resume** *(v)* continue or begin again (after pausing or an interruption). *(s)* back to, restart, recommence. *(ant)* stop.

16 **flustered** *(adj)* agitated and confused. *(s)* unsettled, alarmed, disconcerted, perturbed. *(ant)* calm.

I must leave now! Cad thought, her heart clashing like **cymbals**[1].

As Cad made a dash for the open door, to her horror, she saw her hand floating in mid air, her emerald ring now dull in the candlelight. Her time was up. She was reappearing, and Sir Robert, parchments now gathered in his arms, was heading straight for her, his eyes black and ravenous like those of a shark.

As she watched her hand grow in size, she jigged on the spot, torn between which way to go. Evans was almost upon her. Cad was cornered. Her heart hammered in her chest, then immediately sank like a stone as she realised she was **scuppered**[2]. She must hide; it was her only choice. Hide and hope that before dawn, a slim chance to slip back to her dungeon might arise.

In **defeat**[3], Cad made to dive beneath the four-poster's **draperies**[4], when a **cacophony**[5] of confusion rising from the corridor stopped her. Evans wailed and the guards grunted and groaned **amid**[6] sounds of clattering and chaos. Evans **howled**[7] again, his parchments spewing back across the floor. Cad, seeing her chance, fled out through the open door. Her arm, now fully visible, and akin to a **dismembered**[8] limb, floated unaided through the air like a **ghoul**[9] with no body.

What in heaven? Cad thought, as she darted unnoticed past the **tumult**[10] in the passageway.

A short, tri-coloured terrier had attached itself to Sir Robert's rear, and was hanging on by its teeth. As Cad **scooted**[11] by, the dog loosened its grip, and then, like a miniature **greyhound**[12], it **hared**[13] along the passage before the guards or Robert Evans could catch it.

Cad didn't recognise the wire-haired dog that had saved her skin. And just thankful for

---

1 **cymbals** *(n)* round metal disks which are brought together in a clashing motion to make a sound.

2 **scupper** *(v)* prevent from working or succeeding. *(s)* ruin, thwart, foil. *(ant)* help.

3 **defeat** *(n)* loss. *(s)* failure, losing. *(ant)* win, triumph.

4 **drapery** *(n)* cloth which hangs in loose folds, especially curtains and clothes. *(s)* hanging.

5 **cacophony** *(n)* an unpleasantly harsh mix of sounds. *(s)* din, racket, noise. *(ant)* harmony.

6 **amid** *(prep)* surrounded by, in the middle of. *(s)* among, amidst, between, during. *(ant)* outside.

7 **howl** *(v)* make a howling (crying) sound. *(s)* yowl, groan, wail, shriek.

8 **dismember** *(v)* cut off the limbs of something. *(s)* disjoint.

9 **ghoul** *(n)* a phantom or spirit, especially an evil one. *(s)* bogeyman, fiend, ghost. *(ant)* angel.

10 **tumult** *(n)* a confused and loud noise. *(s)* commotion, chaos, disturbance. *(ant)* peace.

11 **scoot** *(v)* go somewhere quickly. *(s)* hasten, hare, dash. *(ant)* stroll, amble.

12 **greyhound** *(n)* a tall slender, speedy dog used since ancient times for hunting but now bred for racing.

13 **hare** *(v)* run with great speed and agility. *(s)* race, bolt, sprint, fly. *(ant)* dawdle.

its liking of Sir Robert's **rear**[1], she sprinted down the passageway to the stairs leading to the opposite tower. Then panting like the dog that had just saved her, two at a time, she climbed the steps to her cell. As she reached her door, clutching a stitch in her side, like paint brushed onto a blank **canvas**[2] in smoothly applied strokes, her body reappeared like a **masterpiece**[3] before her very eyes.

---

1 **rear** *(n)* backside. *(s)* bottom, bum, rump, butt, buttocks.

2 **canvas** *(n)* a pale-coloured cloth used as a surface for a painting.

3 **masterpiece** *(n)* an outstanding work of artistry, workmanship or skill. *(s)* sensation, showpiece.

CHAPTER NINE

Disappeared

'Master Cad, wake up! Wake up!'

Disorientated, Cad shot upright to see Goodwife Hughes's plump figure bustling into the cell, her face dough-like, her **demeanour**[1] **agitated**[2].

'What is it?' Cad asked, gathering her unruly thoughts, her eyes half-lidded in sleep.

After returning from her foray in the castle, she had not long been **abed**[3], and her fuzzy brain and **bleary**[4] eyes struggled to follow Goodwife Hughes's **blathering**[5].

'Oh, Master Cad, it is **dire**[6]. Our poor ruler. What terrible troubles he must bear,' she sobbed, making a noise like a distressed goose, her body **heaving**[7] in dismay.

That **statement**[8] roused Cad at once. Where was Llywelyn?

'What is it, woman?' Cad barked, **instant**[9] regret halting her meanness as she **vaulted**[10]

---

1 **demeanour** *(n)* outward bearing or behaviour. *(s)* appearance, attitude, conduct.

2 **agitated** *(adj)* appearing or feeling nervous or troubled. *(s)* ruffled, perturbed, disconcerted. *(ant)* relaxed.

3 **abed** *(adv)* in bed.

4 **bleary** *(adj)* unfocused and dull from sleeping. *(s)* hazy, blurry, weary, unclear. *(ant)* lively, clear.

5 **blather** *(v)* talk boring nonsense. *(s)* babble, prattle, gabber, jabber, blether.

6 **dire** *(adj)* serious or urgent. *(s)* terrible, dreadful, appalling, frightful. *(ant)* favourable.

7 **heave** *(v)* rise and fall. *(s)* roll, billow.

8 **statement** *(n)* a clear or definite expression of something. *(s)* declaration, divulgence, utterance.

9 **instant** *(adj)* happening at once. *(s)* immediate, instantaneous. *(ant)* delayed.

10 **vault** *(v)* leap or spring by supporting or propelling oneself with one's hands. *(s)* jump, bound.

out of bed. 'Plain speak,' she urged, her tone softer.

'It is … It is, the baby,' cried Goodwife Hughes.

'Goodwife, calm.' Cad gently took her by the shoulder. 'Calm. What is it?'

'The baby. Prince John. Someone took him.'

'Took him?' Cad snapped. 'What do you mean "took him"?' It was she who now **rambled**[1] in shock.

'It is a mystery, like the devil's work.' Goodwife Hughes fussed with her kirtle as if bothered by fleas.

Cad ducked her chin in a 'go on' gesture, her patience waning fast.

Seemingly finding her **wits**[2], Goodwife Hughes continued. 'Sir Robert stationed several guards outside the prince's bedchamber, but no one entered or left. Nurse Joan slept by his crib in her **truckle bed**[3] until dawn, when she raised the alarm. She is **distraught**[4]. It seems Prince John … well, it seems he just vanished.'

Cad's mind raced, her stomach watery with nerves. If magic was **afoot**[5], then it must be the Gwalch Gem bracelet. Babies do not vanish. She touched the emerald ring hidden in her tunic. When she had returned in the early hours, the wax seal to her door was **intact**[6]. No spies lurked. At least she didn't need to worry about that problem – yet.

'From where did they snatch Prince John?' Cad asked.

'He was in the high keep. In the opposite tower from here. By Sir Robert's rooms.'

Cad realised she might have been outside Prince John's bedchamber just before, or after, his kidnapping, assuming he *was* **abducted**[7], that is.

With her mind fighting to find a solution, Cad thought to beg Evans for **mercy**[8], to release her

---

1 **ramble** *(v)* talk at length in a confused manner. *(s)* chatter, blather, babble, gabble.

2 **wits** *(n)* good sense. *(s)* common sense.

3 **truckle bed** *(n)* (also known as a trundle bed) a bed on wheels that can be stored underneath a bigger bed.

4 **distraught** *(adj)* extremely worried and upset. *(s)* distressed, desperate. *(ant)* calm, serene.

5 **afoot** *(adj)* in preparation or progress. *(s)* happening, underway.

6 **intact** *(adj)* not impaired or damaged. *(s)* complete, unbroken. *(ant)* broken.

7 **abduct** *(v)* take away by force. *(s)* kidnap, seize. *(ant)* release.

8 **mercy** *(n)* forgiveness and compassion. *(s)* clemency, pity, sympathy. *(ant)* cruelty.

from this **wretched**[1] dungeon, where she was **utterly**[2] useless. He knew her secret, and thus her **inevitable**[3] desperation to search for her baby brother. But a **niggle**[4] inside warned her to stay covert, that using the ring might be the best way to find John. After all, with good behaviour, she might be released early. And if the **culprits**[5] thought her locked up, perhaps their vigilance might **falter**[6].

To the best of Cad's knowledge, no one but Llywelyn, Dylan, Siân and perhaps Dewi knew she possessed the ring – at least she hoped it was just them. With the ring, she could **surveil**[7] the castle unseen. It wasn't ideal, but sneaking would work so long as she was swift, and speedier than last night when she'd reappeared too soon. If that **wiry**[8] little terrier had not bitten Sir Robert's rear, he'd have caught her for sure.

'What is being done to ensure Prince John's return?' Cad asked, her thoughts whirring.

'The castle is in **turmoil**[9]: guards **ransacking**[10] every **nook**[11] and cranny in search of the **infant**[12]. Robert Evans has **dispatched**[13] a fast rider to bring Prince Llywelyn back from his quest.'

As Mrs Hughes uttered those words, a realisation struck Cad. If Llywelyn returned early because of Prince John's **abduction**[14], then Siân and Dewi would have more chance to escape Llywelyn's realm.

'Who did Sir Robert send, do you know?' Cad asked.

'I do, for this is how I learned they dispatched a messenger.'

---

1 **wretched** *(adj)* extremely unfortunate. *(s)* desolate, cheerless, bleak. *(ant)* cheerful.
2 **utterly** *(adv)* to an extreme degree. *(s)* absolutely, completely, totally. *(ant)* somewhat.
3 **inevitable** *(adj)* certain to happen. *(s)* inescapable, unpreventable. *(ant)* avoidable, uncertain.
4 **niggle** *(n)* a trivial annoyance or discomfort. *(s)* worry, concern.
5 **culprit** *(n)* a person or thing responsible for a misdeed. *(s)* offender, criminal, baddie. *(ant)* victim.
6 **falter** *(v)* lose momentum or strength. *(s)* stall, waver, diminish. *(ant)* rally, continue.
7 **surveil** *(v)* keep under surveillance (watch closely). *(s)* observe, monitor.
8 **wiry** *(adj)* resembling wire in texture or form. *(s)* coarse, rough, bristly. *(ant)* soft, sleek.
9 **turmoil** *(n)* a state of confusion, disturbance or uncertainty. *(s)* chaos, disorder. *(ant)* order.
10 **ransack** *(v)* search thoroughly, causing damage or harm. *(s)* rifle, comb, turn over.
11 **nook** *(n)* a corner or recess. *(s)* alcove, niche, cranny. *(ant)* open space.
12 **infant** *(n)* a baby or very young child. *(s)* babe, bairn, little one. *(ant)* adult.
13 **dispatch** *(v)* send off for a purpose. *(s)* consign, direct. *(ant)* bring back.
14 **abduction** *(n)* the action of taking someone against their will, often using force. *(s)* kidnap, seizure.

'Goodwife Hughes, pray tell,' Cad said with **burgeoning**[1] impatience. The woman was clearly not telling all.

'I am aware because Sir Robert sent my son, Hugh. His apprentice.'

Cad watched as Mrs Hughes stared into space; her expression wrought with concern.

'Goodwife, please continue,' Cad **coaxed**[2]. 'Why does this bother you so?'

The woman's eyes **misted**[3], and her chest heaved as if **stifling**[4] a wail. Cad forced patience and a sympathetic expression, encouraging the goodwife to speak.

'Many skilled squires remain in the castle,' the woman eventually muttered. 'There are **myriad**[5] expert horsemen, yet Evans sent Hugh off on Master Dewi's battle **destrier**[6]. Hugh will struggle to handle that beast of a horse. I fear he will come to harm.' The woman made an odd noise – a cross between a **foraging**[7] hog and an angry goose – one Cad now recognised when the goodwife became over-emotional.

Cad, surprised that Dewi's **stallion**[8] still remained in the castle stables, pondered the woman's comments. Even though he cared nothing for animals, Dewi **prided**[9] himself on his jet-black destrier, Midnight, for he was indeed a magnificent beast. Taller than all other **steeds**[10] in the stables, the stallion was a **bold**[11] horse and not for the **faint-hearted**[12]. Goodwife Hughes's boy was an architect's apprentice. Why in heaven had Sir Robert sent *him* out on that stallion?

Why send Hugh at all? Cad wondered.

Surely, the squire, Bryn Davis, would have been the obvious choice? Davis prevailed in the tilt yard. To Cad's chagrin, Davis was the most skilled rider of all the squires. She **mulled**[13] over

---

1 **burgeoning** *(adj)* growing or increasing rapidly. *(s)* mounting, ballooning. *(ant)* dwindling.

2 **coax** *(v)* persuade gently to do something. *(s)* cajole, urge. *(ant)* force, compel.

3 **mist** *(v)* (of the eyes) fill up. *(s)* moisten. *(ant)* dry.

4 **stifle** *(v)* restrain a reaction or stop oneself acting on an emotion. *(s)* suppress, repress, curb. *(ant)* encourage.

5 **myriad** *(adj)* extremely great in number *(s)* many, numerous, multiple. *(ant)* few.

6 **destrier** *(n)* a heavy-set, large medieval knight's war horse. Also known as the Great Horse due to its importance.

7 **forage** *(v)* search widely for (often food). *(s)* seek, hunt, rummage, scour, grub, root.

8 **stallion** *(n)* a male horse that has not been gelded (neutered).

9 **pride** *(v)* be proud (happy with) of one's skill or quality. *(s)* congratulate, boast. *(ant)* feel ashamed.

10 **steed** *(n)* a horse that one can ride.

11 **bold** *(adj)* lacking fear. *(s)* courageous, brave, daring. *(ant)* timid, scared.

12 **faint-hearted** *(adj)* a person who lacks courage (bravery). *(s)* timid, craven, cowardly. *(ant)* bold, brave.

13 **mull** *(v)* think about. *(s)* ponder, muse, reflect. *(ant)* disregard.

Evans's actions. The boy, Hugh, was an odd choice – a risk. He may be thrown from his **mount**[1] and never arrive. Little wonder Goodwife Hughes was so distraught.

'Please, do not fret so. I am sure Sir Robert had good reason to send your son. He must place great trust in his abilities,' reassured Cad, placing her arm around the woman's heaving shoulders. 'Come now. Dry your tears.'

The woman took a **grubby**[2] handkerchief from her pocket and mopped away her sniffles with a honk.

'Thank you, Master Cad. You are a kind **soul**[3].' And with that, she blew, honking again.

'Now, now,' said Cad. 'When did your son leave? What was his **destination**[4]?'

'Sir Robert sent my son at once, but I know not where. Why did Sir Robert not search for Prince John before **alerting**[5] Prince Llywelyn? It's all something of a **stew**[6] really,' the woman cried, wiping her eyes again.

Why indeed? Cad wondered.

'I guess Sir Robert had no choice but to alert Llywelyn. Our prince may wish to return without delay,' Cad replied, **unconvinced**[7]. With a forced half-smile, Cad tried her best to comfort the **fraught**[8] lady and win her trust.

'You are right, Master Cad,' said Goodwife Hughes, somewhat calmer. She pointed to Cad's desk. 'I brought you some breakfast, and I will return at **midday**[9] with your proper meal and a ewer of fresh drinking water.' Then, pointing at Cad's face and wrinkling her nose, she said, 'I think perhaps you need a wash. You smell like roast hog.'

Cad put her hands behind her back, remembering the pork scraps she'd **hurled**[10] earlier for

---

1 **mount** *(n)* a horse that is suitable for riding.

2 **grubby** *(adj)* dirty. *(s)* grimy, soiled, unwashed. *(ant)* clean.

3 **soul** *(n)* figuratively, a person. *(s)* individual, human being.

4 **destination** *(n)* the place where someone or something is going to. *(s)* objective, target. *(ant)* starting point.

5 **alert** *(v)* warn of a problem or danger. *(s)* notify, tell, forewarn. *(ant)* keep silent.

6 **stew** *(n)* a state of difficulty. *(s)* mess, muddle, predicament. *(ant)* boon, benefit.

7 **unconvinced** *(adj)* not sure something is true or reliable. *(s)* uncertain, unsure. *(ant)* convinced.

8 **fraught** *(adj)* stressed and extremely anxious. *(s)* tense, apprehensive, troubled. *(ant)* calm.

9 **midday** *(n)* the middle of the day. *(s)* noon. *(ant)* midnight.

10 **hurl** *(v)* throw with force. *(s)* fling, lob, launch, pitch. *(ant)* hold, catch.

the dogs, surprised they'd not all followed her **scent**[1] back to the tower.

'Indeed,' replied Cad, abashed – she stank.

When Goodwife Hughes finally left, Cad sponged her hands and face, then ate a **hunk**[2] of bread, cheese and apple, all washed down with cool water from the castle's well. Although a pee-pot sat in her room, she would visit one of the better **privy**[3] **garderobes**[4] when she ventured out.

Now brimming with concern, Cad flopped onto the bed, her **gritty**[5] eyes desperate to close. Regardless, she forced them open, pondering the goodwife's **revelations**[6]. Why had Robert Evans jumped to dispatch a fast rider so soon? And one so inexperienced as Hugh Hughes? This problem was an odd sum – one that did not **tally**[7].

Unable to come to any **conclusions**[8], Cad contemplated Sir Robert, who she'd known all her life. Llywelyn had invited Evans into the magical order of the Knights Hawk, bestowing upon him the powers of Instinct and longevity. Sir Robert's presence at Cadwaladr Castle had been constant. Cad was aware Evans had **counselled**[9] Llywelyn *against* her knight's training, warning that Llywelyn's **flagrant**[10] **breach**[11] of rules would **sully**[12] his reputation if discovered. Evans was **bitterly**[13] disappointed when Llywelyn had **subsequently**[14] ignored that **counsel**[15]. Llywelyn had **overruled**[16] Sir Robert, allowing, as Cad was then, his only child to conceal her

---

1 **scent** *(n)* a distinctive smell (often a pleasant one). *(s)* trace, whiff, aroma. *(ant)* stench, stink.

2 **hunk** *(n)* a large piece of something, often food. *(s)* chunk, wedge, portion. *(ant)* morsel, scrap.

3 **privy** *(adj)* private. *(s)* separate. *(ant)* shared, communal.

4 **garderobe** *(n)* a toilet situated in a medieval building.

5 **gritty** *(adj)* covered with or containing grit (dirt or earth of some sort). *(s)* sandy, grainy.

6 **revelation** *(n)* a previously unknown fact that has been disclosed (revealed) to others. *(s)* divulgence. *(ant)* concealment.

7 **tally** *(v)* add up, agree or correspond to. *(s)* match, work.

8 **conclusion** *(n)* a decision reached by thought and reasoning. *(s)* judgement, opinion, verdict.

9 **counsel** *(v)* give formal advice to someone. *(s)* advise, direct, instruct.

10 **flagrant** *(adj)* offensively and without regret. *(s)* blatant, obvious. *(ant)* slight.

11 **breach** *(n)* the act of breaking rules, the law or a code of conduct. *(s)* violation, contravention.

12 **sully** *(v)* damage the integrity (honesty) of. *(s)* tarnish, taint, stain. *(ant)* purify.

13 **bitterly** *(adv)* to a great degree. *(s)* extremely, deeply, fiercely. *(ant)* happily.

14 **subsequently** *(adv)* after something has happened. *(s)* later, afterwards. *(ant)* previously.

15 **counsel** *(n)* formal advice. *(s)* recommendation, guidance, input.

16 **overrule** *(v)* use one's authority to reject or disallow something. *(s)* invalidate, veto. *(ant)* approve.

identity and break with all **custom**[1] and **convention**[2]. The **unorthodoxy**[3] **unsettled**[4] the Knight Hawk, Evans.

Cad often wondered if Sir Robert might be jealous of her. Before Llywelyn had rescued Cad from the well, Evans had been closer to the childless couple than even the prince's own brother, Dewi. Most courtiers realised Llywelyn **confided**[5] more in Evans, placing his standing over that of Dewi's. Thus, Cad wondered if Dewi was jealous of Evans – it was complicated.

Now older, Cad understood the complex web of emotions that governed relationships. Apart from her hot-headed temper, her father said Cad read people well for one aged around ten – they knew not her precise birth date. And right now, something told her she should pay closer attention to those maps in Sir Robert's rooms.

With no time to lose, Cad removed the hairpin from its leather sheath. She **whipped**[6] the glinting ring from the secret **lining**[7] of her tunic and placed it on her left thumb. Then, she pulled out one hair from the longest part of her pageboy's haircut and pinched it hard lest she drop it. With her ear pressed to the dungeon's door, she placed the emerald hawk into the lock and held her breath. Again, like a knife slicing through butter, the lock turned. Cad grasped the pin to ensure its invisibility along with hers, then she pressed her right thumb onto the emerald hawk. In a dazzling flash of vivid green, she was gone.

I must hurry. I cannot risk reappearing.

Counting in her head, Cad left the cell and, as gently as its size allowed, closed the door behind her. This time, Cad had no candle wax to use, so she must **improvise**[8]. Falling to her knees, still holding the **strand**[9] of hair, she stuck her little finger into her ear. Careful not to

---

1 **custom** *(n)* a traditional (regular) and accepted way of behaving. *(s)* practice, convention. *(ant)* departure.

2 **convention** *(n)* the way that something is usually done. *(s)* rule, standard, custom. *(ant)* innovation.

3 **unorthodoxy** *(n)* someting different to what is accepted, usual and traditional. *(s)* unusual. *(ant)* orthodoxy.

4 **unsettle** *(v)* cause to feel uneasy or anxious. *(s)* disturb, upset, perturb. *(ant)* settle.

5 **confide** *(v)* trust someone enough to tell them about a private or secret matter. *(s)* entrust, disclose. *(ant)* withhold.

6 **whip** *(v)* snatch suddenly and quickly. *(s)* tear, grab.

7 **lining** *(n)* a layer of material which covers the inside of something.

8 **improvise** *(v)* work with whatever means you have available at the time. *(s)* concoct, devise, rig.

9 **strand** *(n)* a thin lock or single piece of hair. *(s)* wisp, tress.

probe[1] too deeply, she scooped out a blob of earwax and fixed the hair across the door with the goo. Once satisfied the hair had stuck in place, she stood, turned and scooted down the stone steps, knowing that if on her return the hair was gone, then someone was indeed spying on her.

1 **probe** *(v)* dig. *(s)* explore, prod, examine, poke.

CHAPTER TEN

Foul Fowl Feathers

The castle's guards, probably searching for baby John, were not stationed at their usual posts, so, **taking liberties**[1], Cad used the royal privy as quickly as possible. Invisible, she was now in the opposite tower of the high keep, near Sir Robert's rooms, and armed with morsels of hard cheese to **ward off**[2] the dogs.

As the sun rose, leaving the sky pink behind it, she guessed it was a little after dawn. The **cockerels**[3] **crowed**[4], and the castle, for this time of day, was **frantically**[5] busy, and an air of panic **pervaded**[6]. She must move quicker than last night, and if Dewi was gaining control of the bracelet, then her magic jewellery may **cease**[7] working altogether.

Clinging to the hope that the distant power from the Gwalch Gem bracelet had **sufficiently**[8] refilled the ring, Cad counted in her head, knowing she could not risk reappearing in the bustle of the day. When the bracelet had been close by, the hawk's **telling**[9] sparkle resumed in no time

1 **take liberties** (phrase) take advantage of someone or something. *(s)* show disrespect, act with overfamiliarity.

2 **ward off** *(v)* stop someone or something from harming one. *(s)* repel, fend off, keep off.

3 **cockerel** *(n)* a young male chicken (cock).

4 **crow** *(v)* (referring to a male chicken) utter its cry. *(s)* squawk, screech, caw.

5 **frantically** *(adv)* in a frantic (disorganised) way. *(s)* desperately, madly. *(ant)* calmly.

6 **pervade** *(v)* spread throughout, be present and apparent. *(s)* penetrate, encompass. *(ant)* evacuate, drain.

7 **cease** *(v)* stop, end or finish. *(s)* halt, quit, discontinue. *(ant)* start, continue.

8 **sufficiently** *(adv)* in a way that is sufficient (enough). *(s)* adequately, appropriately. *(ant)* insufficiently.

9 **telling** *(adj)* having a revealing effect. *(s)* significant, giveaway, powerful. *(ant)* insignificant.

at all, but now, Cad must risk using the ring when it still remained somewhat dull, for she had not the time to wait. How would she explain invisibility to Sir Robert, who she hoped did not know she possessed Siân's ring? Although he had probably been the one to **design**[1] it for Siân.

Now **confident**[2] of **foul play**[3] surrounding John, Cad headed straight for Sir Robert's chambers hoping that Prince John's room would be adjacent to them. Surely Sir Robert would have **housed**[4] her baby brother close by to watch over him along with his nurses? Goodwife Hughes had said no one had entered or left those rooms. The stationed guards had seen nothing.

Cad moved through the tower as swiftly as she could while remaining silent. Three court ladies, looking oddly **bedraggled**[5], huddled into a corner in the stone passageway leading to Sir Robert's quarters. One **wept**[6]. Cad stopped as close by as she could and cocked an ear towards them.

'There are rumours that the baby has truly been devoured by a great wolf this time,' the lady sobbed. Cad's ears pricked up. 'There is blood in his crib and on the sheets,' she added, pointing to an open door beyond Sir Robert's rooms.

'But how would such a beast enter and leave carrying a baby?' asked another of the three. 'The guards heard or saw nothing. No one entered or left. Three men **corroborate**[7] this story.'

Cad's stomach knotted as she inched past the ladies and into the baby's room. Thankfully it was empty. She could search it **unhindered**[8] as the guards and servants toiled, scouring the castle and its grounds for Prince John.

Fear flooded her thoughts as she approached the ornate **canopied**[9] crib and pulled back its **silken**[10] **drapes**[11].

---

1 **design** *(v)* plan or draw an object before it is then made. *(s)* make, invent, create, produce, fashion.

2 **confident** *(adj)* feeling certainty about something. *(s)* sure, convinced. *(ant)* doubtful, unsure.

3 **foul play** *(n)* criminal behaviour. *(s)* villainy, crime, wrongdoing.

4 **house** *(v)* provide space for or accommodate (keep in a certain place). *(s)* hold, retain. *(ant)* evict.

5 **bedraggled** *(adj)* dishevelled (messy). *(s)* unkempt, rumpled. *(ant)* neat.

6 **weep** *(v)* cry tears (past tense: wept). *(s)* sob, mewl, wail, blub.

7 **corroborate** *(v)* give support or confirm something. *(s)* agree, verify, validate. *(ant)* disprove, deny.

8 **unhindered** *(adj)* not hindered (obstructed). *(s)* unobstructed, unhampered. *(ant)* hindered.

9 **canopy** *(v)* cover with a canopy. *(s)* enclose, shroud. *(ant)* expose, open.

10 **silken** *(adj)* made of silk (a fabric produced by silkworms).

11 **drape** *(n)* curtain.

'Heaven above!'

A chill **scudded**[1] through her. Feeling **unmoored**[2], she gasped in horror at the sight of the bloody scene. She'd seen blood many times, but to see it here in her brother's crib, staining his white sheets **crimson**[3], she **retched**[4], but thankfully nothing came up. No wonder Goodwife Hughes had been so distraught and had kept the **horrific**[5] detail from Cad. It took all Cad's strength to suppress a scream; a cry that would have raised even more havoc amongst the ladies huddled outside.

Awash[6] with **grief**[7] and sinking **dismay**[8], Cad realised that she'd forgotten to count the time since entering the room. She must hasten. Mustering up **courage**[9], she scoured the bedchamber for anything untoward. She checked the nurse's truckle bed which lay by the crib but saw nothing suspicious.

There must be something, she thought, scanning the room.

Befitting[10] for a prince, beautifully polished **wainscoting**[11] adorned the walls, exquisitely **woven**[12] rugs covered the stone floors. A proud looking washstand stood to one side of the luxurious room, piled high with linens and blankets for the baby. A wooden **chest**[13] sat adjacent. Cad opened it. The smell of fresh **lavender**[14] filled her nose, and the pain of losing John ripped at her heart.

---

1 **scud** *(v)* move fast and in a straight line as if driven by the wind. *(s)* speed, streak, race.

2 **unmoor** *(v)* cause to feel unsure or confused. *(s)* unsettle, disconcert. *(ant)* settle.

3 **crimson** *(adj)* a rich red colour with hues of purple.

4 **retch** *(v)* make the motion and sound of vomiting. *(s)* heave, gag, convulse.

5 **horrific** *(adj)* causing horror. *(s)* ghastly, atrocious, grisly. *(ant)* pleasant.

6 **awash** *(adj)* containing a large amount of. *(s)* swamped, overwhelmed, drenched.

7 **grief** *(n)* intense sorrow because of a loss or death. *(s)* heartbreak, desolation, distress. *(ant)* comfort.

8 **dismay** *(n)* concern or distress. *(s)* alarm, dread, trepidation. *(ant)* contentment.

9 **courage** *(n)* the ability to do something frightening. *(s)* bravery, pluck. *(ant)* cowardice.

10 **befitting** *(adj)* suitable to the occasion. *(s)* right, apt, proper. *(ant)* unsuitable, inappropriate.

11 **wainscoting** *(n)* panels (often wooden) that decorate the walls of a room, especially the lower parts.

12 **weave** *(v)* interlace thread to form cloth (past participle: woven). *(s)* intertwine. *(ant)* unravel.

13 **chest** *(n)* a strong, often large, box. *(s)* trunk, coffer, casket, case.

14 **lavender** *(n)* a scented evergreen shrub with bluish-purple flowers used as perfume and medicinally.

Within the **elegantly**[1] **carved**[2] **coffer**[3], John's baby clothes lay in neatly folded piles. She stroked the pale silks, gently **caressing**[4] them between her finger and thumb. But there was no time for **sentiment**[5] now – the sands of time trickled away.

The scene horrified her, but while the chance remained, she decided to search Evans's rooms again. She doubted Sir Robert would be there with the search for John in full force, so she tiptoed towards the door to leave as the ladies **consoled**[6] each other in the passageway. Taking one last glance behind her, she stepped across the **threshold**[7] but suddenly leaped backwards, landing with a dull thud on her sore backside yet again. Like a crab, Cad **scurried**[8] sideways and out of the path of the man into whom she'd almost crashed headlong. Her heart hammered as he entered the room then limped across to John's crib and began stripping its sheets, stuffing them into a woven sack.

Why in heaven was the turnkey, Peggy, stripping Prince John's sullied bed linen? This **menial**[9] task was not a man's work – nor should he be allowed up here; no wonder the ladies had scattered from the passageway. His **stench**[10] would have stunned a bull.

Cad, breathing as quietly as the shock of seeing Peggy would allow, got to her feet and crept as close to him as possible. His task seemed innocent enough: simply stripping **soiled**[11] sheets from the crib – nothing untoward, and her view of him was perfect. Perhaps he'd been sent to save the female servants from the sorry sight of her brother's blood?

On witnessing her brother's bloodied sheets, Cad realised Llywelyn must now return to Catrin immediately. Regardless of the Gwalch Gem bracelet, he would want to know about John and find his son's body. Cad swallowed hard at that thought, suppressing a sob. What if no body

---

1 **elegantly** *(adv)* in an elegant (stylish) manner. *(s)* attractively, tastefully. *(ant)* poorly.

2 **carve** *(v)* cut a hard material to make an object or design. *(s)* sculpt, form.

3 **coffer** *(n)* a strong container, especially for holding valuables. *(s)* chest, trunk, casket.

4 **caress** *(v)* touch gently. *(s)* feel, rub. *(ant)* beat, hit, strike.

5 **sentiment** *(n)* strong feelings of sadness, tenderness or nostalgia. *(s)* emotion. *(ant)* antipathy.

6 **console** *(v)* give comfort and reduce grief. *(s)* soothe, relieve, cheer. *(ant)* upset, distress.

7 **threshold** *(n)* a doorway or other point of entrance.

8 **scurry** *(v)* move quickly with short, hurried steps. *(s)* scamper, scuttle, hasten. *(ant)* saunter, amble.

9 **menial** *(adj)* (of a job) not needing much skill and not highly regarded. *(s)* routine, dull. *(ant)* skilled.

10 **stench** *(n)* a strong and horrid smell. *(s)* stink, reek, malodour. *(ant)* perfume, fragrance.

11 **soil** *(v)* make dirty. *(s)* foul, sully, stain. *(ant)* cleanse.

remained: eaten by a wolf? As that invisible axe hacked her chest again, Cad prayed that was not the case.

Devastated[1] by what she now knew, Cad was about to leave the chamber when something caught her eye. What was Peggy doing? Why was he shaking out the sheets so? Surely he would want to stuff the **gory**[2] items into the sack and be off as soon as possible. Even the likes of this hardened henchman would surely not **revel**[3] in the **tragic**[4] death of a harmless infant.

Not making a sound, Cad moved back closer to Peggy, who stooped to pick up something from the floor. What was it? Cad hadn't moved quickly enough to see what he'd secreted into his pocket. She must risk getting closer to him – within smelling distance.

Her nose wrinkled in disgust as he bent again and picked up a **wisp**[5] of something he'd shaken from the sheet. Cad's invisible eyes doubled in size. Her heart soared, for what Peggy carefully plucked from the sheets and the floor were **downy**[6] little feathers – chicken feathers. Was the blood on the sheets not her brother's, but that of a slain chicken? Had Peggy been tasked to clean up evidence?

The **cunning**[7] culprit would not have been stupid enough to kill a chicken up here, but whoever had slain that bird had forgotten that those **pesky**[8] downy feathers stick like **burrs**[9] to cloth. The blood was a plant to dupe the court into believing a wolf had killed Prince John – she was sure of it. And she'd bet her life on John being alive and hidden in this castle. These actions were a ruse to bring back her father, allowing Dewi and Siân to escape his kingdom with the Gwalch Gem bracelet. Somehow, she must find Prince John and stop that fast rider, Hugh, reaching her father under false pretences. Dewi and Siân would clearly stop at nothing to keep the Gwalch Gem bracelet from Llywelyn, maybe even **staging**[10] a child's death – Siân's child's death.

---

1 **devastated** *(adj)* feeling overwhelming shock or grief. *(s)* traumatised, overcome. *(ant)* comforted.

2 **gory** *(adj)* covered with blood. *(s)* grisly, gruesome, ghastly, macabre.

3 **revel** *(v)* enjoy. *(s)* celebrate, make merry. *(ant)* mourn.

4 **tragic** *(adj)* causing extreme distress or sorrow. *(s)* dreadful, devastating, woeful. *(ant)* cheerful.

5 **wisp** *(n)* a small amount or piece of something. *(s)* shred.

6 **downy** *(adj)* soft and feathery. *(s)* light.

7 **cunning** *(adj)* having skill in achieving one's objectives by deceit (cheating). *(s)* sly, devious, wily. *(ant)* honest.

8 **pesky** *(adj)* annoying. *(s)* irritating, irksome, vexing. *(ant)* welcome.

9 **burr** *(n)* a prickly seed that sticks to animal fur or clothing.

10 **stage** *(v)* fake an incident to make it look real. *(s)* falsify, set up, feign.

Fury filled Cad's throat as she watched Peggy pluck the **remnants**[1] of fluffy down from the sheets before putting them into the sack. No doubt the traitors would keep the sheets for Llywelyn – the fake 'proof' of his son's **demise**[2] as no **corpse**[3] remained. Now **convinced**[4] her brother was alive and in this castle, Cad must act fast before he was truly lost.

She rubbed her eye, which twitched with anxiety, and to her **utter**[5] horror, she saw that her hand had reappeared.

No! she thought, a glancing blow of despair striking her. *Not now!*

Now cornered, with Peggy about to see her, as quick as a **cutpurse**[6] Cad grabbed the hairpin from its sheath and stabbed it into Peggy's rear. The man **yelped**[7], whirling around to see what had speared his **rump**[8]. Without hesitation, Cad leaped, landing behind him. Not wanting to injure him seriously, she jabbed his shoulder, her visible hand hidden behind his head, the rest of her still invisible.

Wild-eyed, Peggy whirled as Cad accompanied him in an invisible **waltz**[9], all the while peppering her **unwitting**[10] partner with jabs as she danced. Throughout their caper she kept her ghoulish, floating hand from his view and scoured the room for a suitable hiding place. If she risked running now he'd see her hand flying along in the air. She knew him to be **fond**[11] of strong beer, but even he would baulk at that sight and raise the alarm. To conceal her visible hand, she had little choice but to jab him harder in the **buttocks**[12], and as he performed a dance of pain and **disorientation**[13], she seized her chance. Cad vaulted like an **acrobat**[14], hurling herself beneath the

---

1 **remnant** *(n)* a part of something that is left over. *(s)* remainder, leftover.

2 **demise** *(n)* downfall or death. *(s)* end, expiry, passing. *(ant)* ascent, birth.

3 **corpse** *(n)* the dead body of a person or animal. *(s)* remains.

4 **convinced** *(adj)* sure about something. *(s)* certain, assured, satisfied. *(ant)* unconvinced.

5 **utter** *(adj)* absolute. *(s)* total, complete, downright. *(ant)* partial.

6 **cutpurse** *(n)* a thief, especially one that steals from a person's pocket. *(s)* pickpocket, dipper, finger.

7 **yelp** *(v)* make a short, sharp cry, especially of pain or alarm. *(s)* squeal, yowl, yell.

8 **rump** *(n)* the hind part or backside of a mammal. *(s)* rear, bottom, behind, buttocks.

9 **waltz** *(n)* a dance, especially performed at formal balls.

10 **unwitting** *(adj)* (of a person) not fully aware of all the facts. *(s)* unknowing, oblivious.

11 **fond** *(adj)* having a liking for. *(s)* keen, partial. *(ant)* disinterested, indifferent.

12 **buttocks** *(n)* bottom. *(s)* backside, behind, rump, rear.

13 **disorientation** *(n)* a state of mental puzzlement. *(s)* bewilderment, shock. *(ant)* certainty.

14 **acrobat** *(n)* a gymnastic (highly athletic) entertainer. *(s)* tumbler, aerialist.

washstand's **decorative**[1] skirts. She prayed Peggy had not seen the flying hand which had held the now-visible emerald hairpin.

Peggy **swore**[2], spinning in circles and rubbing his bony backside, his scored face screwed into a baffled frown of bewilderment. Cad watched from beneath the washstand as he contorted his body to **inspect**[3] his backside, poking and patting it for signs of sharp implements. When finally satisfied that nothing protruded from his bum, and shaking his head in **consternation**[4], Peggy shook the sheets once more before stuffing them into the sack. Then he checked the floor for any remaining evidence. For Cad was convinced of that; the feathers he sought *were* indeed evidence of John being alive.

As Peggy **shuffled**[5] about the crib, dragging his **maimed**[6] leg behind him, Cad, seeing her arm now reappear, clutched the downy feather she had grabbed from the floor and hid it in the hem of her rapidly appearing tunic. How she would escape now, she had no idea. Within minutes, Cad's whole body would be visible once more, and at midday, Mrs Hughes would deliver her food to an empty prison cell.

---

1 **decorative** *(adj)* helping to make something more attractive. *(s)* ornamental, beautifying. *(ant)* plain.

2 **swear** *(v)* use bad language (past tense: swore). *(s)* curse, blaspheme.

3 **inspect** *(v)* look at something closely and with care. *(s)* examine, scrutinise, check.

4 **consternation** *(n)* a feeling of dismay or worry. *(s)* distress, concern, trepidation. *(ant)* relaxation, comfort.

5 **shuffle** *(v)* walk with one's feet dragging on the ground. *(s)* shamble, lumber, dodder.

6 **maim** *(v)* injure so as to be irreparably damaged. *(s)* hurt, disable, incapacitate. *(ant)* heal.

CHAPTER ELEVEN

Nine Lives

Now fully visible and still concealed in Sir Robert's rooms beneath the washstand's skirts, Cad squinted through a gap in the **fabric**[1] and listened **intently**[2]. The ghastly Peggy, **hunched**[3] and stooped, still fiddled around John's crib like a scuttling bug. Once he left, she could try to make a run for it, but now she was visible and chances were she would be seen and caught.

Most guards knew of her imprisonment, as they'd been in the hall when she'd bloodied Bryn's **snout**[4]. Cad pictured his face: Bryn Davis didn't have a snout; he was annoyingly handsome. She pushed him from her mind, **vexed**[5] by thinking of him, especially now.

What is Peggy doing? Cad thought, peeking through the stand's skirts, her invisibility ring now secreted away in her tunic with little hope of it refilling before midday. If she were captured, no one would find it or the pin – they were hers to keep. Without budging an **inch**[6], she **swivelled**[7] her eyes, glancing about the room. The window's wooden shutters were sealed closed with iron bars, and even so, whistling for May to carry a note to Dylan would be a **ludicrous**[8] choice.

---

1 **fabric** *(n)* cloth. *(s)* material, hangings, drapery.

2 **intently** *(adv)* in an intent (eager) way. *(s)* closely, attentively. *(ant)* casually.

3 **hunch** *(v)* lift the shoulders and bend the top of the body forward. *(s)* bow, stoop. *(ant)* straighten.

4 **snout** *(n)* the nose and mouth of an animal, especially a mammal.

5 **vexed** *(adj)* annoyed. *(s)* irked, riled, irritated. *(ant)* pacified, calm.

6 **inch** *(n)* a unit of measurement which is equal to one twelfth of a foot.

7 **swivel** *(v)* turn around a point. *(s)* rotate, pivot, spin.

8 **ludicrous** *(adj)* so foolish, stupid or unreasonable as to be amusing. *(s)* absurd, ridiculous. *(ant)* sensible.

As she **observed**[1] Peggy draw the string at the neck of his sack, then limp towards the door to leave, she thought again of how someone could have accessed and kidnapped a possibly crying baby and then left unseen. It was an unlikely feat, and surely all three guards stationed outside were not **complicit**[2] in John's abduction.

Cad forced her mind to order what she'd just seen, and **deflated**[3], decided she must wait until the passageway quietened and then make a blind run for it. At best, she might make it back before Goodwife Hughes discovered an empty cell. At worst, she would be caught, but Goodwife Hughes would also be in trouble for allowing the escape, for Cad couldn't admit she'd been invisible. Cad must think, for she would not have an innocent blamed for her folly.

As Peggy dragged his gammy leg and pin-pricked buttocks from the room then left, Cad manoeuvred herself into a better position beneath the skirts and flopped back against the wood-panelled wall.

'Ouch!' she yelped, flinging her hand to her mouth in annoyance. Cad, totally **misjudging**[4] her position, had walloped her head, a lump immediately **swelling**[5] as she massaged it.

As the pain eased, something occurred to her: on **impact**[6], the wainscoting behind her head had sounded distinctly **hollow**[7]. Balling her fist, she tapped the panel with her knuckle. An empty sound **reverberated**[8]. She budged to her right, rapped again, and yes, it seemed that the panelling wasn't quite as **robust**[9] as it had first appeared. Peeping around the stand's skirt, she crawled a little further and tapped again. This time the sound was dull and hard – solid.

From beyond the room, approaching footsteps and voices forced her sudden **retreat**[10]. Fear nudged her ribs as she watched two **burly**[11] knights, carrying swords, march past the door, which

---

1 **observe** *(v)* watch carefully. *(s)* see, study, regard. *(ant)* miss, ignore.

2 **complicit** *(adj)* involved in something viewed as wrong. *(s)* guilty, collaborative. *(ant)* innocent.

3 **deflate** *(v)* suddenly lose confidence. *(s)* dispirit, subdue, disappoint. *(ant)* boost.

4 **misjudge** *(v)* form a wrong opinion of. *(s)* miscalculate, mistake. *(ant)* understand.

5 **swell** *(v)* become larger in size. *(s)* expand, bulge. *(ant)* shrink, contract.

6 **impact** *(n)* an instance of one object hitting another. *(s)* contact. *(ant)* avoidance.

7 **hollow** *(adj)* having an empty space or a hole inside or behind. *(s)* vacant, empty. *(ant)* solid.

8 **reverberate** *(v)* repeat as an echo or pulsating vibration. *(s)* resonate, resound.

9 **robust** *(adj)* strong. *(s)* tough, sturdy. *(ant)* weak, feeble.

10 **retreat** *(n)* the act of withdrawing. *(s)* withdrawal, pull back. *(ant)* advance.

11 **burly** *(adj)* large and strong. *(s)* sturdy, strapping, brawny. *(ant)* puny, weedy, weak.

Peggy had left open in his haste. As they marched, she let out a sigh and slumped, bathed in relief as they passed by without **incident**[1].

To take a second look at the panelling, she crawled out again, gently tapping along the length of wooden wainscoting. If she was **estimating**[2] correctly, the hollow area behind the panels would afford someone of **average**[3] size to crawl through. If there were a secret opening here, that would explain how someone had snatched her brother from under the guards' noses. The more Cad **reflected**[4], the more she thought that Prince John's apparent abduction was a ruse to distract her father and bring him back from his quest before he could find the stolen Gwalch Gem.

Deep in thought, she spotted something on the floor.

What in heaven?

A ghastly notion slithered into her head. To get a better view, Cad moved closer, **prodding**[5] the spots with her **forefinger**[6]. A thickish red-brown **substance**[7] **transferred**[8] to her fingers; it was drying blood. Her heart tore in two as that invisible axe hacked at her chest again. She prayed the bloodstains on the floor and her fingers were that of the unfortunate chicken and not her brother.

With her chest tight, Cad followed the marks from the crib to the wainscoting. Could this **spatter**[9] of blood signal a secret exit, a covert passageway from this room to another? On all fours, she tapped the gleaming wood, then ran her fingertips over every angle and corner, but felt or saw nothing. After what felt like ages of searching, grunting and punching the wood in **frustration**[10], she surrendered to this dead end. As before, she would have to wait for a chance to run back to her dungeon having found nothing at all to **bolster**[11] her **theory**[12].

---

1 **incident** *(n)* an event or occurrence that happens. *(s)* occurrence, occasion.

2 **estimate** *(v)* roughly judge or calculate. *(s)* guess, evaluate. *(ant)* know precisely.

3 **average** *(adj)* neither overly large nor small in size. *(s)* normal, typical.

4 **reflect** *(v)* think carefully about. *(s)* contemplate, ponder, consider.

5 **prod** *(v)* poke with something. *(s)* jab, push, nudge.

6 **forefinger** *(n)* the first finger (the one next to the thumb). *(s)* pointer, index finger, indicator.

7 **substance** *(n)* a particular thing. *(s)* material, matter, stuff.

8 **transfer** *(v)* move from one place to another. *(s)* transmit, spread.

9 **spatter** *(n)* a splash or spray of something, especially onto another surface. *(s)* splatter, spray.

10 **frustration** *(n)* the feeling of annoyance at something that one cannot change. *(s)* exasperation. *(ant)* satisfaction.

11 **bolster** *(v)* support or strengthen. *(s)* assist, prop, shore up. *(ant)* weaken, hinder.

12 **theory** *(n)* an idea based on something that needs proving. *(s)* supposition, notion. *(ant)* fact.

Boots **galumphing**[1] down the passageway caught Cad's ear as she readied to flee. She waited. As if she had **fleas**[2], she fidgeted, fingering the notes concealed in the hem of her tunic; the **stock**[3] 'Come and rescue me' notes she'd written earlier in case of emergencies. Messages that May could deliver to her friends if need be. She thought of her stray pup, Fishy, and the little terrier who had **serendipitously**[4] bitten Sir Robert's buttocks. Cad loved animals, and as that thought comforted her, the **whiskery**[5] face of a **soot**[6]-black kitten popped through the skirts of the washstand giving her such a fright she jumped, walloping her head again and yelping with shock.

'I'm such a noddle-head,' she muttered, hoping no one passing by had heard her cry out in pain.

As she calmed her breaths and her **pulse**[7] rate steadied, Cad whispered to the cat. 'Where did you come from, little puss?'

The kitten just blinked, its stunning yellow-green eyes peering at Cad as if they'd been friends for years. With a grin on her face, Cad reached out to stroke it, but the kitten swished its tail, and appearing bored by its new find, turned and walked away.

Typical cat! Cad thought, glancing towards the room's open door and expecting the kitten to leave, but in perfect **feline**[8] **fashion**[9], it continued to **prowl**[10], its tail waving in **serpentine**[11] swirls.

Seeming indifferent, the cat arched its back, wandered to the other side of the room, and pushed at a portion of the wainscoting with its nose. As if on a **hinge**[12], the panel floated open. Within seconds, Cad, her eyes the size of **ducats**[13], watched the cat's tail vanish in a twirl and the panel quietly lower behind it.

---

1 **galumph** *(v)* move in a clumsy or noisy manner. *(s)* clomp, stomp. *(ant)* tiptoe.

2 **flea** *(n)* a tiny insect that feeds on the blood of mammals and birds.

3 **stock** *(adj)* something (often a phrase or expression) used so often it becomes automatic. *(s)* expected. *(ant)* unexpected.

4 **serendipitously** *(adv)* in a serendipitous (lucky) manner. *(s)* fortuitously, coincidentally.

5 **whiskery** *(adj)* having lots of stiff hairs on the face. *(s)* spiky, scratchy.

6 **soot** *(n)* a black powdery residue left over from burning organic matter.

7 **pulse** *(n)* the rhythm of one's blood pulsating through one's arteries, typically at the wrists or neck.

8 **feline** *(adj)* resembling a cat. *(s)* catlike, slinky, graceful, stealthy.

9 **fashion** *(n)* a way of doing something. *(s)* style, manner.

10 **prowl** *(v)* move about stealthily, often in search of prey. *(s)* lurk, patrol, skulk. *(ant)* parade.

11 **serpentine** *(adj)* wavy or twisting, like a serpent or snake.

12 **hinge** *(n)* a movable joint or mechanism that a gate or door is hung upon. *(s)* link, pivot.

13 **ducat** *(n)* a gold coin formerly used for trading in Europe from the Middle Ages.

Before Cad forgot which part of the wainscoting the kitten had vanished through, she crawled at speed, praying no one would appear. Then she **butted**[1] the very same piece of panelling with her nose. As if by magic, the flap lifted smoothly, and like the cat before her, Cad squeezed herself through the opening with no regard whatever as to where it might lead her.

1 **butt** *(v)* strike against something with the head. *(s)* bump, ram, shove.

CHAPTER TWELVE

Into the Void

As soon as the flap in the wainscoting closed behind her, Cad froze. Fear filled her stomach. And now enveloped by blackness, a **dank**[1] smell of **must**[2] pinched her nostrils. She coughed, inhaling **mouldy**[3] grit which fell from the roof of the **suffocatingly**[4] small space. Her hands **groped**[5] at the soil, and sweat crept over her body like a rash. For what felt like a lifetime, she stared into the darkness, paralysed.

Then, like a spooked horse **lashing**[6] out with its hooves, she kicked at the flap over and over but it did not yield. Above the thuds, she heard the screams of a trapped animal and, realising they were hers, stopped. Her breaths **rasped**[7], her sobs were constant, and the kitten had vanished into the darkness. With all choices burned, she inched forward. Her heart punched her ribs, and although it was cold and **damp**[8], sweat dripped into her eyes. Surely the cat wouldn't crawl to its death; even though rumour had it they enjoyed nine lives.

As she crawled, the tunnel reminded Cad of the well Llywelyn had rescued her from all

---

1 **dank** *(adj)* cold and damp. *(s)* musty, unaired, fusty. *(ant)* warm, dry.

2 **must** *(n)* dampness or mould. *(s)* mildew.

3 **mouldy** *(adj)* covered with a fungal growth (mould) that causes decay. *(s)* rotten, festering. *(ant)* fresh, new.

4 **suffocatingly** *(adj)* in such a way to make one feel trapped or oppressed. *(s)* horribly. *(ant)* pleasantly.

5 **grope** *(v)* feel or search about for blindly with the hands. *(s)* fumble, scrabble, fish. *(ant)* withdraw.

6 **lash** *(v)* move quickly and violently. *(s)* kick, thrash, strike.

7 **rasp** *(v)* make a harsh sound. *(s)* croak, grate. *(ant)* soothe.

8 **damp** *(adj)* a little wet. *(s)* moist, dank. *(s)* dry.

those years ago. While leaving a battlefield and watering his horse, Llywelyn had heard a baby's cries coming from the depths of the village's well. Llywelyn and his fellow knight, Owain, had **dismounted**[1] their horses and found something tied to the **shaft's**[2] side. She, a tiny baby, had been attached to the end of that rope. The two Knights Hawk had lifted Cad to safety. But, unable to find Cad's mother, Llywelyn had taken her to Cadwaladr Castle. Although she had no real memory of her rescue, its scars remained, and enclosed spaces had **petrified**[3] her for as long as she could remember.

While her imagination **tortured**[4] her, Cad wondered what supported the **cramped**[5] tunnel. Why didn't it cave in on her head? Then she remembered the maps she'd seen in Sir Robert's rooms. Was this tunnel on those plans, so small only a child or an animal might crawl through them? If a page such as she had been tasked with the kidnapping, carrying a baby through here would be arduous, yet not impossible.

In complete darkness and with no sign of the cat returning, panic strangled her again. But if she were to succeed, the only way now was ahead. As she continued to force herself forward, Cad prayed the cat knew what it was doing. Then her heart almost stopped. She faced a horrific **dilemma**[6]. **Terror**[7] choked her, and no one heard her scream. Before her, she could just make out a **fork**[8] in the tunnel. A choice – an impossible choice. If she took one path, then another, and another, tracking back **whence**[9] she came would be impossible. Her father would return to find not only his son **presumed**[10] dead at the jaws of a wolf, but his daughter also vanished. Cad refused to die down here and put Llywelyn through that double **trauma**[11]. She had no choice but to back up, kick open the flap and risk capture.

---

1 **dismount** *(v)* get off something that one rides. *(s)* descend, alight. *(ant)* mount.

2 **shaft** *(n)* a long, narrow hole that gives access to something. *(s)* borehole, tunnel.

3 **petrified** *(adj)* made so frightened as to be unable to move. *(s)* terrified, horrified. *(ant)* reassured.

4 **torture** *(v)* to inflict pain or suffering. *(s)* punish, torment. *(ant)* relieve.

5 **cramped** *(adj)* uncomfortably small or restricted. *(s)* confined, tight, limited. *(ant)* comfortable.

6 **dilemma** *(n)* a difficult situation where a decision must be made. *(s)* predicament, plight. *(ant)* breeze, cinch.

7 **terror** *(n)* great fear. *(s)* horror, dread, trepidation.

8 **fork** *(n)* a route that divides into two parts. *(s)* split, branch, divergence. *(ant)* convergence.

9 **whence** *(adv)* from where. *(s)* wherefrom, from what place.

10 **presumed** *(adj)* appearing to be something but without certainty. *(s)* assumed, supposed. *(ant)* confirmed.

11 **trauma** *(n)* a distressing occurrence or experience. *(s)* agony, anguish, hurt, upset. *(ant)* benefit.

About to **reverse**[1], Cad suddenly jumped, bashing her head on the tunnel and **simultaneously**[2] biting her tongue. 'Ouch!' she yelped, staring at the two yellow-green **almond**[3] shapes before her face.

'Miaow,' **mewled**[4] the kitten, turning and swishing its tail right across the front of her nose and tickling it before turning to face her once more. Cad rubbed her nose, blinking at the peculiar eyes that bored into hers. How in heaven could a cat's eyes glow in the dark thus? Then she remembered the ring that had made her invisible and the emerald hairpin which opened locks.

The cat's eyes twirled in a **figure of eight**[5], its tail brushing her nose each time it did. Then it slowly prowled forward, its eyes lighting the way, as it took the right-hand fork. Cad squinted, but no longer seeing its eyes; she was blind. Then, from nowhere, those almond-shaped yellow lanterns were before her nose again. The kitten let out such an ungodly mewl that Cad immediately realised: the cat wanted her to follow. It was leading the way. Without hesitation, Cad reached out, rubbed the cat's neck and said, 'Let's go,' and with that, she followed the kitten, its tail brushing her face for **guidance**[6] and comfort.

Trying to ignore the dank smell of earth, and the taste of soil in her mouth, Cad followed her feline friend, hoping the interminable crawl would soon end. The air was thin, and her breaths rapid and shallow as she tried to fill her lungs with much-needed **sustenance**[7]. Without its eyes as lanterns, the cat's outline was just visible, its tail doubling as a guide. So long as that tail swished her nose, she knew the cat was just in front, and she now knew that the cat had led her down here deliberately.

Without warning, the cat abruptly stopped, and the two yellow-green eyes faced her once more. 'What is it?' asked Cad. The cat turned away, mewled, and then a crack of light appeared before them. Cad saw the cat standing stock-still, gently sniffing the air. He didn't budge, and

---

1 **reverse** *(v)* move backwards. *(s)* retreat. *(ant)* advance.

2 **simultaneously** *(adv)* at the same time. *(s)* concurrently, instantaneously. *(ant)* separately.

3 **almond** *(n)* the edible oval seed of an almond tree; the shape of an almond. *(s)* oval.

4 **mewl** *(v)* make a high-pitched cry. *(s)* mew, miaow, yowl.

5 **figure of eight** *(n)* something that is shaped like the number 8.

6 **guidance** *(n)* information aimed at solving a problem. *(s)* instruction, direction, advice.

7 **sustenance** *(n)* something regarded as a source of strength. *(s)* nourishment.

Cad realised she was holding her breath. She must trust this animal. He had led her here. If the cat was waiting for something, then so should she.

It was hard to ignore the thudding at her ribs as she waited for the cat's next move. The tunnel was deadly silent, yet her breaths and heart thundered in her ears. The cat's paw lifted, scratching and clawing at the tunnel's side. And in the same way they had accessed this crawl space, a flap rose outwards and the cat pounced through it.

Once through, the cat turned back to face Cad and mewled again. Weak with relief, Cad inched forward into the glow. At the threshold, she stopped, her pupils **adjusting**[1] to the light flooding into the dark tunnel. Cad realised her hands were trembling so much she planted them both onto the ground by her knees. She must steel herself for who or what awaited her on the other side of this opening. There was absolute silence as, **precariously**[2], Cad crawled through the flap and out of the grimy tunnel.

The sight before her stopped her in her tracks; she was utterly **astonished**[3]. But her eyes ached, struggling to focus, until, blinking and quickly scanning the **vicinity**[4], she realised where she was: under a four-poster bed as big as a boat. A bed she recognised well. These beds were for dignitaries only: she was in the royal wing and the bedchamber of Sir Robert Evans.

It made sense that a secret tunnel might exist between Prince John's room and Evans's. But the **unfathomable**[5] questions, the ones racing around her head, **jostling**[6] for attention, were why would a trail of chicken's blood exist between both, and why was Peggy clearing up feathers? Someone wanted her father back from his quest before he could recover the bracelet. If this trail led into Sir Robert's private quarters, could he be connected in some way? Her father's closest **ally**[7].

Still **shrouded**[8] by the bed, Cad had ample time to scan the scene. She couldn't see any feet walking about, nor could she hear anyone in the room. Looking up, Cad saw the bed wasn't

---

1 **adjust** *(v)* change to achieve a desired outcome. *(s)* alter, modify, regulate.

2 **precariously** *(adv)* in a precarious (dangerous) way. *(s)* shakily, unsteadily. *(ant)* securely, steadily.

3 **astonished** *(adj)* extremely surprised or impressed. *(s)* astounded, staggered. *(ant)* indifferent.

4 **vicinity** *(n)* surrounding or nearby areas. *(s)* proximity, locale. *(ant)* distance.

5 **unfathomable** *(adj)* not capable of being understood. *(s)* indecipherable, puzzling. *(ant)* fathomable, clear.

6 **jostle** *(v)* hustle, push, or bump into something. *(s)* fight, struggle, compete.

7 **ally** *(n)* a person that helps another in a task. *(s)* aide, associate, supporter. *(ant)* opponent.

8 **shroud** *(v)* envelop or cover to prevent from being seen. *(s)* conceal, mask, hide. *(ant)* reveal.

bowed[1], so **deemed**[2] it empty. With the emerald ring tucked safely away, it would be hours before the Gwalch Gem bracelet **remotely**[3] refilled it to full power. And now the gem was more distant, that could be even longer than usual. Waiting was not an option. If Cad was to return before Goodwife Hughes found her gone: she must run. Either way, she was probably scuppered, along with Goodwife Hughes's job as a turnkey.

Cad drew in a deep breath and **edged**[4] from under the bed towards the room, slithering snake-like on her stomach. She was sure she was alone – the kitten had vanished – so counting one, two, three, Cad slid out, and with stiff knees, wobbled to her feet, with her hairpin placed in her tunic pocket where she could grab it if need be.

To her utter relief, the room was empty, and its door was closed. The large table in the room's centre was now clear save for a few precious books and one parchment. Cad picked it up and studied it, expecting it to be another of Evans's maps, but it wasn't. She stared at it, baffled. It seemed to be some sort of cipher, a code the likes of which she'd never before seen. Cad folded it carefully and tucked it beneath the folds of her tunic; she would study it later when she had ample time. Right now she must find her kidnapped brother and halt Goodwife Hughes's fast-riding son.

Cad's eyes scoured the room. There was no sign that Prince John had ever been here. The bed was **immaculately**[5] made, the floors swept, and nothing seemed untoward, no different from when she'd entered this room last night in search of John. Surely if they'd brought John through here there would be some sign of it. She checked the floors for feathers and drops of blood but saw nothing. She checked beneath the washstand and looked inside the wardrobes. If John had been here, then they had deftly cleaned away the evidence. It would be impossible to search further for John until the ring refilled and she could escape that damned dungeon again. But first, she must return to it.

As she readied to leave, she hoped all the guards were occupied searching for John's body, and that she might dash to the adjacent tower unseen. She didn't even have any treats to distract the

---

1 **bow** *(v)* bend under pressure. *(s)* distort, sag, curve. *(ant)* straighten.

2 **deem** *(v)* consider, judge or regard in a specified way. *(s)* assume, reckon, suppose. *(ant)* misjudge.

3 **remotely** *(adv)* from a distance and without physical contact.

4 **edge** *(v)* move slowly in a gradual way. *(s)* creep, inch, steal. *(ant)* rush, career.

5 **immaculately** *(adv)* done in an immaculate (perfect) manner. *(s)* flawlessly, impeccably. *(ant)* defectively.

dogs. Why had that kitten led her here if there was nothing to find? Maybe she'd **misread**[1] the cat's signs. Perhaps the cat was returning to its master, but she was sure Evans didn't have a cat. Indeed, she remembered him not caring for animals at all.

With her heart **fluttering**[2] like that of a **terrified**[3] bird, she crept towards the door and placed her ear to it. About to open it, she froze. Her heart **somersaulted**[4] as footsteps approached. She glanced about the room; where could she hide? Then, thankfully, she heard the deep-throated bark of a hound, and the footsteps **fading**[5]. Almost faint with relief, her body relaxed a tad as she turned to leave again. But to her absolute horror, as she did so, the **latch**[6] to the enormous door clanged. Someone was entering the room. Springing like a **fawn**[7] on the run from a hunter, Cad, with one giant leap, turned and dived headlong under the hanging skirts of the vast four-poster bed.

---

1 **misread** *(v)* interpret or judge a situation wrongly. *(s)* misinterpret, misunderstand. *(ant)* understand.

2 **flutter** *(v)* move with a light, irregular or trembling motion. *(s)* beat, quiver, tremble.

3 **terrify** *(v)* cause to feel great fear. *(s)* scare, horrify, petrify. *(ant)* calm, soothe.

4 **somersault** *(v)* perform a flip. *(s)* overturn.

5 **fade** *(v)* slowly become faint. *(s)* wane, decrease, subside. *(ant)* increase.

6 **latch** *(n)* a bar (especially metal) with a lever and a catch used for fastening a gate or door closed.

7 **fawn** *(n)* a deer in its first year of life.

CHAPTER THIRTEEN

Too Late

As Cad peered from beneath the skirts of Sir Robert's **regal**[1] bed, her eyes nigh on doubled in size. Why on earth was Peggy accompanying Sir Robert into his bedchamber, and what was he carrying for him? Peggy was Dewi's man, and **escorting**[2] a Knight Hawk such as Evans was most peculiar.

'Place them on the table,' Sir Robert said to Peggy. 'And be gentle with them.'

Sir Robert spoke as if he addressed an associate and not one of Dewi's **vile**[3] henchmen.

'Sire, do we know how long remains?' Peggy asked.

'Not yet. It is too soon,' replied Evans, his voice quiet, his snake's eyes scanning the room.

Cad **recoiled**[4] further beneath the bed skirts, the blood rushing through her ears and **drowning**[5] the men's voices. The whooshing seemed so loud, she feared they might hear her heart beating.

'When does the rider arrive?' Peggy asked.

Cad flinched – something was afoot. Why would Peggy know of the fast rider? This was

---

1 **regal** *(adj)* fit for a ruler. *(s)* royal, grand, majestic. *(ant)* humble.

2 **escort** *(v)* accompany (go with) someone somewhere. *(s)* partner. *(ant)* abandon.

3 **vile** *(adj)* very unpleasant. *(s)* nasty, foul, horrid. *(ant)* pleasant.

4 **recoil** *(v)* suddenly spring or flinch back in horror or disgust. *(s)* withdraw, retreat. *(ant)* confront.

5 **drown** *(v)* make another sound inaudible (unable to be heard) by being much louder. *(s)* deaden, muffle. *(ant)* louden.

absurd[1] – it seemed Evans now confided in this foe, and she must find out why.

'Weather **permitting**[2], he should arrive soon,' Evans replied. 'Thank you, Hari. You may continue your duties.'

Hari, Cad thought, astonished. Why was Sir Robert on first-name terms with Peggy?

'Sire,' Peggy replied, with a deep bow. Then Dewi's henchman left the room, closing the door behind him.

From beneath the bed, Cad couldn't see what Peggy had placed on the table when he'd entered the room, but Evans was ignoring it. Instead, he walked over to his washstand, tipped some water into a bowl, rinsed his hands, and dried them on a crisp linen cloth. Then he poured himself some beer from a metal ewer and rested at his writing desk, which stood against the wall adjacent to the ornate bed. Cad hoped Evans would hurry his work and leave the room, but to her dismay, he picked up his quill, dipped it in ink and began scratching on a piece of parchment.

Stiff, uncomfortable, and with her stomach growling like a dog, she contemplated crawling out from beneath the bed and **concocting**[3] a tall story for Evans, who was after all, her father's friend. But what good would that do? She dared not lose the ring or hairpin to him and there was no guarantee he would let her keep them. Deflated and frustrated, she had little choice but to sit this out and hope he might leave soon. Either way, she'd be scuppered once Goodwife Hughes raised the alarm.

In an attempt to ease her cramped position without alerting Evans, she slid onto her side and tried to settle; but her slingshot and stones, hidden in her tunic, poked into her side. Cad fidgeted, watching as Evans scribbled away, when an idea flashed through her head.

It might just work, she thought.

Now somewhat **heartened**[4], Cad **weighed up**[5] where his ink pot sat. She couldn't swing her sling from here, but if she yanked it back hard enough, and managed to stretch and lever it simultaneously, it might just work. If it didn't, he'd catch her, but either way, she'd be caught.

---

1 **absurd** *(adj)* something ridiculous or very unreasonable. *(s)* ludicrous, preposterous. *(ant)* reasonable.

2 **permit** *(v)* allow to do something. *(s)* enable. *(ant)* prohibit.

3 **concoct** *(v)* devise or create a story or plan. *(s)* fabricate, invent, conceive.

4 **hearten** *(v)* make confident or cheerful. *(s)* encourage, boost. *(ant)* dishearten.

5 **weigh up** *(v)* assess something or someone carefully. *(s)* evaluate, gauge. *(ant)* calculate.

Also, he might write like this for hours, and she couldn't leave her hidey-hole unseen by him. It was, **literally**[1], worth a shot.

As quietly as she could, she manoeuvred herself into a **sniping**[2] position. Now on her side, propped up on her elbow, she closed one eye and fixed the other on the ink. Then with pinpoint accuracy she positioned her sling and waited for Evans to dip his quill into the wooden pot. For her **stunt**[3] to work, he must blame himself for his **clumsiness**[4].

Cramp **threatened**[5] her arms and legs as she watched and waited. How many words could a man write before needing more ink, she asked herself. Then her chance came. The moment his hand lifted from the parchment, Cad **catapulted**[6] the stone straight at Sir Robert's ink pot.

Wide-eyed, Cad watched. Had Evans seen the incoming projectile as he'd **immersed**[7] his quill into the pot, or did he blame the fact that his face was now dripping in ink on his **sheer**[8] **ungainliness**[9]. Holding her breath, Cad hoped it was the latter. If the former, he'd explode like a volcano – she knew that his temper, when **riled**[10] enough, was explosive.

For what felt like **aeons**[11], Evans sat unmoving, either in a state of utter **disbelief**[12] or **contemplation**[13]. In the grim shadow of the skirts, Cad waited for Evans to spin around, venture forth and drag her from beneath the bed, but he didn't.

As a slow smile parted her lips, Cad suppressed an **incongruous**[14] **desire**[15] to giggle at Sir

---

1 **literally** *(adv)* in a literal (exact) manner or sense. *(s)* really, truly. *(ant)* figuratively.

2 **snipe** *(v)* shoot from a hiding place. *(s)* fire.

3 **stunt** *(n)* an action showing daring or skill. *(s)* feat, exploit, caper, deed.

4 **clumsiness** *(n)* the characteristic of being careless in one's movements. *(s)* ungainliness. *(ant)* carefulness.

5 **threaten** *(v)* cause danger to. *(s)* jeopardise, endanger. *(ant)* help.

6 **catapult** *(v)* hurl, propel or launch. *(s)* shoot, project, slingshot.

7 **immerse** *(v)* dip in a liquid. *(s)* dunk, plunge, soak. *(ant)* dry.

8 **sheer** *(adj)* absolute. *(s)* pure, utter, total, downright, outright.

9 **ungainliness** *(n)* the carriage of someone moving in an awkward manner. *(s)* clumsiness, ineptitude. *(ant)* elegance, grace.

10 **rile** *(v)* annoy or irritate someone. *(s)* vex, bother, irk, anger. *(ant)* please.

11 **aeon** *(n)* an indefinite and long time. *(s)* eternity, forever. *(ant)* moment, jiffy, flash.

12 **disbelief** *(n)* the refusal to believe that something is true. *(s)* incredulity. *(ant)* belief.

13 **contemplation** *(n)* deep thought. *(s)* reflection, consideration, pondering.

14 **incongruous** *(adj)* unusual or out of keeping in some way. *(s)* inappropriate. *(ant)* appropriate.

15 **desire** *(n)* a strong feeling. *(s)* want, impulse, fancy.

Robert's face, dripping with tar-black ink. With a **furious**[1] grunt, rising, the knight grabbed his handcloth, wiped off the **excess**[2] ink and then rubbed at his face. But his efforts proved futile. He would need hot water and more cloths to remove the stains. With unrepeatable **curses**[3], he threw the cloth to the floor, picked up the items Peggy had placed onto the table, opened the door and **stomped**[4] out of the room, leaving the door wide open behind him.

The moment Evans left, those two yellow-green eyes appeared next to Cad again; she almost **shed**[5] her skin with fright. The cat stared at her, mewled quietly, turned in a figure-of-eight, then **slunk**[6] out from beneath the bed.

Without hesitation, Cad wriggled out too, vaulted to her feet and made for the door, where the black kitten stood. Reminding herself she was now visible, Cad held onto the door's vast frame with trembling hands and poked her head around its **jamb**[7]. **Fortuitously**[8], the passageway was clear. Cad made to head towards the other tower and her cell, but the cat sprang in front of her, hissing. She **shifted**[9] to dodge past, but it arched its back, spitting like a vexed snake. Then it darted past her in the opposite direction, hissing again.

Cad's attention suddenly jerked towards the sound of a voice she recognised well: Bryn Davis. *What is he doing here?* she thought, her heart sinking into her belly.

Not waiting for her answer, she turned and fled in the opposite direction, the black cat **scampering**[10] ahead of her. She was **done for**[11] now, and she was no nearer to finding her brother. Bryn was about to see her when the cat stopped outside one of the smaller chambers and let out that devilish howl again. With nothing to lose, and hearing Bryn's footsteps closing in, Cad opened the door and followed the cat inside the room.

---

1 **furious** *(adj)* extremely angry. *(s)* enraged, infuriated, fuming, seething. *(ant)* calm, mild.

2 **excess** *(adj)* more than a desirable amount. *(s)* unwanted, excessive. *(ant)* wanted.

3 **curse** *(n)* an unpleasant and offensive word. *(s)* expletive, profanity.

4 **stomp** *(v)* step heavily and noisily, especially to show anger. *(s)* stamp, pound. *(ant)* creep.

5 **shed** *(v)* discard. *(s)* lose, cast off. *(ant)* keep, adopt.

6 **slink** *(v)* move smoothly and quietly in a stealthy way (past tense: slunk). *(s)* slip, steal. *(ant)* stomp.

7 **jamb** *(n)* a post at the side or surface of a doorway. *(s)* frame, pillar.

8 **fortuitously** *(adv)* in a fortuitous (by chance) way. *(s)* luckily, serendipitously.

9 **shift** *(v)* move a short distance. *(s)* reposition. *(ant)* remain motionless.

10 **scamper** *(v)* run with light, quick steps. *(s)* scurry, scoot. *(ant)* dawdle, stroll.

11 **done for** *(adj)* prevented from succeeding. *(s)* thwarted, foiled, defeated.

Only when she had gently closed the door behind her did Cad think about what might await her on the other side, and to her great relief, it was nothing. The room was empty save for a simply made bed, a washstand and a large chest. Cad approached the washstand, where a jug stood containing water. She dipped her finger into the ewer. The water was **tepid**[1], not cold like when it **gurgles**[2] up from the mountain streams. Only royals and dignitaries benefited from warmed washing water. There was also a **waft**[3] of fresh lavender hanging in the air, which was used for freshening the royals' clothes, especially that of their children.

With **conflicting**[4] hope and **dread**[5], Cad flew over to the coffer and lifted its heavy lid. Inside lay piles of clean **swaddling**[6], sponges and linen: **necessities**[7] for a baby. All were clearly for John, but where was he? The room was average-sized and probably used for visiting dignitaries, **stewards**[8] or **officials**[9].

The stewards of royals often slept with their masters in case of illness or **threat**[10]. Cad walked over to the wood-panelled walls. They were **uniform**[11] and simple-looking. A **continuous**[12] wall of wainscoting and nothing out of the ordinary, their design being the same as most in the high keep. But Cad now knew that if royalty slept here, they might well have an adjoining door, a secret passage to the adjacent room. Perhaps John was hidden there?

Cad began her search in one corner, working from chest height down to the floor. To ensure she missed nothing, she **systematically**[13] checked each panel for signs of an opening. Apart

---

1 **tepid** *(adj)* slightly warm. *(s)* lukewarm, warmish, temperate. *(ant)* icy, boiling.

2 **gurgle** *(v)* make a bubbling sound. *(s)* burble, babble, splash.

3 **waft** *(n)* a gentle movement or current of air. *(s)* wave, puff, gust, draught.

4 **conflicting** *(adj)* two things that vary from each other in some way. *(s)* contradictory, clashing. *(ant)* harmonious.

5 **dread** *(n)* fear. *(s)* apprehension, trepidation. *(ant)* confidence.

6 **swaddling** *(n)* cloth or garments used to wrap someone, especially a baby.

7 **necessity** *(n)* something that is needed absolutely. *(s)* essential, prerequisite. *(ant)* luxury.

8 **steward** *(n)* a person employed to look after another or their property. *(s)* manciple, butler.

9 **official** *(n)* a person appointed by a public office to represent a governing body. *(s)* dignitary, appointee.

10 **threat** *(n)* something or someone likely to cause damage. *(s)* risk, hazard, peril. *(ant)* benefit, boon.

11 **uniform** *(adj)* remaining the same. *(s)* unvarying, identical. *(ant)* different, varied.

12 **continuous** *(adj)* without interruption. *(s)* uninterrupted, constant, unbroken. *(ant)* sporadic, intermittent.

13 **systematically** *(adv)* in a systematic (according to a plan or system) way. *(s)* methodically, consistently. *(ant)* haphazardly.

from the decorative **beading**[1], which lay in **parallel**[2] squares along the panels, the walls were flat and smooth. She would feel a crack or line if a hidden hinge lay **embedded**[3] in the wooden wainscoting. Determined, she ran her finger along each section, missing not an inch.

As she searched, her sweaty clothes clung due to the tower's rising **temperature**[4], and she guessed it was nearing midday. Goodwife Hughes would be readying Cad's dinner. Sweat trickled down her **torso**[5] as she continued her **fruitless**[6] search. The kitten sat quietly in one corner, its yellow-green eyes fixed on Cad. Cad walked over to where it sat and gently moved it sideways. It had led her here, and maybe it was sitting by this panel as a **clue**[7]. But Cad searched to no avail. She could not find a covert exit. Cad had been convinced John might be in the adjacent room. Now frustrated, sweating and exhausted, she sank to the floor, flopping back with a hard grunt.

'Ow!' she cried, as the back of her head walloped the floor so hard, silver lights swirled in her head and her teeth **gnashed**[8] with a loud clack. She rubbed her neck, disorientated, and it took her several moments to understand her **whereabouts**[9]. Ever grateful her tongue had escaped intact, she realised she was staring at the adjoining room's ceiling. There had been a secret panel after all. One so well hidden, it was **undetectable**[10] except to the **discerning**[11]. She held her breath, waiting for an oncoming **tirade**[12] from whoever might be in this room, but none came. All was quiet. She pushed herself through the panel, wriggled onto her front and closed it behind her.

Still on all fours, she scanned the room. It was fit for a royal, with a privy garderobe, a grand writing desk, and an **elaborate**[13] washstand. But what caught Cad's eye was the beautifully ornate

---

1 **bead** *(n)* a type of decorative woodwork used to soften edges and protect against splitting.

2 **parallel** *(adj)* side by side, having equal distance between. *(s)* aligned, lateral. *(ant)* perpendicular.

3 **embedded** *(adj)* fixed deeply in a surrounding mass. *(s)* implanted, inserted, lodged.

4 **temperature** *(n)* the degree or intensity of heat measured in someone or something.

5 **torso** *(n)* the trunk (body without head or limbs) of a human. *(s)* upper body.

6 **fruitless** *(adj)* not achieving the desired results. *(s)* useless, pointless, futile. *(ant)* fruitful.

7 **clue** *(n)* a piece of information about something, especially a crime. *(s)* sign, indication. *(ant)* evidence.

8 **gnash** *(v)* (the teeth) grind together. *(s)* clench, grit, grate, clash.

9 **whereabouts** *(n)* the place where something or someone is. *(s)* position, location.

10 **undetectable** *(adj)* unable to be detected, seen or noticed. *(s)* invisible, unnoticeable, unseen. *(ant)* obvious.

11 **discerning** *(adj)* someone who has or shows good judgement or knowledge. *(s)* knowing. *(ant)* undiscerning.

12 **tirade** *(n)* a lengthy, angry speech, criticism or accusation. *(s)* outburst, rant. *(ant)* praise.

13 **elaborate** *(adj)* detailed in design. *(s)* fussy, extravagant, ornate. *(ant)* plain, simple.

crib, its curtains drawn. It sat adjacent to the four-poster bed, a nurse's truckle bed **flanking**[1] it.

Cad found her feet and crept over to the cot. Unable to stem her trembling, she gently drew back the curtains, and, holding her breath, fully expected to find her brother lying there. Disappointment hit her like a falling axe; it was empty. Even worse, she could smell him. The scent of a baby, a **faint**[2] **whiff**[3] of lavender, and the linen sheets, still warm to the touch. He had been here, and recently. Someone was moving her brother around the castle. Someone who wanted her father to return to Catrin to allow Dewi and Siân to flee with the Gwalch Gem bracelet.

To bolster her resolve, Cad grabbed the **discarded**[4] swaddling which lay in the crib, tore off a scrap and hid it away in her tunic. She chewed her lip as her eyes quickly scanned the room for any **concrete**[5] evidence of her brother, but found none. With time running away from her, she sat at the writing desk and scribbled a note to Dylan. Her hand shook, her letters a **scrawl**[6]. Fortunately, probably to air the room, the wooden window shutters were open.

Then as quietly as possible, but in as high a **pitch**[7] as she could muster, Cad whistled for May. Within seconds, the blind hawk swooped in and settled on Cad's shoulder. Cad fed May her last morsel of cheese, tied the note to her **scrawny**[8] leg, and commanded, 'Master Dylan. Master Dylan. Now. Go.'

As May soared away, Cad **willed**[9] Dylan to be outside practising his **archery**[10] skills at the **butts**[11]. Finally, she scribbled a note to her father, begging him to ignore the fast rider and imploring him to continue his quest to recover the Gwalch Gem bracelet. Nothing must stop him, for that is what the traitors desired. But for now, she tucked that note safely away in her tunic; before she alerted Llywelyn, she must find her brother, Prince John – alive.

---

1 **flank** *(v)* be on each side or on one side of.

2 **faint** *(adj)* (of a smell, sight or sound) not strong. *(s)* vague, subtle, weak. *(ant)* strong.

3 **whiff** *(n)* a smell that is only smelled briefly or faintly. *(s)* trace, hint, suggestion. *(ant)* saturation.

4 **discarded** *(adj)* thrown aside, as no longer useful or desirable. *(s)* abandoned, dumped. *(ant)* retained.

5 **concrete** *(adj)* something that exists in material form. *(s)* real, physical, tangible. *(ant)* abstract.

6 **scrawl** *(n)* an example of careless or hurried writing. *(s)* scribble.

7 **pitch** *(n)* the highness or lowness of a sound. *(s)* tone, timbre.

8 **scrawny** *(adj)* bony and thin. *(s)* skinny, scraggy, spindly. *(ant)* fat, plump.

9 **will** *(v)* mentally hope for something to happen or someone to do something.

10 **archery** *(n)* shooting with a bow and arrow.

11 **butt** *(n)* an archery shooting target or range.

CHAPTER FOURTEEN

Saving a Squire

Still stuck in the room where she'd found evidence that her brother was alive, Cad knew she must act fast lest it be too late for John. **Skittish**[1] with anxiety, visible and about to be caught, Cad trembled as she pushed open the chamber door. As its stiff hinges **protested**[2] with a groan, she peeked into the passageway; all seemed quiet. Perhaps folks were still frantically searching for her brother's 'body' and had already ransacked the high keep's twin towers. Or maybe the masters of their **wild goose chase**[3] had sent them elsewhere; someone in Catrin was lying about her brother.

On tiptoe, in a cautious half-walk half-run, Cad headed along the passageway and back down towards her dungeon in the opposite tower, her body **taut**[4] with **stress**[5]. She curled around a bend, and when she had climbed one floor and entered a stone corridor which led her towards more stairs, footsteps and voices drifted towards her. Like a startled fawn, Cad sprang into a stone **alcove**[6], a window seat where courtly ladies could admire the gardens during **inclement**[7]

---

1 **skittish** *(adj)* nervous. *(s)* jumpy, fidgety, edgy. *(ant)* calm, collected, composed.

2 **protest** *(v)* express an objection to something. *(s)* object, complain. *(ant)* agree.

3 **wild goose chase** *(n)* a useless search or pursuit of something that cannot be achieved.

4 **taut** *(adj)* tight, with no slack. *(s)* stiff, rigid, tense. *(ant)* slack, loose.

5 **stress** *(n)* mental or emotional strain. *(s)* worry, anxiety, distress. *(ant)* relaxation.

6 **alcove** *(n)* a recess (hollow or indentation) in a wall. *(s)* niche, nook, bay. *(ant)* protrusion.

7 **inclement** *(adj)* (of the weather) unpleasant. *(s)* bleak, wintry, cold, chilly.

weather. Fighting to ignore her hammering heart, she curled up like a hedgehog in **hibernation**[1]. Armed with her hairpin, which quivered in her fingers, she pushed her back into the stone **recess**[2] until it hurt.

When three silken-gowned ladies bustled by, all huddled together and gossiping of the 'tragic incident', Cad's body **sagged**[3] with relief. Counting her heartbeat, she **stowed**[4] the hairpin and waited for silence. So close to safety, she hopped down from the **bay**[5] and hastened towards the higher floors and her dungeon. Sweat soaked her body. Unsure whether it was heat or nerves, she mopped her **brow**[6] on her tunic sleeve. The towers now **sweltered**[7] in the **blistering**[8] sun, its position overhead a dire warning of her **tardiness**[9]. She might even bump into Goodwife Hughes carrying her dinner along with her. That would prove an interesting **conversation**[10].

On seeing the stairs up to her cell, Cad hastened. She was almost there; the stone steps lay just feet away. But to her utter dismay, more footsteps and voices approached, and one was that of the squire, Bryn Davis.

Thank goodness the tower looks onto the gardens, she thought as she stopped and leaped up into another window seat recess, hiding herself away.

With an angry twist of her mouth, Cad wondered why Bryn was in the tower and right at the base of the stairs leading to where she was captive? With his master, Dewi, absconded and a traitor, surely he should be out at his **beloved**[11] archery butts or practising in the tilt yard in preparation for training with a new knight.

Cad **thrust**[12] her back so tightly into the nook she could barely breathe, and willed the **bully**[13]

---

1 **hibernation** *(n)* the condition or period that an animal spends dormant (inactive) during the winter.

2 **recess** *(n)* a small corner or hollow place, usually in a wall. *(s)* alcove, bay, niche. *(ant)* protrusion.

3 **sag** *(v)* slump, sink, subside or bulge downwards under pressure or lack of strength. *(s)* droop. *(ant)* rise.

4 **stow** *(v)* store, pack or keep neatly in a specific place. *(s)* stash, secrete. *(ant)* remove.

5 **bay** *(n)* a space by a window. *(s)* alcove, nook, hollow, recess.

6 **brow** *(n)* forehead.

7 **swelter** *(v)* to become overly hot. *(s)* burn, boil, heat. *(ant)* cool.

8 **blistering** *(adj)* intense heat. *(s)* fierce, ferocious, scorching. *(ant)* cold.

9 **tardiness** *(n)* lateness. *(s)* delay. *(ant)* timeliness, punctuality.

10 **conversation** *(n)* a talk between two or more people. *(s)* discussion, chat, dialogue, exchange.

11 **beloved** *(adj)* much loved. *(s)* adored, favourite, treasured.

12 **thrust** *(v)* move forcefully. *(s)* shove, propel, drive.

13 **bully** *(n)* a person who harms or intimidates others whom they see as vulnerable. *(s)* tyrant, persecutor.

Davis to walk right past her. His voice sounded vexed, almost **menacing**[1], and it **loudened**[2] as he approached. She didn't recognise the voice with whom he argued, but it snapped back in **hostile**[3] tones. Her heart boxed her ribs with painful thumps because if Bryn found her here, she was utterly done for. As they neared, **trepidation**[4] rose like **nausea**[5], and overwhelmed by fear of being found, her limbs felt floaty. She forced even breaths, but they didn't work.

With little time, and gauging quickly, Cad clutched her hairpin as the voices approached from the passage. She prayed they'd move swiftly in the heat of their **quarrel**[6]. But to her horror, the footsteps stopped. The **ensuing**[7] silence pressed down on her like a **lead**[8] weight. With burning cheeks and her body prickling with sweat, she braced herself for fight, flight or capture, when a dull **thwacking**[9] sound from the passageway shocked her.

Thwack! It happened again, followed by a groan and what sounded like a body bouncing off the wall. Neither man spoke nor yelled – only animal-like grunts ensued. Then a pained cry **proceeded**[10] another cruel-sounding **blow**[11], but she could not discern whose pained voice groaned.

Fists hitting **flesh**[12], feet kicking bones, and the scuffle of **wrestling**[13] bodies left Cad in no doubt: that **brute**[14], Davis, was beating on someone, and badly. Should she peep and risk **exposure**[15]? Should she run? They might not see her and she'd escape if she did. But when she

---

1 **menacing** *(adj)* threatening or dangerous. *(s)* intimidating, fearsome. *(ant)* reassuring.

2 **louden** *(v)* become or make something louder. *(s)* increase. *(ant)* quieten, decrease.

3 **hostile** *(adj)* unwelcoming or showing opposition. *(s)* harsh, unfavourable, unpleasant. *(ant)* friendly.

4 **trepidation** *(n)* anxiety or fear about what may happen. *(s)* dread, apprehension. *(ant)* assurance.

5 **nausea** *(n)* a feeling of sickness. *(s)* queasiness, biliousness. *(ant)* wellness.

6 **quarrel** *(n)* an argument. *(s)* row, dispute, altercation, disagreement. *(ant)* agreement.

7 **ensuing** *(adj)* happening afterwards due to something else. *(s)* resulting, consequent. *(ant)* preceding.

8 **lead** *(n)* a dense and heavy metal, but one that is soft.

9 **thwack** *(v)* hit hard with a sharp blow. *(s)* strike, pound, thump, smack.

10 **proceed** *(v)* originate. *(s)* follow, result, derive.

11 **blow** *(n)* a strike with a weapon, hand or hard object. *(s)* punch, thump, thwack.

12 **flesh** *(n)* the muscle and fat of a human or an animal. *(s)* tissue.

13 **wrestle** *(v)* force or fight by grappling (tussling). *(s)* struggle, brawl, battle, scuffle.

14 **brute** *(n)* a violent person. *(s)* barbarian, thug, savage, bully.

15 **exposure** *(n)* the uncovering of something secret. *(s)* discovery, detection.

heard the sickening sound of skull bashing stone, she could resist no longer, **compelled**[1] to peek around the alcove's edge.

'Lord save us all!' Cad mouthed **aghast**[2], her eyes widening with disgust. A stout man, whom she'd never seen before, clutched Bryn's head by his hair and was bashing it against the stone floor with such force that the **subsequent**[3] blows might kill him.

With one leap, Cad flew, and now clung to the man's back, her arms around his neck, her legs gripping his midriff like a tree monkey. He let go of Bryn, who fell to the floor, and before the man could blink, Cad stabbed him hard in one shoulder with the hairpin, and then sank it even deeper into the other. He **wheeled**[4], trying to cast her off, but she held on and pricked him with the pin again and again, wherever she could reach him with its tip.

Flailing, the man whirled, stumbling and almost **toppling**[5] with Cad still on his back. Then, **regaining**[6] his balance and crashing backwards with what felt like full force, he **crushed**[7] Cad into the wall. His **tactic**[8] worked; her head cracked cruelly against stone. Pretty lights swam before her eyes; sparks of white and silver swirled along in time to the rhythm beating her skull.

Cad cried out in shock. She blinked over and over, shaking her head, her grip loosening around the man's neck. She must not black out. She must not **succumb**[9] to the pretty stars glittering into her vision. She must hold on. She could have stabbed his neck and killed him right there, but she refused to **stoop**[10] to that level yet. She would be an honourable Knight Hawk: **fatal**[11] **wounding**[12] would be her **last resort**[13].

---

1 **compel** *(v)* force or oblige someone to do something. *(s)* impel, drive.

2 **aghast** *(adj)* shocked or horrified. *(s)* astounded, stunned, appalled. *(ant)* unaffected.

3 **subsequent** *(adj)* occurring after something in time. *(s)* ensuing, following. *(ant)* prior, former.

4 **wheel** *(v)* turn around rapidly to face another way. *(s)* veer, circle, rotate, swing.

5 **topple** *(v)* overbalance and fall. *(s)* tumble, keel, collapse.

6 **regain** *(v)* recover something. *(s)* repossess, recapture.

7 **crush** *(v)* squeeze to the point of damaging. *(s)* squash, compress, press.

8 **tactic** *(n)* an action to achieve something specific. *(s)* plan, strategy, ploy.

9 **succumb** *(v)* give in or give way. *(s)* yield, submit, surrender, capitulate. *(ant)* withstand.

10 **stoop** *(v)* lower one's standards enough to do something bad. *(s)* sink, resort, descend.

11 **fatal** *(adj)* causing death. *(s)* lethal, deadly. *(ant)* harmless.

12 **wound** *(v)* cause an injury. *(s)* harm, maim, hurt, damage. *(ant)* heal.

13 **last resort** *(n)* the last action after all else has failed.

Cad, now **sandwiched**[1] between the man's back and the wall, her left arm **garrotting**[2] his neck, swiftly speared again, managing to **puncture**[3] his fleshy thighs repeatedly. He was strong, but eventually Cad let go, because with high-pitched yelps, the man danced across the passageway, crashing to his knees. Cad seized her chance; she ran at him and landed an almighty kick to the back of his neck. His hands flew towards the blow. He turned to look at Cad, the **hatred**[4] in his eyes shocking her, then like a **drunk**[5], he lurched forward, landing face first on the floor.

Thank goodness for my short boots, she thought, now forgiving their noisiness, and for **good measure**[6], in turn, she stuck the pin deep into both his buttocks. The hairpin **inflicted**[7] **minor**[8] damage, but the soreness would **hinder**[9] his escape once he came to, and she **figured**[10] that might be quite soon.

'Bryn, Bryn,' she said, crouching down next to him. 'Bryn.'

A surge of panic gripped her limbs. Was she too late? 'Bryn,' she hissed in his ear. She shook him hard. 'Wake up, you lazy **hare brain**[11],' she cried, shaking him again.

The **insult**[12] seemed to work: he stirred.

'Mmm,' Bryn groaned, but his already bruised eyes remained shut.

'Bryn, you're hurt, and we have no time. **For all our sakes**[13], wake up,' she urged, shaking his shoulders.

Now terrified he was **fading fast**[14], Cad lifted Bryn's head. Sticky blood stained her fingertips,

---

1 **sandwich** *(v)* uncomfortably squash between two other people or things.

2 **garrotte** *(v)* restrict someone's breathing with something around the neck.

3 **puncture** *(v)* make a hole in something. *(s)* pierce, stab, prick, spike.

4 **hatred** *(n)* great dislike. *(s)* hate, loathing, detestation. *(ant)* love.

5 **drunk** *(n)* a person who habitually drinks too much alcohol. *(s)* drunkard. *(ant)* teetotaller.

6 **good measure** (phrase) something that is done in addition to other things to enable a good outcome.

7 **inflict** *(v)* cause or impose pain or suffering. *(s)* create, make. *(ant)* relieve.

8 **minor** *(adj)* not important. *(s)* slight, unimportant, insignificant. *(ant)* major, important.

9 **hinder** *(v)* make difficult, hamper, obstruct or slow down. *(s)* delay, impede. *(ant)* help.

10 **figure** *(v)* believe to be the case. *(s)* suppose, think, expect.

11 **hare brain** *(n)* a foolhardy person. *(s)* fool, crackpot, dope.

12 **insult** *(n)* a rude or unkind remark. *(s)* dig, jibe, abuse. *(ant)* compliment.

13 **for (someone's) sake** (phrase) for the well-being and success of.

14 **fade fast** *(v)* to become weak or fail very quickly. *(s)* worsen, decline, deteriorate. *(ant)* improve rapidly.

but it wasn't **gushing**[1] and was already **congealing**[2] and **matting**[3] his hair. From experience of injuries, Cad knew this was a good sign.

'Bryn Davis, if you don't wake up now, I will tell everyone about this. Do you understand me? Wake up.'

She took the hairpin and pricked his bottom. His eyes suddenly snapped open. With an overwhelming relief, she glared at him.

'Davis, listen to me. You must leave before this man comes to.'

Bryn stared at her, his eyes **puffed**[4] and **glassy**[5].

'Wake up,' she hissed again, **manhandling**[6] his dead weight up to a sitting position and **concerned**[7] he might vomit.

'What, what?' he **murmured**[8], his eyes fighting to widen as he scanned the scene. Then, he jerked into life. 'What in heaven? You!' he exclaimed, his bruised eyes swivelling from Cad to the **prone**[9] man and back again. 'You?'

'Yes, it's *me*,' she snapped. 'Now listen. I don't know what you're up to, but I just saved your skin, and if you want that kept secret, you never saw me here. You understand?'

Bryn remained **mute**[10], but Cad caught the look lurking in his puffy eyes.

'I'm going that way.' She lifted her chin to point towards her dungeon. 'And you're going that way, she gestured with her eyes. And I'd be quick, lest he wakes first.'

Tight-lipped[11], Davis nodded.

Cad helped him to his feet. He swayed like a **scarecrow**[12] in a gale, clearly struggling to stand.

---

1 **gush** *(v)* flow quickly. *(s)* pour, spill, stream. *(ant)* trickle.

2 **congeal** *(v)* begin to become solid. *(s)* clot, set, harden. *(ant)* liquify, soften.

3 **mat** *(v)* become tangled. *(s)* knot, snarl.

4 **puffed** *(adj)* bigger than normal. *(s)* swollen. *(ant)* shrunken, normal.

5 **glassy** *(adj)* (of the eyes) showing no interest. *(s)* glazed, blank, expressionless. *(ant)* expressive.

6 **manhandle** *(v)* move someone roughly. *(s)* jostle, shove, push, maul.

7 **concerned** *(adj)* worried. *(s)* anxious, troubled, perturbed. *(ant)* happy, content.

8 **murmur** *(v)* say something softly. *(s)* mumble, mutter. *(ant)* shout, declare.

9 **prone** *(adj)* lying flat, particularly face downwards. *(s)* prostrate, horizontal. *(ant)* upright, supine.

10 **mute** *(adj)* remaining speechless. *(s)* silent, taciturn, quiet. *(ant)* vocal.

11 **tight-lipped** *(adj)* with the lips closed as a sign of keeping quiet or hiding emotion. *(s)* taciturn, reticent. *(ant)* talkative.

12 **scarecrow** *(n)* a figure made to look human set up to scare birds away from crop-growing fields.

'You never saw me, Bryn, did you?' she **reiterated**[1], worried his battered head would lose her words the minute she left him.

Like a drunk, Bryn still stared into the distance, his eyes bleary, his mouth open. The man on the floor groaned, shifting slightly.

'Heavens,' Cad muttered again. 'Bryn, unless you want the **entire**[2] castle to know a lowly page saved your **hide**[3], then you do as I say. You never saw me.' She almost spelled out each word with a wave of her hand. 'Have you got that, Davis?'

Without uttering a sound, he gave the slightest nod.

'I would hurry,' she added, glancing at the rousing man **heaped**[4] on the floor.

And with that, Cad turned and fled up the stone stairwell to her cell, praying she would beat Goodwife Hughes to it.

---

1 **reiterate** *(v)* say again for emphasis or clarity. *(s)* repeat, persist, restate, recap.

2 **entire** *(adj)* with nothing or no part left out. *(s)* whole, complete. *(ant)* partial.

3 **hide** *(n)* the skin of an animal. *(s)* pelt.

4 **heap** *(v)* collect in a pile or bundle. *(s)* clump, lump, arrange.

CHAPTER FIFTEEN

Spies and Lies

Having hared up the steep steps two at a time, Cad locked her cell door behind her, and trembling with **fatigue**[1], hunger and relief, flopped onto her bed, panting like a dog. The sun beamed above the towers, blazing down on Catrin Castle – affording her no **respite**[2].

When she'd caught her breath, Cad realised she'd actually beat Goodwife Hughes back to the dungeon. To quell any suspicion from the woman, Cad rose, quickly washed her face, combed her **dishevelled**[3] hair, smoothed down her bedraggled tunic and perched at her desk, awaiting Mrs Hughes's imminent arrival. Cad was so **drained**[4] of energy, her hands trembled, but she managed to re-read the note she dearly hoped May the hawk would be delivering to her father sometime later today. Cad would dispatch May with the message once she'd found her brother alive.

Earlier, Cad had considered sending May the moment she'd felt the warmth of the sheets in that empty crib. But if by some tragic turn of events Cad were to find her brother dead, her father would want to return, and she could not live with the **prospect**[5] of spoiling that by sending him the note too soon. She must find her brother first, and only then could she send May to tell Llywelyn that the fast rider brought lies, not news. She prayed Hugh Hughes had

---

1 **fatigue** *(n)* extreme tiredness. *(s)* exhaustion, weariness, weakness. *(ant)* refreshment.

2 **respite** *(n)* a period of rest or relief from something difficult. *(s)* break, interval. *(ant)* continuation.

3 **dishevelled** *(adj)* (hair or clothes) made untidy. *(s)* mussed, messy, tousled. *(ant)* tidy, groomed.

4 **drain** *(v)* take away or stop someone's energy. *(s)* deplete, deprive, deny. *(ant)* fill.

5 **prospect** *(n)* a future or anticipated event. *(s)* thought, idea, contemplation.

not yet reached her father, for if he had, Llywelyn would already be returning.

A clunking of keys pulled Cad's attention to the door, which creaked open on its **parched**[1] hinges. Goodwife Hughes's face was **blotchy**[2], her eyes puffy.

Why has she been weeping? Cad thought, but did not ask.

'Goodwife Hughes, do we have any further news of Prince John? Have they … Have they found a body?' Cad asked.

'No, Master Cad,' replied Goodwife Hughes, placing a food platter next to Cad, 'they have not.' The woman **stuttered**[3] as she spoke, a sob rising in her throat.

'Then perhaps all is not lost,' said Cad, standing to reassure the woman and hiding her note as she did so. 'Perhaps they may find my … Prince John alive yet.'

I must be more careful, thought Cad, having almost uttered the word 'brother' to Mrs Hughes.

'Oh, I do hope they find something soon, Master Cad. It would seem that wolf got clean away.' The woman's arms sailed into the air as she wailed again.

That thought turned Cad's stomach, and she refused to believe it.

'Thank you for the food,' Cad said, trying to distract the goodwife and hoping she would leave soon. 'I did not sleep at all well last night, and I am **famished**[4]. I shall eat and then nap.'

Goodwife Hughes busied herself tidying the wash **utensils**[5] and filling up a water ewer as Cad tucked into cheese, fruit and bread. As Cad just about finished, Mrs Hughes made to leave. 'I'll be back with supper later. And I will bring better candles: beeswax, not those cheap tallow things. You'll see your scholarly studies better tonight.'

'Thank you,' Cad replied. 'You are most generous.'

'I know you're a good page, Master Cad,' Mrs Hughes said as she left, and locked the dungeon behind her.

Cad was exhausted, but sleep would **elude**[6] her, for she was too anxious and wanted to return to the castle to find baby John. But what perturbed her even more was that the hair she'd sealed

---

1 **parched** *(adj)* dried up from lack of water or hydration. *(s)* dehydrated, unlubricated. *(ant)* lubricated.

2 **blotchy** *(adj)* covered with blotches (marks or spots). *(s)* patchy, blemished. *(ant)* clear.

3 **stutter** *(v)* struggle to say one's words. *(s)* stammer, falter, hesitate. *(ant)* enunciate.

4 **famished** *(adj)* very hungry. *(s)* ravenous, starving. *(ant)* full, sated, satiated.

5 **utensil** *(n)* a tool, container or article used for jobs. *(s)* apparatus.

6 **elude** *(v)* avoid or escape. *(s)* evade, shun. *(ant)* embrace, pursue.

across her doorjamb before leaving had been gone when she'd returned to her cell. Unless it had fallen off accidentally, which she doubted, as she had fixed it **firmly**[1] in place with earwax, then someone had entered her cell whilst she was out in the castle. Someone knew Cad had means of escape, and who that someone was, she would dearly love to know.

With **reluctance**[2], Cad tucked the note she'd penned to her father in her new, clean tunic, and flopped down on her bed, thinking of what had happened. She shuddered: revisiting the fight with Bryn shook her deeply. Not only had she risked so much in revealing herself, but she'd also hated stabbing the man. But even stranger, who was he, and why had he fought so **viciously**[3] with Bryn? Was his presence linked to the theft of the Gwalch Gem bracelet and her brother's disappearance?

Bryn's brain would be **addled**[4] from the blows, but no doubt once he recovered, he'd be wondering how she'd escaped her cell, and she knew he'd not stop until he found out. Once Bryn got the **bit between his teeth**[5], he **rarely**[6] let it go.

The blistering heat now roasted her cell. Cad glanced up at the arrow slit; pondering the sun's position, she gauged it was early afternoon. She hoped Dylan had received the note from May and could meet her where she'd requested: where they'd hidden Fishy beneath the keep. By chance and good fortune, they had concealed the pup close to where Cad knew she must now search for baby John.

With the reduced, unclear amount of time the ring now afforded her, Cad would need Dylan's help to find her brother, but that was not the only reason she sought his **assistance**[7]. As a tingle of dread and disgust slithered down her spine, Cad pictured the task ahead of her. Without a doubt, she knew she could never enter that hideous place alone – the place buried in the deep depths of Catrin Castle's keep where Cad suspected someone now imprisoned her baby brother, Prince John.

---

1 **firmly** *(adj)* in a firm (solid) manner. *(s)* soundly, thoroughly. *(ant)* weakly.

2 **reluctance** *(n)* not really wanting to do something. *(s)* unwillingness, hesitation. *(ant)* eagerness.

3 **viciously** *(adv)* in a vicious (cruel or violent) manner. *(s)* brutally, ferociously. *(ant)* gently.

4 **addle** *(v)* make someone unable to think properly. *(s)* confuse, muddle, stupefy, daze.

5 **bit between one's teeth** (phrase) do something with extreme enthusiasm and determination.

6 **rarely** *(adv)* not often. *(s)* seldom, scarcely. *(ant)* frequently, often.

7 **assistance** *(n)* the act of helping someone or something. *(s)* aid, support, service.

CHAPTER SIXTEEN

Feeding Fishy

Armed with her hairpin, the note for her father and invisible cheese scraps to ward off the guards' dogs, and not fixing a trap across the doorjamb this time, Cad **descended**[1] the keep's stairs in twos, knowing a spy loomed. Nor did she bother to count the time passing by, for when the ring failed her, as it inevitably would, she would face the ensuing consequences. Finding her brother and **preventing**[2] her father's unnecessary return was **crucial**[3], and she would risk all to ensure both.

When she reached the foot of the stairs, there was fortunately still no guard at the bottom. However, extra vigilant, Cad waited, and watched a while. The passageways seemed quiet save for the odd servant **milling about**[4], fetching ewers of water and platters of food for the ladies up in their chambers. The corridors were narrow, Cad must be careful lest she scare a servant half to death if she accidentally brushed by one.

When the coast finally cleared, rather than **bearing**[5] left and out into the main bailey, she **veered**[6] right and headed down the corridor she knew led towards Dewi's secret and forbidden,

---

1 **descend** *(v)* move or fall downwards. *(s)* go down. *(ant)* ascend, climb.

2 **prevent** *(v)* stop something from happening. *(s)* block, halt. *(ant)* cause, permit.

3 **crucial** *(adj)* of absolute (complete) importance. *(s)* critical, vital, key. *(ant)* trivial.

4 **mill about** *(v)* move around. *(s)* rove, wander.

5 **bear** *(v)* turn and take a particular direction. *(s)* veer, move.

6 **veer** *(v)* suddenly change direction. *(s)* turn, divert, swerve.

underground dungeons beneath the keep. When searching for a safe place to hide the pup they had rescued, she and Dylan had happened upon their ghastly discovery by chance. Neither had explored nor verified their fears, but Cad was now certain of what lay deep below Catrin Castle. At the **mere**[1] thought of it, Cad's skin **bristled**[2], and a tingle pricked her spine. As she descended, she hoped the torches below would be lit. She would need to remove one and carry it down to that unspeakable place. What a sight that would be: a burning torch floating through the air as if **conjured**[3] by a **demon**[4] lighting the pathway to hell.

To stop terrifying herself with those visions, Cad quashed her fear, and as when she woke from a nightmare, forced lighter thoughts into her head. She pictured Fishy's imminent greeting: the happy **yaps**[5], the whirring tail, the sloppy kisses – **unconditional**[6] love. Cad's heart lifted at the thought of the **whelp**[7] she had rescued from the water. If ever she discovered who had thrown Fishy into the moat …

Now moving swiftly, Cad **navigated**[8] the last few **dingy**[9] twists and turns, and finally reached the narrow corridor that housed the storage area for old **armaments**[10] and battle **miscellany**[11]. Thankfully a torch burned here, so she could see well. With a welcome wave of excitement, Cad opened the door and entered. She pushed past various items – things she must use once knighted – and, lifted by the prospect of seeing Fishy, she made to the back of the room, from where **whimpering**[12] and high-pitched yaps now rose. Hastening, Cad reached behind a stack

---

1 **mere** *(adj)* no matter how small the significance. *(s)* just.

2 **bristle** *(v)* recoil or react defensively. *(s)* prickle, shiver, flinch. *(ant)* accept.

3 **conjure** *(v)* make something appear unexpectedly or from nowhere. *(s)* summon, raise, rouse. *(ant)* dispel.

4 **demon** *(n)* a bad spirit. *(s)* devil, fiend. *(ant)* angel.

5 **yap** *(n)* a high-pitched bark. *(s)* yelp, woof.

6 **unconditional** *(adj)* without question. *(s)* unlimited, unreserved. *(ant)* conditional.

7 **whelp** *(n)* a puppy. *(s)* pup. *(ant)* adult dog.

8 **navigate** *(v)* find the way, guide or steer. *(s)* journey, negotiate.

9 **dingy** *(adj)* drab and gloomy. *(s)* dismal, sombre, dim, dark. *(ant)* bright, clean.

10 **armament** *(n)* military equipment and weapons. *(s)* arms, munitions.

11 **miscellany** *(n)* a group or mixture of different items. *(s)* assortment, collection. *(ant)* uniformity.

12 **whimpering** *(n)* low, feeble sounds expressing displeasure. *(s)* whining, mewling. *(ant)* rejoicing.

of large **barrels**[1], removed some **sacking**[2], and lifted up the **trap door**[3] to reveal her pup's **crate**[4].

'Fishy,' she cried. The little dog barked, her tail wagging but her eyes full of bewilderment. 'Fishy,' Cad said again, opening the crate and letting the pup out. But the dog whirled in strange circles backing away from Cad, its behaviour **flummoxing**[5] her.

'Oh, Fishy, what a hare brain I am. I forgot you cannot see me. How confusing for you. You can smell me, touch me, but you cannot see me.'

Cad grabbed Fishy and flopped onto her backside as the young pup covered her invisible face with soggy-wet licks. When Fishy calmed, Cad's mind turned to Dylan. Where was he? He should have been here by now. Cad had requested he feed Fishy early, in good time to meet her down here.

Worried about Dylan's tardiness and **resigned**[6] to being visible soon, Cad waited, playing with Fishy to distract her thoughts. But as time rushed by, Cad's **uneasiness**[7] gained **pace**[8]. Perhaps Dylan had not been in the tilt yard or at the butts when May had searched for him. Or maybe the note had fallen from her leg. Maybe he could not leave his duties. What if she was wrong about everything and they had already found baby John without her knowing?

Stop it, Cad. He will come.

But waiting alone in the dungeon **sapped**[9] her **spirits**[10] and drained her resolve. Little light came in through the crack she'd left open in the door, and she knew her wait was over. She glanced down at her limbs. She was still invisible. If she were to visit the **oubliette**[11] alone, then her best chance of getting there would be now, before she reappeared.

'What would you do, Fishy?' she whispered in the pup's **velvety**[12] ear, but her question was

---

1 **barrel** *(n)* a cylindrical container usually wider around the middle. *(s)* cask, keg, vat, tub, drum.

2 **sacking** *(n)* bags or sacks made from coarse fabric called sackcloth.

3 **trap door** *(n)* a removable (often hinged) panel in a ceiling, roof or floor. *(s)* escape hatch.

4 **crate** *(n)* a wooden case used for containing or transporting things. *(s)* box, trunk.

5 **flummox** *(v)* perplex or bewilder. *(s)* baffle, puzzle, mystify. *(ant)* clarify, demystify.

6 **resigned** *(adj)* accepting what cannot be avoided. *(s)* acceptive, unresisting. *(ant)* resistant.

7 **uneasiness** *(n)* a feeling of worry or discomfort. *(s)* anxiety, apprehension. *(ant)* ease.

8 **pace** *(n)* speed. *(s)* rapidity, swiftness, quickness.

9 **sap** *(v)* gradually weaken, erode, destroy or deplete power. *(s)* drain, debilitate. *(ant)* bolster.

10 **spirits** *(n)* feelings and mood. *(s)* energy, enthusiasm, morale.

11 **oubliette** *(n)* an underground dungeon, often in a medieval castle, with access only through a trapdoor in the ceiling.

12 **velvety** *(adj)* like velvet cloth. *(s)* soft, smooth, silky. *(ant)* rough, coarse, uneven.

rhetorical[1]. Dylan wasn't coming, and even if he was, she must move now – alone. To wait would make her too late: she might be seen in a passageway once visible.

'Come on, Fishy,' she said, swooping up the pup. I'm sure Dylan will be down with some goodies soon. Cad put the puppy back into her crate and gave her a handful of **pork crackling**[2] from the **stash**[3] she and Dylan had saved for her. She filled up Fishy's water bowl from the ewer and closed the trap door, putting the sacks back over it, arranging them in such a way that when Dylan arrived, he would know she had visited Fishy and was still down here alone.

'I'll be back for you the moment I'm released, and no one will take you from me,' Cad said to the pup as she left, pulling the storeroom door closed behind her.

---

1 **rhetorical** *(adj)* asked for effect or to make a statement rather than to get an answer.

2 **pork crackling** *(n)* roasted or fried pork (pig) skin, especially served as a crispy snack.

3 **stash** *(n)* a secret store of something. *(s)* cache, hoard, stockpile.

CHAPTER SEVENTEEN

To Forget

As Cad left the room where Fishy lived, every part of her yearned to ascend to the towers above her in the high keep.

How is it I want for a prison cell so much? she wondered, but knowing the answer.

But instead of fleeing, she gathered herself, **pivoted**[1] on her heel and descended further towards the **spiral**[2] stairs to Dewi's secret and forbidden place. The ghastly hole called the oubliette, whose name **derived**[3] from the French *oublier*, meaning *to forget*. With her brother missing, Cad would not rest until she'd checked what was beyond that locked door in the depths of Catrin Castle.

Cad thought of how easily she could have been forgotten as a baby and shuddered. Llywelyn had reassured her, promised her, that when he and Owain had pulled on that rope, drawing her from the bottom of that well, they had been certain that her **concealment**[4] had intended to preserve her life and not take it. The actions of a desperate mother trying to save her child from the hideous **inevitability**[5] of war. Llywelyn had searched for Cad's mother, to no avail. No one had remained alive in her village. To this day, Cad knew not if her mother had lived or died.

---

1 **pivot** *(v)* turn as if on a pivot (central point). *(s)* rotate, revolve, swivel, whirl, pirouette.

2 **spiral** *(adj)* winding in a continuous curve. *(s)* curling, helical, coiling.

3 **derive** *(v)* come or arise from something specific. *(s)* acquire, attain.

4 **concealment** *(n)* the act of hiding something or someone. *(s)* secretion. *(ant)* revelation.

5 **inevitability** *(n)* the characteristic of being sure to happen. *(s)* certainty. *(ant)* doubtfulness, uncertainty.

Now with burgeoning trepidation, Cad inched her way forward, her steps tentative, her hand gripping the flaming torch she'd grabbed from outside the storeroom. How ghoulish the floating flames looked, **illuminating**[1] the darkness with their **amber**[2] glow. The torch was a necessity; it was so heavy it hindered her progress, yet without it, she would see nothing. No daylight found its way down here.

As the passageway **steepened**[3] and the temperature **plummeted**[4], a dank, musty smell nipped at her nostrils. She faltered, wishing with all her heart that Dylan was here with her. But convinced Prince John would be in the oubliette, she pushed on through the grimy tunnel. She winced as the walls **shrank**[5] closer, **encroaching**[6] with their glistening dampness, the floors treacherous with slime.

Now below the level of the moat, trickles of **telltale**[7] water occasionally splashed from the roof onto her cheeks. Invisible or not, her **senses**[8] still worked perfectly, and presently, they began to torment her. The drip, drip sound of water, the faint echoing of her footsteps, the **sinister**[9] shadows shimmering on the walls, their long twig-like fingers poking their accusing bones her way. All these eerie **silhouettes**[10] gathered here to **haunt**[11] her.

Cad swallowed hard, struggling to ignore the detail the torch drew from the darkness. Her invisible limbs felt floaty, her head light, her breaths shallow and rapid as she fought to calm her mind. All proved to be an arduous task, but she forced her eyes forward, taking careful steps lest she trip and fall. Every part of her **longed**[12] to turn and run, but she edged on towards the door which concealed the steep steps down to the cell rumoured to exist.

'Arrgh!'

---

1 **illuminate** *(v)* light up. *(s)* brighten, lighten. *(ant)* darken, dim.

2 **amber** *(n)* a golden-yellow colour typical of amber resin.

3 **steepen** *(v)* get or cause to become steeper (more of an incline). *(s)* decline. *(ant)* flatten, level.

4 **plummet** *(v)* fall or drop straight down at high speed. *(s)* dive, tumble, decrease. *(ant)* climb, rise.

5 **shrink** *(v)* make or become smaller (past tense: shrank). *(s)* contract, narrow. *(ant)* expand.

6 **encroach** *(v)* advance gradually but beyond desirable limits. *(s)* intrude, invade. *(ant)* keep distant.

7 **telltale** *(adj)* indicating or revealing something. *(s)* giveaway.

8 **sense** *(n)* a faculty of the body that perceives the external environment. *(s)* awareness, perception.

9 **sinister** *(adj)* giving a feeling that something bad may happen. *(s)* menacing, threatening. *(ant)* innocent.

10 **silhouette** *(n)* a visible, dark shape and outline. *(s)* contour, form, shadow, figure.

11 **haunt** *(v)* (of the supernatural) to appear. *(s)* spook, scare, visit.

12 **long** *(v)* to have great want. *(s)* yearn, ache, desire. *(ant)* hate, despise.

Cad suddenly screamed, her hands **batting**[1] her head, snatching and grabbing at her hair as the torch dropped to the ground at her feet. She shrieked again as a scorching pain **seared**[2] through her foot. From her **violent**[3] kick, the torch flew away from her, **plunging**[4] her into almost darkness. Her arms wheeled like **windmills**[5] as she **collided**[6] with the wall.

'What on Earth?' she cried, as two rats scurried down the passageway, the waning torch lighting up their **scraggy**[7] bodies.

'What a wantwit I am!' she exclaimed as the **rodents**[8] scuttled away to safety. The rats had not seen her because she was invisible, and they'd dropped from the roof's low **beam**[9] and landed right on top of her head.

'Oh no!' Cad cried, realising the scant light in the tunnel was fading further and rapidly so. She pounced on the torch, swooping it up from the floor. Then **cupping**[10] her free hand around it, she blew gentle breaths onto its faltering flames in a desperate bid to **rekindle**[11] it.

'Please, please,' she murmured into the dying flame. 'Please.'

If that flame died, Cad's **mission**[12] would fail along with it. She would be forced to retreat and return tomorrow with a new torch. But that would be too late for John. A baby would soon perish in these temperatures without food and his mother's love. That thought rocked Cad, for in that moment, regardless of the outcome, she realised this infant might never know his mother's touch again.

Cad blew on the torch as gently as she might treat any **babe in arms**[13] and vowed to make up for John's loss. He and she were both without a mother now.

---

1 **bat** *(v)* hit something or someone with one's hand. *(s)* swipe, knock.

2 **sear** *(v)* scorch or burn with intense heat. *(s)* streak, flash. *(ant)* cool, freeze.

3 **violent** *(adj)* using damaging physical force. *(s)* vicious, fierce, wild. *(ant)* weak, gentle.

4 **plunge** *(v)* suddenly bring into a specified condition or state. *(s)* thrust, force, throw.

5 **windmill** *(n)* a building with large sails that converts wind power into energy.

6 **collide** *(v)* come into contact with (usually forcefully). *(s)* bump, crash, ram, run into. *(ant)* miss.

7 **scraggy** *(adj)* bony and thin. *(s)* skinny, scrawny. *(ant)* fat, plump, rotund.

8 **rodent** *(n)* a gnawing mammal such as rats, mice, squirrels, etc.

9 **beam** *(n)* a strong piece of wood or metal used to support structures in a building or house. *(s)* joist, strut.

10 **cup** *(v)* form one's hands into a curved cup shape. *(s)* curl, wrap. *(ant)* uncurl.

11 **rekindle** *(v)* (of a fire) relight. *(s)* revive, revitalise. *(ant)* snuff, smother, extinguish.

12 **mission** *(n)* an important job of work. *(s)* undertaking, operation, quest.

13 **babe in arms** (phrase) a young baby. *(s)* infant.

How absurd Cad felt whispering, 'Please light, please light,' to a dying flame, but as it **dwindled**[1] to hardly a glow, she knew she would be forced to abandon her search. Nothing in this dank prison would serve as **fuel**[2] to this flame; even her clothes were too damp. Then in a desperate, **last-ditch**[3] attempt, she yanked viciously at her invisible hair, and with a loud 'Ouch!' tore out a great **clump**[4] in her fist.

Sheltering[5] the dying torch with a cupped hand, she offered up several strands of hair, gently blowing at the torch's glowing remains, wishing it would **reignite**[6], but to no avail – the torch was dead.

'No!' she bellowed at the top of her lungs, not caring a jot if anyone heard. '*No!*'

But it would seem that blowing gently on the torch had been the wrong **tack**[7] to take, for suddenly, thanks to the **gusts**[8] of air from her **blaring**[9] shouts, a lone flame flickered from its club-like tip.

'What?' Cad cried, quickly offering up the remaining hair as fuel. With the reassuring stench and hissing crackles of the burning hair, Cad's heart soared as the flames danced around the torch's end.

'Yes, yes, yes!' she said, weak with **gratitude**[10] and relief. And so thankful that the torch now burned, she **gathered her wits**[11] and moved on, scolding herself for fearing two scrawny rats. After all, what could really harm her in the **confines**[12] of this tunnel? Then, in the distance, at the dead end of the passageway, she saw the **squat**[13] metal door before her. At

---

1 **dwindle** *(v)* lessen in size or strength. *(s)* decrease, fade, diminish. *(ant)* increase.
2 **fuel** *(n)* something that is burned to produce heat or power. *(s)* combustible.
3 **last-ditch** *(adj)* a final attempt when all else has failed. *(s)* desperate, frantic.
4 **clump** *(n)* a mass or collection of something. *(s)* bunch, bundle.
5 **shelter** *(v)* protect or shield from harm. *(s)* preserve, conserve. *(ant)* expose.
6 **reignite** *(v)* cause to ignite (burn) again. *(s)* relight, rekindle. *(ant)* extinguish.
7 **tack** *(n)* a direction or course of action.
8 **gust** *(n)* a strong and sudden rush of wind or air. *(s)* rush, blast.
9 **blare** *(v)* make a loud sound. *(s)* boom, roar, bellow. *(ant)* murmur, whisper.
10 **gratitude** *(n)* the quality of being thankful and showing appreciation. *(s)* thanks, gratefulness. *(ant)* ingratitude.
11 **gather one's wits** (phrase) to gather and calm oneself after a shock or surprise.
12 **confines** *(n)* restrictive boundaries and limits of the surrounding region. *(s)* limitations, margins.
13 **squat** *(adj)* short and broad (wide). *(s)* solid, chunky. *(ant)* puny, small.

once, the dread resurfaced, hitting her like a blow from a **blunt**[1] lance.

Now at the entrance to what she thought was the oubliette, her hand shook as she tried the door. Of course, it was locked. Cad had foreseen that, and now her hairpin danced between her fingers, the torch swaying in her other hand. She forced her limbs to calm as the emerald hawk turned the lock with ease. Even though her body was as tense as taut rope, she sighed a long-held breath of relief. Then with care, she removed her pin from the lock, pushed open the heavy door and stepped forward an inch. As she peered down the stairwell, an almost **vertical**[2] drop into darkness, just like the well whence she was rescued as a baby, terror **crippled**[3] her, threatening **victory**[4] this time.

I can't do it, she thought, about to flee to find Dylan. *I just can't do it.*

Nausea swirled in her guts as she **teetered**[5] on the **brink**[6] of bolting back to her room. She pictured baby John. Her mouth turned sandy, her pulse boxing her ears as she stepped forward and placed one foot atop the first stone step. Before taking another, she glanced over her shoulder into the jet-black passageway, hoping that **miraculously**[7], Dylan might appear. Knowing he wouldn't, Cad turned, and with the most **daunting**[8] clanging sound she had ever heard, the metal door slammed closed behind her.

---

1 **blunt** *(adj)* not sharp. *(s)* dulled, rounded. *(ant)* sharp, pointed.

2 **vertical** *(adj)* at right angles to a horizontal plane. *(s)* perpendicular, plumb. *(ant)* horizontal.

3 **cripple** *(v)* cause to become unable to move properly. *(s)* immobilise, paralyse.

4 **victory** *(n)* a win. *(s)* success, triumph. *(ant)* defeat.

5 **teeter** *(v)* be unable to decide between things or actions. *(s)* waver, falter, see-saw. *(ant)* decide.

6 **brink** *(n)* the point at which something unwelcome is about to happen. *(s)* edge, threshold.

7 **miraculously** *(adv)* in a remarkable and welcome way. *(s)* astoundingly, unbelievably. *(ant)* unremarkably.

8 **daunting** *(adj)* seeming difficult to face. *(s)* unnerving, unsettling. *(ant)* reassuring, comforting.

CHAPTER EIGHTEEN

Trapped

With each step Cad took, the temperature plummeted, yet hers soared along with her quickening heart. Even though she was light-headed and sweating, shivers rippled through her body; her skin was cold and her bones ached. Relying on the **meagre**[1] light from the waning torch to punctuate the dark, she prayed the climb down the spiral stone stairs would be short.

But after what felt like an **eternity**[2], with no end in sight, and seeing the eerie torch float alone in the air like an **apparition**[3], an iron fist of fear gripped her, refusing to let her go.

Her legs froze, and her arms weakened, no longer listening to her mind's commands. A strangled sound, so unlike that of her voice, escaped her throat. Whether fatigue or fear were at fault, Cad's legs gave up, and her knees **buckled**[4] beneath her.

Even as she tumbled, and her free hand grasped air, her other clutched the torch, for to be plunged into darkness now was **unthinkable**[5]. The stone steps **grazed**[6] her legs, **skinning**[7]

---

1 **meagre** *(adj)* inadequate or scant. *(s)* measly, paltry, insufficient. *(ant)* plentiful.

2 **eternity** *(n)* infinite or unending time. *(s)* forever, endlessness. *(ant)* instant, jiffy.

3 **apparition** *(n)* a ghost or ghostlike image. *(s)* phantom, spectre, ghoul.

4 **buckle** *(v)* bend and give way under strain or pressure. *(s)* crumple, fold. *(ant)* straighten.

5 **unthinkable** *(adj)* too horrid to be thought possible. *(s)* unimaginable, inconceivable. *(ant)* desirable.

6 **graze** *(v)* cause a slight injury to the skin. *(s)* scrape, abrade, scuff.

7 **skin** *(v)* remove the skin off something. *(s)* flay.

her **shins**[1] and elbows as she battled to **break**[2] her fall with her feet. Thank goodness her head escaped **unscathed**[3], and the torch stayed just about alive as she finally came to an ungainly stop.

Disorientated, Cad felt like she'd been pulled through a **mangle**[4]. So she took a moment and peered into the **abyss**[5] to gain her **bearings**[6]. However, she could not yet see the bottom, and gripping her torch as though it were **priceless**[7], she prayed to God it would last the **descent**[8].

As she braced herself to continue, her ears caught a noise in the distance: a cry so faint, so **feeble**[9], it might have been the mewl of a newborn kitten. Stunned, she calmed her **quaking**[10] and cocked her head, listening intently. There it was.

What is that? she thought, on high alert.

'Ouch!' she yelped, trying to stand on a twisted ankle. It, too, felt like it was being turned in a mangle, but she blanked the pain, leaning on the foot. Her breaths so loud in the silence, she sounded like a panting mastiff.

In agony, Cad struggled to bear her weight, and with her free hand now **buttressed**[11] against the damp wall for support, she listened again. There it was, the sound a kitten might make. As she fathomed her whereabouts, she saw she had tumbled down the last few remaining steps and now stood on firm ground; thankfully, the torch was still burning.

Stock-still[12], she listened again, but *plop, plop, plop* was all she heard. No mewling. No crying. She remembered she was beneath the moat, its water leaking and trickling about her, always finding its lowest **course**[13].

---

1 **shin** *(n)* the bony front of the leg below the knee.

2 **break** *(v)* interrupt an action or thing. *(s)* stop, halt.

3 **unscathed** *(adj)* without suffering, harm or injury. *(s)* safe, unhurt. *(ant)* injured, harmed.

4 **mangle** *(n)* a machine with two rollers turned by hand to squeeze water from laundry.

5 **abyss** *(n)* a deep hole or chasm. *(s)* pit, depth, void.

6 **bearing** *(n)* direction or position. *(s)* orientation, location, course.

7 **priceless** *(adj)* so precious that a value cannot be put on it. *(s)* rare, high-priced. *(ant)* worthless.

8 **descent** *(n)* an act of moving downwards. *(s)* climb down, drop. *(ant)* ascent, climb.

9 **feeble** *(adj)* lacking strength. *(s)* weak, frail, infirm. *(ant)* forceful.

10 **quake** *(v)* tremble or shake. *(s)* shudder, wobble, vibrate, rock.

11 **buttressed** *(adj)* placed for support. *(s)* braced, bolstered, propped.

12 **stock-still** *(adj)* without motion. *(s)* immobile, unmoving. *(ant)* mobile, moving.

13 **course** *(n)* a route followed by something. *(s)* way, path, channel.

Plop, plop, plop.

In this deafening silence, she wondered if she'd ever heard the sound at all, her imagination duping her into hearing what she so wished to hear. The torch hovered before her eyes, her body still invisible. She blinked, blanking the pain of her ankle and taking in the empty **hovel**[1] where she now found herself. It was cramped, nothing but a hollowed-out, den-like space, its **domed**[2] roof supported by wooden beams, its walls **rough**[3] yet angular, as if **hacked**[4] by a child with a **chisel**[5]. Her heart sank: she had been wrong. The only things that now faced her were emptiness, silence and some sort of metal **grille**[6] beneath her feet which covered a drainage hole, probably there to **siphon**[7] flood water from the moat.

Cad **surveyed**[8] the **barren**[9] space, devastated with disappointment; hot tears rolled down her invisible cheeks. Then as if to be doubly cruel, she noticed the hand that held the torch was beginning to reappear as if painted with elegant brush strokes. Now her time was up; she must leave quickly lest the torch burn out and force her to navigate her journey in the dark, visible to the castle folks. About to face the climb out, her ankle throbbing and swelling, she stopped in her tracks. Her head jerked upright and her breathing stilled. The sound was not a cry as such, but more a **snuffling**[10] and, most oddly, the smacking of lips.

'What in heaven?' she cried.

Then, without **hesitation**[11], she dropped to her knees and peered through the grille in the floor. The torch flame struggled to illuminate what lay beneath, so with all her might, she **heaved**[12] at the metal grille which **barred**[13] her view. To her utter amazement, it shifted, and although it was

---

1 **hovel** *(n)* a small room or dwelling. *(s)* hole, rathole. *(ant)* palace.

2 **dome** *(n)* a rounded space forming part of a structure. *(s)* arched roof, hemisphere.

3 **rough** *(adj)* not smooth or level. *(s)* bumpy, stony, uneven. *(ant)* smooth, flat.

4 **hack** *(v)* cut with rough haphazard (random) blows. *(s)* chop, hew. *(ant)* shape.

5 **chisel** *(n)* a tool used for carving and shaping materials such as wood, stone or metal.

6 **grille** *(n)* a screen or grating of metal bars or wires placed in front of something to allow ventilation or observation.

7 **siphon** *(v)* extract over a period. *(s)* draw off, drain. *(ant)* flood.

8 **survey** *(v)* look closely at or examine. *(s)* study, inspect, assess, evaluate. *(ant)* overlook.

9 **barren** *(adj)* lifeless and bare. *(s)* bleak, empty. *(ant)* warm, welcoming.

10 **snuffle** *(n)* a noisy inhalation. *(s)* sniffle.

11 **hesitation** *(n)* pause. *(s)* delay, waiting, dithering. *(ant)* certainty.

12 **heave** *(v)* lift with great effort. *(s)* haul, pull, raise. *(ant)* push.

13 **bar** *(v)* prevent. *(s)* prohibit, obscure. *(ant)* allow, permit.

heavy, she lifted it a tad and slid it off to the side, kneeling and poking the torch through the hole to light her way.

'What on Earth?' she mouthed.

Several feet below, directly beneath the **grid**[1], she saw the outline of a small carry crib. 'John,' she said. 'John, is that you?'

But he made no sound, nor did she see any movement from within the crib. Now, with her body half-visible, she manoeuvred herself into a position where she could drop into the hole and hopefully land on her feet beside the crib. It seemed someone had lowered John into this **pit**[2], like she had been lowered into the well, but for **wholly**[3] different reasons. Whoever had abandoned John here in this hideous oubliette intended just that – for Prince John to be trapped – forgotten.

Cad turned her feet so they now faced the hole. Then, lying flat on her stomach, and wriggling backwards, she teetered at the edge of the short drop. With the torch in one hand, she slithered back further until her hips allowed her legs to dangle down into the hole. **Craning**[4] her neck, she looked down at the crib, gauging where best to land.

I must time this just right.

An unwelcome storm swelled inside her as she balanced and readied herself for the one-chance drop into the space. She counted, 'One … two …' and was about to drop into the oubliette when a shadow **glancing**[5] from the stairs stopped her.

What was that? Her eyes darted about the dim space. Her body jerked and her stomach heaved as she held her breath and listened. She waited, but all was silent and still: just her mind spooking her. She took a deep breath, gathering up her courage and resolve along with it. She would drop into the oubliette, and from her **estimation**[6], would be able to pass that crib back up through the opening. Then, she must pull herself up and out, just like exercising on the bars

---

1 **grid** *(n)* a framework of bars that provides a covering. *(s)* grille, grating, mesh.

2 **pit** *(n)* a big hole in the ground. *(s)* cavity.

3 **wholly** *(adv)* completely. *(s)* entirely, totally. *(ant)* partially.

4 **crane** *(v)* stretch one's body or neck to see something. *(s)* extend. *(ant)* retract, shrink.

5 **glance** *(v)* hit something and bounce off it. *(s)* bounce.

6 **estimation** *(n)* an approximate calculation. *(s)* evaluation, assessment. *(s)* calculation.

in the yard and climbing trees in the woods. She must be like a squirrel on the fly, **nimble**[1] and agile.

I can do this, she told herself, her throat as dry as hot sand.

Holding the torch as best she could, she wiggled back and, with a grunt, pushed herself down through the hole. The drop was short, but she landed hard on her feet.

'Ouch,' she yelped as a sharp pain shot up through her ankle, which had turned again on impact. She gave it a quick rub, and although it was sore, she didn't think it broken. With an empty sensation in her stomach, she approached the crib. She knew her brother was in there, but what petrified her was the silence. Not a sound came from where he lay, and the faint outline of the **swaddled**[2] baby did not move.

With each sharp breath, **fetid**[3] air filled her throat, and a pulse **stamped**[4] her neck as she leaned towards the baby's bed, the torch held **aloft**[5]. Her brother, Prince John, swaddled in white linen, lay there before her, a peaceful look on his **cherubic**[6] face. Her breath caught in a gasp. Her left hand now hovered above his face: the anticipation of what it would feel paralysing her. She forced the back of her hand to touch the baby's cheek, which, although cool, was not cold.

'John,' she whispered, as she removed the **woollen**[7] cap he wore and cupped his tiny head in her hand. It was warm, and she saw the pulse, albeit faint, beneath the child's **fontanelle**[8] pushing rhythmically against his **delicate**[9] skin.

'John, you're alive,' she cried, lifting him from his crib and holding him against her chest. He snuffled, his eyes fluttering, his lips smacking together in search of his mother's milk. But he didn't cry. That was not a good sign; Cad knew this. When close to death, babies became quiet and **withdrawn**[10]. How long he'd been here in this hellhole without food, she didn't know, but she

---

1 **nimble** *(adj)* light and quick in movement. *(s)* agile, sprightly, lithe, deft. *(ant)* awkward, clumsy.

2 **swaddle** *(v)* wrap tightly in cloth, especially a baby. *(s)* sheathe, bundle, bind. *(ant)* unwrap.

3 **fetid** *(adj)* smelling extremely unpleasant. *(s)* putrid, rank, malodorous. *(ant)* fresh.

4 **stamp** *(v)* push on with pressure. *(s)* impress, beat, pulse.

5 **aloft** *(adv)* overhead. *(s)* high, upwards. *(ant)* low, down.

6 **cherubic** *(adj)* like a young, pretty child. *(s)* angelic, cute, adorable. *(ant)* devilish.

7 **woollen** *(adj)* made from wool, partly or wholly.

8 **fontanelle** *(n)* the soft area of a baby's skull which is yet to close over with bone.

9 **delicate** *(adj)* fine in structure. *(s)* dainty, fragile. *(ant)* strong, durable.

10 **withdrawn** *(adj)* quiet. *(s)* unresponsive, remote, distant. *(ant)* outgoing.

read the signs: his grey **pallor**[1], the ominous blue **tinge**[2] about his lips, his silence.

Cad lowered him back into the crib and secured him as best she could before moving to lift him up and out of this most disgusting chamber – Dewi's oubliette.

Her head buzzed as if tormented by a fly. She shuddered. The faster she moved now, the better the **outcome**[3] would be. Time was not on her side. On tiptoe and with her arms at full stretch, she should be able to offer one edge of the crib up onto the **lip**[4] of the opening, and then with a jump, push it through. To climb out of the oubliette and preserve the torch without burning John would prove tricky, but she knew that with care she could do it.

Her hand trembled as she placed the torch on the floor and lifted the crib. Fortuitously, it weighed little, and she lifted it with ease.

'Don't worry, John, we'll have you warm and fed soon,' she said.

Cad's capture now mattered not. She must save her brother and stop their father from returning from his quest. Cad's quaking hands gripped the crib's base. With her arms fully outstretched, and ignoring the **gripe**[5] of her ankle, she **flexed**[6] her feet, pushing herself onto the very tips of her toes. She moved with **stubborn**[7] difficulty and, wobbling, just about steadied herself, feeling for the right moment to push one edge of the crib over the top and slide it to safety. As she became accustomed to this **pose**[8], she **extended**[9] a little more until she could stretch no further. Then, suddenly, with an almighty scream, she wobbled again, lost her footing and almost dropped the crib.

But it wasn't Cad's clumsiness or lack of balance at fault. It wasn't a **miscalculation**[10] or **misjudgement**[11] in timing that scuppered her attempts. It was the outline of a **monk's**[12]

---

1 **pallor** *(n)* a pale and unhealthy appearance. *(s)* sallowness, pastiness. *(ant)* rosiness.

2 **tinge** *(n)* a hint of colour. *(s)* shade, tone, hue, cast.

3 **outcome** *(n)* the way something turns out. *(s)* result, conclusion.

4 **lip** *(n)* the edge of an opening. *(s)* brink, brim, boundary. *(ant)* centre.

5 **gripe** *(n)* a pain. *(s)* grumble, protest, groan.

6 **flex** *(v)* move or extend through muscle contraction. *(s)* activate, stretch. *(ant)* relax, retract.

7 **stubborn** *(adj)* difficult to overcome. *(s)* persistent, lingering. *(ant)* fleeting.

8 **pose** *(n)* a particular position. *(s)* stance, posture, attitude.

9 **extend** *(v)* straighten at full length. *(s)* stretch, reach.

10 **miscalculation** *(n)* an act of not calculating (working out) correctly. *(s)* mistake, blunder. *(ant)* calculation.

11 **misjudgement** *(n)* an act of poor judgement (decision making). *(s)* misinterpretation, blunder. *(ant)* understanding.

12 **monk** *(n)* a member of a religious community. *(s)* brother, friar.

hood shrouding a face, and bony hands holding the grille and sliding it back into place that caused Cad's tumble. Just as she was about to rescue John, someone dressed as a monk had sealed the oubliette shut with the metal grille.

Like an **axed**[1] **sapling**[2], and with a murderous cry, Cad crumpled into a heap on the floor, her brother's crib beside her lit by the waning torch. Wide-eyed with disbelief, she stared at the metal grille now fixed above her head. As hope **bled**[3] from her body, weak with fear and her mind in frantic tangles, she regarded her **ailing**[4] brother. Her magic ring and the emerald hairpin could do nothing: they were both futile now. It was over. Her eyes scoured the **austere**[5] dungeon. There was nothing here. Nothing to stand on. Nothing to use as a **lever**[6] to lift open the grille. No food, no water, and very soon, no light. A taste as **sour**[7] as vinegar flooded her mouth.

Now trapped, the realisation of their **plight**[8] **crushed**[9] her, for that was the entire point of an oubliette – to forget.

---

1 **axe** *(v)* cut or strike with an axe (strong, sharp, handled blade used for chopping wood). *(s)* chop, fell.

2 **sapling** *(n)* a young tree.

3 **bleed** *(v)* cause something to flow or drain (especially blood) (past tense: bled). *(s)* ooze, flow.

4 **ailing** *(adj)* in poor health. *(s)* sickly, weak, feeble, frail. *(ant)* well, healthy.

5 **austere** *(adj)* having a plain appearance. *(s)* bleak, unadorned. *(ant)* ornate.

6 **lever** *(n)* a bar used to move or lift something heavy. *(s)* jemmy, crank.

7 **sour** *(adj)* possessing a taste like vinegar or lemon. *(s)* acid, bitter, tart. *(ant)* sweet.

8 **plight** *(n)* a difficult or dangerous situation. *(s)* predicament, bind, dilemma.

9 **crush** *(v)* make someone feel incredibly embarrassed or disappointed. *(s)* humiliate, devastate. *(ant)* cheer.

CHAPTER NINETEEN

Final Chance

Barely able to stand on her pained ankle, and with the torch threatening to die at any moment, Cad forced her mind to order what she'd just seen, but couldn't. Instead she kicked, scratched and clawed at the crumbling walls, now their **impending**[1] **tomb**[2].

Like John's, her tears had dried.

Even though her limbs felt like clay, she frantically scraped, yet found nothing but rock, earth and stone. Cad crawled about the floor, patting, gouging and digging until her fingernails flaked and broke away, beads of blood appearing around their tips. Her hands, now **raw**[3] and black with **filth**[4], **pummelled**[5] the earth.

The grille. I must try to ***dislodge***[6] *it.*

She stretched and vaulted, and with every leap, she pushed at the metal grid which sat above her head like a dead weight. Cad knew it was like pushing a **boulder**[7] up a mountain, yet if only she had something to stand on, she might be able to **assert**[8] enough force to push it up. But there

---

1 **impending** *(adj)* about to happen. *(s)* imminent, looming, approaching. *(ant)* receding.

2 **tomb** *(n)* a large (often underground) vault (strong room) for burying the dead. *(s)* crypt, sepulchre.

3 **raw** *(adj)* painful and red. *(s)* sore, inflamed, abraded. *(ant)* healed, healthy.

4 **filth** *(n)* extreme dirt. *(s)* grime, muck, mud. *(ant)* cleanliness.

5 **pummel** *(v)* strike at repeatedly with the fists. *(s)* beat, thrash, pound, batter.

6 **dislodge** *(v)* force or knock out of position. *(s)* displace, move, shift.

7 **boulder** *(n)* a large rock. *(s)* stone.

8 **assert** *(v)* apply. *(s)* exert, use, employ.

was nothing, and any remaining thoughts of hope dissolved like a puff of smoke.

Cad's imagination **reeled**[1] at the thought of their **predicament**[2]. **Steeped**[3] in horror, and as she realised their **fate**[4], a faint snuffling sound dragged her from the nightmare. John was **writhing**[5] against the confines of his swaddling. Judging by the stench coming from the crib, he'd soiled his **clouts**[6]. Unless she changed them, his skin would become raw in no time. Even though she had no water, she must try. She would tear some of his swaddling and wipe away what she could. At least that way, John might be in less pain from his hunger, thirst and the cold.

Cad gently lifted John from his crib. In her arms, he felt as **fragile**[7] as a feather. With care, she removed the cot's thin **mattress**[8] and laid it on the ground, placing her brother on top of it. He stared at her, then blinked slowly in the dim light, his eyes like that of a baby owl's. Misty tears blinded her. Cad would ensure her baby brother would not suffer any more than he already had. As she began to loosen his swaddling, like an arrow to her head, something struck her.

'What a wantwit I am!' she exclaimed, leaping to her feet and grabbing John's crib. 'Why did I not think of it before!'

Cad began working like a bee. The cot was **flimsy**[9], lightweight, meant for carrying about the castle, but if she were **prudent**[10], it should just about support her weight enough to stand on and push open that metal grating and allow her to climb out. She would need to leave John here, but she could bring help and rescue him if she was quick. Her heart sang with **joy**[11].

'Hang on, John,' she **chirped**[12]. 'I am getting you out of this hellhole if it's the very last thing I do. And once we're out of here, and I'm a knight, I will protect you with my life.'

---

1 **reel** *(v)* feel bewildered and shocked. *(s)* spin, whirl. *(ant)* steady, stabilise.

2 **predicament** *(n)* a difficult situation. *(s)* dilemma, crisis, plight. *(ant)* walkover.

3 **steep** *(v)* immerse in a task or experience. *(s)* absorb, engross, engage. *(ant)* disengage.

4 **fate** *(n)* a future outcome that is out of one's control. *(s)* destiny, lot.

5 **writhe** *(v)* twist and turn, contort the body. *(s)* squirm, thrash. *(ant)* still, relax.

6 **clout** *(n)* an archaic (old) word for cloth or clothing (often a nappy for babies).

7 **fragile** *(adj)* easily damaged. *(s)* delicate, flimsy. *(ant)* sturdy, robust.

8 **mattress** *(n)* a soft fabric case filled with comfortable material, used for sleeping on.

9 **flimsy** *(adj)* light and easily damaged. *(s)* weak, fragile, delicate. *(ant)* robust.

10 **prudent** *(adj)* acting with care. *(s)* cautious, careful. *(ant)* imprudent, careless.

11 **joy** *(n)* great happiness. *(s)* delight, jubilation. *(ant)* misery, unhappiness.

12 **chirp** *(v)* speak in a sing-song way. *(s)* sing, trill. *(ant)* groan.

The torch's flame flickered with ominous **portent**[1], threatening to plunge her into darkness at any moment. That would make her task so **problematic**[2]. Pushing those thoughts aside, she knew the sands of time were trickling by; she must hasten. She placed the upturned crib beneath the metal grille above her head. As she had done previously, Cad knew she could lift the grille, but she needed to push it aside sufficiently to afford her exit. If not, her efforts would be futile. Failure was not an option.

Cad rubbed her eyes and studied the crib. The tricky part would be balancing on its curved base. To perch on there, and push the grille upwards simultaneously, would be precarious. With a wince of pain, she removed her boots for better purchase. Then, **barefoot**[3], Cad stepped gently onto the upturned crib's base, placing her feet wide enough to ease her wobbling.

Easy does it, girl, she thought, her mind brimming like an overfilled cup.

As she reached up to push away the grille, one foot slipped, and she stumbled off, twisting her ankle even further. Ignoring the immediate throbs, she placed her good foot back onto the crib, and gently brought up the other and stood for several seconds, **acclimatising**[4] her balance to the new challenge.

With her feet apart, Cad stretched upwards and applied even pressure to both edges of the metal grid. As she pushed, it barely budged, just **grating**[5] a little against the sides of the hole. She must push harder and lift it, releasing it from the confines of the **grooves**[6] which held it firmly in place.

'Hang on, John,' she said, as she planted her feet even harder on the curves of the crib's base, and blocking out the **intense**[7] pain shooting through her ankle. With all her might, Cad gave a steady upward push, and letting out a huge grunt, lifted and released the grate from its holdings.

Her heart flipped with joy as she cried, 'Yes!'

But then, with a cruel crack, her firm footing vanished, and she dropped to the floor, both

---

1 **portent** *(n)* a sign or warning that something bad is about to happen. *(s)* indication, foreboding.

2 **problematic** *(adj)* being a problem. *(s)* difficult, tricky. *(ant)* easy.

3 **barefoot** *(adj)* wearing nothing on one's feet. *(s)* unshod.

4 **acclimatise** *(v)* become accustomed (used) to. *(s)* adapt, adjust. *(ant)* misadjust.

5 **grate** *(v)* rub against and make a sound. *(s)* grind, scrape, scratch.

6 **groove** *(n)* a long, narrow cut in a hard substance. *(s)* channel, hollow.

7 **intense** *(adj)* of great strength. *(s)* severe, fierce, extreme. *(s)* mild.

ankles **absorbing**[1] the impact with full force. The crib had collapsed beneath her weight with the grille pushed only slightly aside.

Unable to hold back tears, and now on all fours, she crawled to inspect the crib. There were no second chances. The crib's base had given way and would no longer even hold a baby. **Numb**[2], she gently picked John up. She cleaned him best she could and tightened his swaddling, and, strangling a sob in her throat, leaned against the damp wall, hugging him so tightly to her chest that he **squirmed**[3] in her grip.

Cad had tried her very best, but Lady Luck had **spurned**[4] them. There was simply no way on this earth she could hang from the lip of the opening and push back the grille simultaneously. It would be a truly impossible feat. Yet, still loath to capitulate, she placed her brother back onto the floor and tried and tried. Not only was it **inconceivable**[5], but her ankle, now throbbing and swelling, **impeded**[6] her further. Hopelessness smothered her as fate played its cruel hand.

She picked John up, realising there was no point in trying anymore. A huge stone settled in the pit of her stomach. Cad had fought **gallantly**[7] but now she must allow the **current**[8] to carry them both away. With an incongruous feeling of calm, Cad closed her eyes, cuddling her brother in close. As she drifted off into a comfortable numbness, finally spent of fuel, the flame died beside her, gently sputtering away to join her in the darkness.

---

1 **absorb** *(v)* physically or figuratively take in. *(s)* consume, experience.

2 **numb** *(adj)* being unable to think or feel. *(s)* paralysed, stupefied. *(ant)* feeling.

3 **squirm** *(v)* twist and move the body. *(s)* writhe, wriggle. *(ant)* still.

4 **spurn** *(v)* reject with disdain (dislike). *(s)* snub, rebuff, ignore. *(ant)* accept.

5 **inconceivable** *(adj)* something so bad it cannot be imagined or considered. *(s)* unbelievable. *(ant)* conceivable.

6 **impede** *(v)* delay or prevent by obstructing. *(s)* hamper, hinder. *(ant)* facilitate.

7 **gallantly** *(adv)* in a gallant (brave) manner. *(s)* boldly, fearlessly, heroically. *(ant)* cowardly.

8 **current** *(n)* the flow of a body of water. *(s)* tide, stream, undertow.

CHAPTER TWENTY

Bad Dreams

'Cad. Cad. Wake up.'

Cad's eyes flickered, trying to open, but capitulating to the darkness and cold, she **clamped**[1] them closed and clutched John closer to her chest. She didn't know if he still breathed. She dared not check, but she would not let him go. Even while she'd dozed, she'd held him. And what cruel games one's dreams played. In her **stupor**[2], she'd heard Dylan calling her, waking her to a summer's morning, where chores seemed easy and a day in the tilt yard beckoned. How cruel indeed.

Ocean-deep in despair, like a **mirage**[3], she saw her friend's face once more as she shivered against the dungeon's bone-chilling air. He urged her to wake, his voice sharp with impatience. All these pictures **fused**[4] together as she shook her head and squeezed her eyes tightly shut, burying the callous images away.

'Cad. Wake up,' the voice **intruded**[5] again. 'Wake up,' it implored.

'Go away,' she muttered, shaking her head to **erase**[6] the dream and the black scorch marks it burned inside her mind.

---

1 **clamp** *(v)* fasten shut. *(s)* secure, press, hold. *(ant)* release.

2 **stupor** *(n)* a state of near unconsciousness or unawareness. *(s)* daze, torpor, blankness. *(ant)* consciousness.

3 **mirage** *(n)* an optical illusion, unrealistic hope or wish. *(s)* vision, hallucination, fantasy. *(ant)* reality.

4 **fuse** *(v)* join to form one. *(s)* blend, combine, merge. *(ant)* split, separate.

5 **intrude** *(v)* disrupt without invitation. *(s)* interrupt, interfere, invade. *(ant)* withdraw, avoid.

6 **erase** *(v)* remove or rub out. *(s)* delete, eradicate, eliminate. *(ant)* preserve.

Time contracted as she clutched her brother, and finally **solace**[1] came when some **semblance**[2] of sleep smothered her exhausted thoughts. But she was too quickly snatched from drifting on a calm sea, as the familiar voice sliced through the silence.

'Cad. *Wake up now!*'

Her eyes fluttered open to darkness.

Where am I? she thought, then remembered with crashing despair, and checked that she was still holding John. Like **lichen**[3] to a rock, Cad clung to the baby and would not let go until the last breath left her body.

Then suddenly, her eyes now the size of saucers, and in an ungodly pitch, she shrieked, 'The Lord save us all!' and almost dropped John onto the floor.

It can't be, she thought, as her eyes adjusted to the change, and myriad questions formed queues in her head.

Cad blinked hard, and with her mouth **gaping**[4] in disbelief, peered up at a faint light flickering from the hole above her.

'Master Cad, it's me,' someone whispered, but it was not Dylan's voice she heard.

Cad's eyes, almost doubling in size, stared in shock. Though her vision was **blurred**[5], she saw that the face poking through the grille above her head, lit by a meagre torch, was Rhys Price's.

'Rhys,' she whispered, then placing John onto the floor, she vaulted to her feet.

'Ouch!' she yelped, wincing as pain shot through her ankle, so she began hopping instead.

'Rhys! What in heaven are you doing here?' But she didn't wait for his answer. 'You must help me get Prince John out of this place before it is too late. He is cold and **frail**[6].'

Cad had no idea how long they'd languished in the dark, but her brother remained alive, just.

'How did you find us?' she asked as she straightened her thoughts.

Rhys hung over the opening, his voice **timid**[7]. 'I followed Dylan down to where … where …

---

1 **solace** *(n)* comfort in a bad situation. *(s)* support, relief, help. *(ant)* aggravation.

2 **semblance** *(n)* resemblance. *(s)* approximation, similarity. *(ant)* reality.

3 **lichen** *(n)* a plant that clings to the things upon which it grows.

4 **gape** *(v)* be or become wide open. *(s)* part, yawn. *(ant)* close, shut.

5 **blur** *(v)* become or make unclear. *(s)* obscure, cloud, fog. *(ant)* clear, focus.

6 **frail** *(adj)* delicate and weak. *(s)* feeble, infirm, fragile. *(ant)* robust, sturdy, strong.

7 **timid** *(adj)* without confidence (self-belief). *(s)* fearful, apprehensive, weak. *(ant)* bold.

you, and he hid your … secret. I felt left out. I had seen you sneak off together before, so today I followed Dylan. When I saw it was just a pup you hid, I wandered down here. The fat door at the top is always locked, but today it was just **ajar**[1], so I came to take a look.'

'Oh, Rhys!' Cad exclaimed, not thinking for a second of how that door had slammed shut behind her when she'd entered the stairs down to the oubliette, and how Rhys might then have subsequently entered. 'How fortunate that you are a spy and an eavesdropper. I have never been more pleased to see anyone in my life. Now move quickly. I will pass John up through the hole. Slide the metal grille out of the way. It's heavy, but you'll manage it.'

Without hesitating, Rhys heaved the grille away from the hole with a grunt, and then beamed a wide grin of victory down at Cad.

Not wanting to **tempt fate**[2] further, Cad said, 'Gently does it.' Then, lifting her brother and wincing again, she stretched onto tiptoe and offered John up through the hole.

'Have you got him tight?' she asked before loosening her grip. 'Don't drop him, for heaven's sake,' she added, finally letting go of the baby.

Rhys took John with ease, holding him tightly in his arms. 'I have him,' said Rhys, moving away from the open hole at his feet.

'Mind that torch stays lit,' Cad said.

'Right you are,' Rhys replied, moving it gently to one side where its flame burned unhindered.

'Put John down carefully. You'll need to haul me out of here. I've hurt my ankle,' she grumbled, still barefoot. 'I cannot bear down on it as I should. As I reach up, take one hand and pull me with all your might. No worry if my arm comes away from its **socket**[3], and I howl. You ignore me and pull, no matter how much it might hurt me. You haul like you've never hauled before.'

'Yes, Master Cad,' Rhys answered with an edge of uncertainty in his voice.

'And drop the "master" **lark**[4]. I am your friend,' Cad reassured him. 'Now. I will count to three; then you pull with all your strength. You hear me, Rhys?' she said. 'As if you are tearing me **asunder**[5].'

---

1 **ajar** *(adj)* slightly open. *(s)* cracked, unfastened. *(ant)* closed, shut.

2 **tempt fate** (phrase) do a risky thing. *(s)* play with fire, live dangerously. *(ant)* play it safe.

3 **socket** *(n)* a hollow into which something fits and turns. *(s)* cavity.

4 **lark** *(n)* a foolish thing. *(s)* caper, business.

5 **asunder** *(adv)* apart. *(s)* in two, into pieces. *(ant)* together.

Cad braced herself for the **intensifying**[1] pain in her ankle, and with a deep **inhalation**[2], extended onto her tiptoes. At full stretch, she grasped the lip of the opening with one hand and reached up to Rhys with the other. Gripping Rhys's bony hand with hers and gritting her teeth against the searing pain in her foot and calf, she commanded, '*Pull!*'

Dragging herself up with her free hand, as Rhys pulled her other, she let out an inhuman grunt – her arm felt it would pop from her shoulder. But she dared not scream lest Rhys drop her for fear of maiming her.

'*Pull harder*,' she snarled through gritted teeth, knowing they both had only the strength to attempt this successfully once. '*Pull*,' she repeated, her voice **hoarse**[3] with agony as her hand slipped from Rhys's grip. '*Pull!*'

Then with a final heave and a dull thud, her chin smacked the stone floor as she plopped down from Rhys's hand like the practice dummy in the tilt yard. Left balancing on her midriff, with her legs still hanging down the hole, she barked at Rhys, 'Come on then, Rhys. Stop gaping at me like a frightened frog. Help me up, and pick up my brother. I will need your shoulder as a crutch.'

Rhys jumped to attention, pulling Cad up and over the final hurdle, and then helped her to her feet. Without another word, he picked up the baby.

Just moments later, Cad, now holding the torch with one hand, and her other arm wrapped around Rhys's neck, said, 'Come on, my friend. Do not drop that child. Let's get out of this ungodly place.'

Rhys nodded, clutching the swaddled infant as if his life depended on it. Cad winced as she walked, her ankle swelling like a full **bladder**[4].

'Oh, and Rhys,' she said, halting to ensure the boy made eye contact, 'You and I. We need to spin a little **yarn**[5] for the powers that be in the castle. You will need to tell a tale and stick to it.' Cad's gaze bored into Rhys's. 'Do you understand?' she asked, her stare, intense.

With a shy half-smile, Rhys nodded but said not a single word.

---

1 **intensify** *(v)* become more intense (stronger). *(s)* increase, strengthen. *(ant)* abate, lessen.

2 **inhalation** *(n)* a breath in. *(s)* gasp, gulp. *(ant)* exhalation.

3 **hoarse** *(adj)* harsh and rough. *(s)* husky, croaky, gruff, gravelly. *(ant)* soft, mellow.

4 **bladder** *(n)* a flexible bag for holding liquid. *(s)* pocket, blister.

5 **yarn** *(n)* a far-fetched story. *(s)* tale, lie, tall story. *(ant)* truth.

With little breath to spare, Cad braced herself for the painful **ascent**[1] out of the oubliette. It would be an arduous climb, especially with her boots lost to the hideous dungeon. She headed for the stairs, her moves awkward, when something yanked at her tunic so hard that she stumbled back, her ankle giving way, and she landed with a thud.

Agog[2] with shock, and **winded**[3], Cad watched as a monk, his **cowl**[4] shrouding his face, snatched her brother from a **blindsided**[5] Rhys. Her poor friend didn't stand a chance against the adult man. With one hand, the monk lifted Rhys from the ground and flung him like a rag across the shadowy room, where he landed against the wall with a sickening thud, slumping into a crumpled heap on the floor. The monk then tucked her brother firmly under one arm, and with a swoosh of his **habit**[6] made for the stairs leading up from the oubliette.

Her pain numbed by shock, Cad vaulted to her feet. In a heartbeat, she grasped the metal grille from the floor and flew across the hovel with it. As the monk made to leave, Cad, finding superhuman strength, took an almighty swing and brought the metal grating down onto the back of the man's head and shoulders. The dull-sounding thud sealed his fate.

Frozen in the moment, Cad watched as the monk's legs wobbled beneath him. Then, as quick as a squirrel, before the man hit the ground like a **felled**[7] tree, Cad snatched her brother to safety. With John in her arms, she sprang over to Rhys, who, although **dazed**[8] and **incapacitated**[9] with shock, stared straight at Cad.

'Are you badly hurt?' she asked, panting and terrified her friend might nod.

Rhys didn't answer, but slowly shook his head.

'Come, then!' she cried, holding John whilst urging Rhys to stand. 'We must leave now, in

---

1 **ascent** *(n)* a climb to the top of something. *(s)* trek, scaling. *(ant)* descent.

2 **agog** *(adj)* keen or curious. *(s)* anxious, intrigued. *(ant)* uninterested.

3 **wind** *(v)* cause someone to have difficulty in breathing because of a blow to the diaphragm.

4 **cowl** *(n)* a large and loose hood, especially that found as part of a monk's habit.

5 **blindside** *(v)* attack unexpectedly. *(s)* ambush, assault, surprise. *(ant)* forewarn.

6 **habit** *(n)* a long, loose overgarment (item of clothing) worn by someone religious such as a monk or nun.

7 **felled** *(adj)* cut down or toppled. *(s)* chopped, axed. *(ant)* raised, righted.

8 **dazed** *(adj)* not able to react or think well. *(s)* bewildered, stunned.

9 **incapacitate** *(v)* prevent from functioning normally. *(s)* debilitate, disable. *(ant)* enable.

case this man comes to.' Although after the **clout**[1] she'd given him, she feared that might never happen.

'Those stairs will be slow going. Come, now.'

But Rhys, wide-eyed and speechless, still didn't budge.

'*On your feet, Rhys!*' she yelled, bending and grabbing him by the sleeve of his tunic.

'You are needed to carry a prince, for I doubt I can,' she said, as a **fiery**[2] agony gripped her lower leg.

Rhys, trembling, teetered to his feet and held out his arms for baby John.

'Are you sure you can manage him?' Cad asked.

Rhys nodded.

Cad rewrapped John's **tatty**[3] swaddling as best she could. Then she carefully handed him over to Rhys and nodded towards the door. 'You first. I will manage, but I may be slower. I want you up ahead. If you tire, sit and wait for me.'

Rhys nodded again.

'Rhys, begin. I am right behind you,' Cad said, lifting her chin to urge him on.

With baby John clutched in his arms, Rhys, eyes like a **snared**[4] **stoat**[5], stepped over the prone man, whose bloodstained cowl hid his face. Then with tentative steps, Rhys began up the steep stone stairs.

Now trembling like linen on a laundry line, her ankle protesting, Cad bent closer to the man, listening for breaths in the deathly quiet of the oubliette. Although he was a foe, Cad was relieved to hear breathing, albeit shallow and **laboured**[6]. Curious, she knelt, and with her fingertips, she lifted the side of his cowl from his bloodied face. She recognised him immediately as the man who had beaten Bryn.

'Who are you?' she whispered, her eyes popping wide. Horrified, she dropped back the hood as though it singed her fingers.

---

1 **clout** *(n)* a heavy strike with the hand or something hard. *(s)* blow, knock, smack.

2 **fiery** *(adj)* like fire. *(s)* raging, hot, burning, scorching. *(ant)* cold.

3 **tatty** *(adj)* worn and ragged. *(s)* shabby, tattered. *(ant)* pristine, new.

4 **snare** *(v)* catch something in a trap. *(s)* bag, net, entrap, ensnare. *(ant)* free, release.

5 **stoat** *(n)* a small furry mammal of the weasel family.

6 **laboured** *(adj)* something done with great difficulty and effort. *(s)* strained, heavy. *(ant)* easy.

She **floundered**[1] to her feet and, making for the exit, glanced back at him. 'Who are you?' she said again.

But as Cad hauled her battered body up the stairs after Rhys, what perturbed her most, sending her mind into turmoil, was not the identity of the man she'd left on the floor, but his hands. For his **stubby**[2] fingers were not the same as the **slender**[3], bony hands that had slid the grille back into place earlier, trapping her and John inside.

1 **flounder** *(v)* struggle physically or mentally. *(s)* falter, blunder, stumble.

2 **stubby** *(adj)* short and thick. *(s)* stumpy. *(ant)* slender.

3 **slender** *(adj)* slim and graceful. *(s)* delicate. *(ant)* chubby, plump, fat.

CHAPTER TWENTY-ONE

We Can Be Heroes

'So, Rhys Price ...'

Sir Robert, eyes like slits, glanced up from his notes, his tiny, mobile pupils stilling as he fixed his gaze on his **quarry**[1]. With a deep inhalation, he took a long, **deliberate**[2] pause to **amplify**[3] further his **intimidation**[4] tactics. Then, with a hard stare like a kick, he continued to pick at his prey, his voice like a cool grey slate.

'You claim you managed to, and I **quote**[5], "borrow" the dungeon's key from Goodwife Hughes. Then you say you let Master Cad ...'

Slowly lacing his fingers as if about to pray, Evans paused again to throw an **accusatory**[6] **leer**[7] Cad's way before resting his snake-eyes back on Rhys.

'Then you say you *freed* Master Cad from his cell because ...?'

Evans chose his words with precision, applying a certain **emphasis**[8] to wound Rhys as much as possible.

---

1 **quarry** *(n)* an animal pursued by a hunter or predator for food. *(s)* prey, victim, target. *(ant)* hunter.

2 **deliberate** *(adj)* careful and unhurried. *(s)* measured, steady. *(ant)* hasty, careless.

3 **amplify** *(v)* increase the impact or sound of *(s)* boost, strengthen, louden. *(ant)* decrease, quieten.

4 **intimidation** *(n)* the act of frightening someone. *(s)* menacing, bullying. *(ant)* reassurance.

5 **quote** *(v)* repeat or copy the words of another. *(s)* recite, retell. *(ant)* misquote.

6 **accusatory** *(adj)* suggest a wrongdoing. *(s)* critical, condemnatory. *(ant)* complimentary.

7 **leer** *(n)* an unpleasant look. *(s)* stare.

8 **emphasis** *(n)* stress given to spoken words to signify particular importance. *(s)* weight, prominence.

Then he lifted his chin, and his gaze, like a **peregrine's**[1], **flitted**[2] between Cad and Rhys, chilling the atmosphere to **glacial**[3]. Cad, her eyes like emeralds, met his **scrutiny**[4], with a look that could cut glass. She knew Evans would taunt the weakest animal for sport – Rhys. The very thought brought rage to her as a brimming fury rose into her throat. But, she held her tongue, feeling all the ugly words piling up inside her.

An agonising silence passed before Evans eventually cleared his throat and continued, clearly **relishing**[5] his performance.

'You say you *freed* him from the tower because you **pitied**[6] him, and so he could feed his *dog*!'

Rhys **quavered**[7] at Sir Robert's **timbre**[8], and both he and Cad now peered at their feet, just as Cad had said they must when facing Sir Robert.

'Whatever you do, Rhys, don't look Evans in the eyes. If you do, like a hound hunting **game**[9], he'll pounce and devour you.'

This she had instructed last night, on their **hobble**[10] up to the keep with the rescued Prince John, for unlike her, Cad knew that Rhys would find it difficult to meet his **interrogator's**[11] gaze.

Cad had been gentle but firm with Rhys. 'Treachery is afoot in this castle, and until we find the culprits, we must remain vigilant and tight-lipped. This story is our secret. Yours and mine, and it will be Dylan's too. Rhys, do you understand?' Cad had implored him to respond. A silent nod from Rhys had reassured her, although she'd felt dreadful **burdening**[12] him with such lies.

Sir Robert, now readying himself to resume his play, and aptly dressed in his **finery**[13], glanced

---

1 **peregrine** *(n)* a powerful bird of prey. *(s)* falcon.

2 **flit** *(v)* move swiftly. *(s)* dart, flick, dance. *(ant)* remain, still.

3 **glacial** *(adj)* (figuratively) unfriendly. *(s)* hostile, cool. *(ant)* friendly, warm.

4 **scrutiny** *(n)* examination. *(s)* observation, study. *(ant)* glance.

5 **relish** *(v)* greatly enjoy something. *(s)* savour, love. *(ant)* dislike.

6 **pity** *(v)* feel sorry for someone. *(s)* sympathise. *(ant)* disdain.

7 **quaver** *(v)* shake or tremble. *(s)* quiver, tremor. *(ant)* steady.

8 **timbre** *(n)* the character of a sound or voice independent of pitch and loudness. *(s)* tone.

9 **game** *(n)* wild animals or birds that are hunted for sport. *(s)* quarry, prey.

10 **hobble** *(n)* an awkward way of walking, especially due to injury. *(s)* limp. *(ant)* run, sprint.

11 **interrogator** *(n)* a person who questions someone closely. *(s)* inquisitor.

12 **burden** *(v)* cause worry, hardship or distress. *(s)* afflict, overload. *(ant)* relieve.

13 **finery** *(n)* fancy, expensive things. *(s)* splendour, glad rags. *(ant)* rags, scruffs.

down at his notes again, clearly **savouring**[1] the torturous silences in the makeshift courtroom. With his face arranged in a **pompous**[2] sneer, his voice **formal**[3], he continued.

'Then you claim you replaced the key without Goodwife Hughes noticing that it had ever been "borrowed". *Then*, after doing so, you both …'

Evans stopped again and **theatrically**[4] waved a dainty finger at the accused pages.

'Then after doing so, you say you just "wandered" into the bowels of the castle and "happened" upon Prince John. But then a "mad monk" tried to steal him, so you—'

His gaze landed upon Cad; heat rose in her chest.

'So you **clubbed**[5] him over the head.'

Cad **cringed**[6] at the absurdity of the tale she had concocted for Rhys, but there had been no time for **flowery**[7] **creations**[8] as they'd limped back through the passageways last night. And, the latter part about the monk was true. Yet, before today's court session had started, Sir Robert had announced that when the guards had entered the oubliette to retrieve the accused monk, it had been empty. No proof of what she said existed.

Cad knew Evans didn't believe their story, not for one minute, nor did she care for the most part. In the eyes of Catrin's **residents**[9], she and Rhys were heroes – Prince John's saviours. For a while, they would do no wrong. But the part that had **nagged**[10] Cad all night, robbing her of sleep, was the monk's hands. And now he'd either miraculously risen unaided, or more likely, someone had shifted him. Who that someone was, would be the key to this whole mystery.

'Well, boy. Cat got your tongue?' Sir Robert's fist bounced off his desk with a *bam!*

'Sorry, sir,' Rhys replied, flinching hard and muttering into his chest.

'Lift your chin, boy. Stop mumbling,' barked Evans with a loud tut and a wave of his hand.

---

1 **savour** *(v)* enjoy and linger over. *(s)* relish, delight in. *(ant)* dislike.

2 **pompous** *(adj)* self-important or affectedly grand. *(s)* pretentious, exaggerated, vain. *(ant)* modest.

3 **formal** *(adj)* official in attitude or appearance. *(s)* aloof, reserved, clipped. *(ant)* informal, friendly.

4 **theatrically** *(adj)* done in a theatrical (dramatic) way. *(s)* arrogantly, pompously. *(s)* modestly.

5 **club** *(v)* hit someone hard with a club (blunt object). *(s)* bludgeon, cudgel.

6 **cringe** *(v)* shiver inwardly with embarrassment or disgust. *(s)* wince, squirm.

7 **flowery** *(adj)* exaggerated, elaborate. *(s)* fancy, flamboyant. *(ant)* plain, simple.

8 **creation** *(n)* the act of bringing something into existence. *(s)* making, design. *(ant)* destruction.

9 **resident** *(n)* a person who lives somewhere. *(s)* inhabitant, dweller, citizen.

10 **nag** *(v)* ask over and over again. *(s)* harass, hound, bother.

Cad, realising that Rhys might capitulate at any moment, **interjected**[1] swiftly. 'Sire, I apologise **wholeheartedly**[2] for Rhys's involvement, but this is not his fault. He is my friend, and I ordered him to help me after I shot the stone at squire Davis when leaving the great hall. Rhys is young, **impressionable**[3] and loyal. He would not dare **disobey**[4] a senior page such as me,' she added, wearing her most **earnest**[5] face, and knowing the word 'senior' was a complete **stretch**[6].

In fact, Cad cared not a jot what Sir Robert believed. What mattered presently was Rhys's discretion and his **liberty**[7] – she would not have him locked away in the tower because of her **escapades**[8] – never. That, along with keeping her hairpin and ring as secret as possible, was what mattered now.

There was never a doubt that she would take all blame for Rhys. Last night, after leaving the oubliette, when she and Rhys had reached the storage room with John, they found Dylan finally tending Fishy. At the time, and **mortified**[9] at his tardiness, he had been delayed emptying **chamber pots**[10] as a punishment for gambling with a guard.

Cad had bitterly scolded Dylan, so disappointed that he'd let her down thus when he'd known how crucial their arranged meeting had been. Even so, she had quickly instructed Dylan to hasten forth and **herald**[11] the news that Cad and Rhys had found Prince John while investigating the dungeons after feeding Fishy. In spreading this joyous news, Cad knew that not only would the castle folks forgive her and Rhys, but they would **laud**[12] and **honour**[13]

---

1 **interject** *(v)* say brusquely as an aside or interruption. *(s)* intervene, comment, cut in, butt in.

2 **wholeheartedly** *(adv)* something done with sincerity (honesty). *(s)* completely. *(ant)* insincerely.

3 **impressionable** *(adj)* easily persuaded or influenced. *(s)* suggestable. *(ant)* unimpressionable.

4 **disobey** *(v)* fail to follow rules or advice. *(s)* defy, oppose, resist. *(ant)* obey.

5 **earnest** *(adj)* serious and sincere. *(s)* solemn, honest. *(ant)* insincere, superficial.

6 **stretch** *(n)* something which is difficult to believe. *(s)* exaggeration, overstatement. *(ant)* understatement.

7 **liberty** *(n)* freedom. *(s)* independence. *(ant)* constraint.

8 **escapade** *(n)* a daring, adventurous or exciting act or incident. *(s)* caper, stunt, exploit, antic.

9 **mortified** *(adj)* embarrassed or ashamed. *(s)* abashed, guilty. *(ant)* pleased, gratified.

10 **chamber pot** *(n)* a bowl in a bedroom used as a toilet during the night.

11 **herald** *(v)* indicate that something is about to happen. *(s)* announce, signal.

12 **laud** *(v)* praise someone highly. *(s)* applaud, admire, commend. *(ant)* criticise, condemn.

13 **honour** *(v)* regard with absolute respect. *(s)* laud, admire, commend. *(ant)* disrespect.

them for finding the prince alive. The castle's courtiers would **celebrate**[1] two **humble**[2] pages for their outstanding bravery in entering the oubliette and risking their lives for Prince John.

Sir Robert cleared his toady throat again. Cad glanced up to see him chewing his words before he spat them out. His eyes were mere cracks as he hissed at Cad, 'Henceforth, *Master Cad*, I will be watching you very closely, very closely indeed. You will be under my eye.'

Cad peered at the floor in feigned **contrition**[3]. Rhys copied her.

'Prince Llywelyn will return by tonight. We will leave your fate in his hands.'

He stopped there to enjoy the effect of those words. Cad, on the razor's edge of a glare, looked Evans square in the eyes but said nothing. She was now more confident than ever that last night's decision to dispatch May with a wax-sealed note for her father, imploring him to remain on his quest, had been the right choice. She had also warned him to **disclose**[4] her **correspondence**[5] to no one – no one at all.

'Well, what say you, boy?'

Sir Robert's barking tore Cad back to the present.

'Yes, sire,' she answered, her voice drenched with regret and **flimsy**[6] pretence. 'The great Prince Llywelyn will **preside**[7] over my punishment.'

As she uttered those words, she pondered two outcomes: Would Evans rage when he realised that Llywelyn would not return, but would continue his search for the Gwalch Gem bracelet? Or would Sir Robert be pleased?

'Prince Llywelyn will indeed,' Evans **declared**[8] with a crabby toss of his head and pushing back his black judgement **robes**[9]. Cad, noting that he **resembled**[10] a crow, and ignoring the

---

1 **celebrate** *(v)* praise publicly. *(s)* laud, honour, applaud, admire. *(ant)* criticise.

2 **humble** *(adj)* unimportant. *(s)* lowly, respectful. *(ant)* important, noble.

3 **contrition** *(n)* a feeling of remorse and penitence (sorriness). *(s)* sorrow, regret. *(ant)* indifference.

4 **disclose** *(v)* make known. *(s)* show, reveal, divulge. *(ant)* hide, conceal, secrete.

5 **correspondence** *(n)* a communication by sending letters. *(s)* writing, note.

6 **flimsy** *(adj)* unconvincing. *(s)* frivolous, lame, feeble. *(ant)* convincing.

7 **preside** *(v)* authorise something at a meeting. *(s)* lead, guide, conduct. *(ant)* follow, obey.

8 **declare** *(v)* say in a serious and clear manner. *(s)* assert, affirm. *(ant)* withhold.

9 **robe** *(n)* a long, loose garment that often covers other clothing. *(s)* cloak, wrap.

10 **resemble** *(v)* look or seem like something else. *(s)* simulate. *(ant)* differ from.

snowstorm of white scales of skin flaked on his shoulders, fixed her face in a mask of calm respect as he fiddled with his parchments.

Drawn by an **escalating**[1] **din**[2], Cad glanced out into the bailey where a small crowd, **spurred**[3] on by Dylan, had gathered, and all but Bryn Davis and his cronies were clapping and **chanting**[4], 'Cad, Cad, Cad! Rhys, Rhys, Rhys!'

Bryn, standing as straight as a reed, his skin milk pale beneath his bruises, glared at Cad through plum-like eyes; their puffiness **conveniently**[5] masking his **stony**[6] expression. The stock story spreading through the castle was that an angry stallion had cornered Bryn in the stables, kicking him full-on in the face with both rear hooves. But rumours also flew that he'd **brawled**[7] in too much beer and received a **royal**[8] **pasting**[9] from another squire whilst **in his cups**[10]. Only Cad, the man dressed as a monk that she'd left in the oubliette, and Bryn knew the truth: how fortunate for Bryn she'd been there. He might otherwise not be here today.

Could Bryn be involved in John's abduction? She'd thought of little more all night, yet somehow, she didn't think so; it was a feeling her gut held on to. But for now, she must be vigilant because Cad knew full well that Bryn Davis suspected something to be **amiss**[11] about her.

Sir Robert stood, snorting as he gathered his parchments. Cad eyed him, filled with numerous **warring**[12] urges, none of which she would **execute**[13]. He regarded neither Cad nor Rhys, but through gritted brown teeth, snarled, 'You are free to tend your daily duties.'

'Thank you, sire,' Cad replied with a deep bow and hiding her half-grin half-sneer. Rhys followed suit.

---

1 **escalate** *(v)* increase quickly. *(s)* develop, grow, mushroom. *(ant)* decrease.

2 **din** *(n)* a loud, irritating and prolonged noise. *(s)* uproar, racket, commotion. *(ant)* silence.

3 **spur** *(v)* encourage. *(s)* urge, motivate, drive, inspire. *(ant)* discourage.

4 **chant** *(v)* say or shout repeatedly in a sing-song tone. *(s)* chorus, repeat.

5 **conveniently** *(adv)* in a trouble-free way. *(s)* efficiently, handily. *(ant)* inconveniently.

6 **stony** *(adj)* showing no sympathy. *(s)* unfriendly, cold. *(ant)* friendly.

7 **brawl** *(v)* fight. *(s)* scuffle, scrap, tussle.

8 **royal** *(adj)* real (informal and used for emphasis). *(s)* complete, total, absolute. *(ant)* trivial, slight.

9 **pasting** *(n)* a beating (informal). *(s)* thrashing, pounding, caning.

10 **in his cups** *(adj)* having drunk too much alcohol (archaic and informal). *(s)* drunk, intoxicated. *(ant)* sober.

11 **amiss** *(adj)* out of place or not right. *(s)* wrong, awry, untoward. *(ant)* right, in order.

12 **warring** *(adj)* opposing. *(s)* conflicting, contending, battling. *(ant)* agreeing.

13 **execute** *(v)* put an order, plan or action into effect, carry out. *(s)* implement. *(ant)* fail.

As Cad straightened, she was astonished to spot Peggy's hunched figure lurking at the doorway.

Why on earth was Peggy eavesdropping on their verdict, and did Evans know he was doing so?

'Be off with you both,' snapped Evans, waving his talon-like hands at Cad and Rhys, who, needing little encouragement, fled the room.

As they left, Cad noticed that Peggy had vanished.

Had Evans spotted him ***loitering***[1] *just now?*

'Well done.' Cad grinned, gripping Rhys's arm. 'You stuck to our story, and bravely so. Evans can be **tyrannical**[2] when vexed like that.'

Rhys smiled his gap-toothed grin, his eyes wide with pride.

'Come on, you nonny,' she joked, ruffling his coppery curls. 'Let's find Dylan and Fishy.'

That proved easy, for as Cad entered the bailey, Dylan, with Fishy in his arms and a grin too broad for his face, placed the pup onto the floor and watched as she bounced over to her master, tripping and **bumbling**[3] over giant paws she would soon grow into.

'Fishy!' cried Cad, bending down to furious wet kisses from the pup's lapping tongue. Cad's heart smiled. 'You're mine now, and the powers that be dare not scold me, not while the court are so grateful for my finding John,' she whispered into the **oblivious**[4] pup's ear.

As she scooped up Fishy in her arms, folks cheering and patting her back, Cad turned towards the castle to see Sir Robert's face turn **puce**[5]. His parchments had flown from his arms and were **gliding**[6] on the morning breeze before fluttering into **haphazard**[7] piles about his feet.

Heaven save us, that man's a ***butterfingers***[8], thought Cad, stifling a grin as she ruffled Fishy's fur.

But as Cad turned away, the crowd's **adulation**[9] distracting her, she did not see the cause of

---

1 **loiter** *(v)* wait around without apparent purpose. *(s)* linger, lurk, skulk. *(ant)* rush, scurry.

2 **tyrannical** *(adj)* be cruel. *(s)* brutal, ruthless, unjust. *(ant)* gentle, kind.

3 **bumble** *(v)* move awkwardly. *(s)* lurch, lumber, shamble.

4 **oblivious** *(adj)* unaware or unconcerned about what is happening. *(s)* ignorant, unconscious. *(ant)* conscious.

5 **puce** *(adj)* dark red or purple-brown in colour.

6 **glide** *(v)* move smoothly and continuously. *(s)* sail, float, drift. *(ant)* hurtle, careen.

7 **haphazard** *(adj)* lacking organisation. *(s)* random, chaotic. *(ant)* methodical.

8 **butterfingers** *(n)* a clumsy person who drops things. *(s)* bungler, fumbler.

9 **adulation** *(n)* extreme praise or admiration. *(s)* awe, worship. *(ant)* indifference, disregard.

Sir Robert's **momentary**[1] **petrification**[2]. Evans, as if faced by a **phantom**[3], his features suddenly ashen, now roused himself from his stupor and **grappled**[4] with his strewn papers. Looking stunned, he gaped as the cloaked and hooded figure, who peered at him from a shaded archway, swirled and turned away. Then as silent as a shadow, with Evans watching agog, the monk disappeared, vanishing into the **murky**[5] passages of Catrin Castle's keep.

To be continued.

1 **momentary** *(adj)* lasting for a short time. *(s)* brief, fleeting, quick. *(ant)* lasting.

2 **petrification** *(n)* a state of such fear that one cannot move. *(s)* immobilisation, paralysis. *(ant)* mobilisation.

3 **phantom** *(n)* a ghost. *(s)* apparition, spirit, spook, wraith.

4 **grapple** *(v)* engage in a struggle. *(s)* wrestle, fight, battle. *(ant)* surrender.

5 **murky** *(adj)* gloomy and dark. *(s)* dim, shadowy, obscured. *(ant)* bright, light, clear.

A SNEAK PEEK!

Thank you for reading *The Cadwaladr Chronicles: Book 1 – Trap*.
I hope you enjoyed reading it as much as I did writing it!

If you did, here's a sneak peek at the first chapter of *Book 2* in *The Cadwaladr Chronicles* series: *Cipher*

S. L. Ager

CHAPTER ONE

Cipher

From beneath a loose hood, two black holes **peered**[1] at her. Below **gaped**[2] the space where a nose should be. **Bared**[3] teeth flashed, no lips left to cover them. The mouth grinned. No eyes **conveyed**[4] emotion, and no **flesh**[5] crinkled or **creased**[6]. Then, as always, the face took shape, **transforming**[7] before her eyes. Whose features would form upon tonight's bare bones? Whose laugh would ring from its cruel mouth? Its face held the **expression**[8] a nightmare wore.

Cad struggled for air. She kicked hard against the **biting**[9] water, the surface rippling above her as she **floundered**[10] in the well where **forsaken**[11] as a baby. Could she breathe before the bones formed flesh; escape the **oubliette**[12] before the skull spoke its **scornful**[13] words? Could Cad

---

1 **peer** *(v)* look with concentration. *(s)* stare, gape, gaze. *(ant)* glance.

2 **gape** *(v)* be or become wide open. *(s)* part, yawn. *(ant)* close, shut.

3 **bare** *(v)* reveal and expose something to view. *(s)* uncover, unveil, display. *(ant)* cover, hide.

4 **convey** *(v)* make known or understandable. *(s)* deliver, exude, communicate. *(ant)* obscure, conceal.

5 **flesh** *(n)* the muscle and fat of a human or an animal. *(s)* tissue.

6 **crease** *(v)* make a line in. *(s)* wrinkle, pucker. *(ant)* smooth, straighten.

7 **transform** *(v)* markedly change something. *(s)* alter, modify, remodel. *(ant)* preserve, sustain.

8 **expression** *(n)* a look that conveys (shows) a certain emotion. *(s)* face, appearance.

9 **biting** *(adj)* extremely cold. *(s)* freezing, bitter, glacial. *(ant)* balmy, warm.

10 **flounder** *(v)* struggle physically or mentally. *(s)* falter, blunder. *(ant)* succeed.

11 **forsake** *(v)* abandon (past participle: forsaken). *(s)* desert, leave, disown. *(ant)* welcome.

12 **oubliette** *(n)* a dungeon, especially in a medieval castle, with access only through a trapdoor in the ceiling.

13 **scornful** *(adj)* showing or feeling contempt (disrespect). *(s)* disdainful, derisive. *(ant)* admiring.

survive the **myriad**[1] mothers, none known to her, **morphing**[2] from skull to skin before her eyes? Or tonight, might she see Siân again? The cold grip of fear **subsided**[3], but in its place burned a hot fire of **despair**[4].

With a gasp, Cad shot upright, wide-eyed. Sweat soaked her body. In a heartbeat, reality **dawned**[5] on her. She had woken in time. Cad had beaten the **ghoul**[6] who invaded her nights, waking before it had fully **manifested**[7]. Tonight, she'd **thwarted**[8] the **fiend**[9] who appeared in her dreams. The cloaked **monk**[10] who had sealed her and John in the **dungeon**[11] to rot away forgotten.

Weak with relief, her chest **heaving**[12], Cad flopped back against her pillows, **grateful**[13] she had not seen Siân's face this time. Then like an **evaporating**[14] mist, the **tension**[15] left the air.

Since Cad's **ordeal**[16] in the oubliette, as though the images were nailed to her memory, she had suffered nightmares. And although they were now less regular, and she more able to wake before they **terrified**[17] her, too often she met that hooded figure **looming**[18] over her bed. Now, as she caught her breath, and dawn crept into her bedchamber, Cad **banished**[19] the **hideous**[20]

---

1 **myriad** *(adj)* many *(s)* numerous, multiple. *(ant)* few.

2 **morph** *(v)* undergo a gradual process of transformation. *(s)* convert, modify, transform. *(ant)* preserve.

3 **subside** *(v)* become less severe or intense. *(s)* diminish, ease, abate. *(ant)* increase.

4 **despair** *(n)* the loss of all hope. *(s)* hopelessness, desperation. *(ant)* hope, joy.

5 **dawn** *(v)* become evident, be perceived or understood by the mind. *(s)* strike, occur. *(ant)* obscure.

6 **ghoul** *(n)* a phantom or spirit, especially an evil one. *(s)* bogeyman, fiend, monster. *(ant)* angel.

7 **manifest** *(v)* appear. *(s)* show, display, present. *(ant)* hide.

8 **thwart** *(v)* successfully oppose. *(s)* foil, stop, defeat, overpower. *(ant)* aid, facilitate.

9 **fiend** *(n)* a cruel or wicked person. *(s)* baddie, monster. *(ant)* hero, angel.

10 **monk** *(n)* a member of a religious community. *(s)* brother, friar.

11 **dungeon** *(n)* a cell or room where prisoners are held. *(s)* prison, jail, oubliette, donjon.

12 **heave** *(v)* rise and fall. *(s)* roll, billow.

13 **grateful** *(adj)* feeling or showing appreciation for something. *(s)* thankful, glad, appreciative. *(ant)* ungrateful.

14 **evaporate** *(v)* dry out. *(s)* disperse, disappear. *(ant)* materialise.

15 **tension** *(n)* stress or unrest. *(s)* agitation, unease, apprehension. *(ant)* calmness.

16 **ordeal** *(n)* a prolonged and horrid experience. *(s)* test, trial, tribulation, trauma, affliction, nightmare. *(ant)* joy.

17 **terrify** *(v)* cause to feel great fear. *(s)* horrify, petrify. *(ant)* calm, soothe.

18 **loom** *(v)* appear over someone or something as a large, often threatening presence. *(s)* tower, rise. *(ant)* recede.

19 **banish** *(v)* get rid of. *(s)* dismiss, eliminate, eradicate, exclude. *(ant)* accept, allow.

20 **hideous** *(adj)* extremely unpleasant. *(s)* ugly, revolting, appalling, monstrous. *(ant)* attractive.

images from her head, turning her thoughts over to the ever-present **cipher**[1] instead.

These days, when awake, she **pondered**[2] little else. **Symbols**[3] and letters formed in her mind, none wanting to be found and all **eluding**[4] her still.

Cad **scoured**[5] the puzzle for the hundredth time, still **stumped**[6]. **Exhaustion**[7] **impaired**[8] her **judgement**[9]. She longed to rip the **parchment**[10] apart, tear it to shreds cheering and whooping as she did so. As **rash**[11] as she was, Cad knew that would lead to regret once the red mist of anger, **fuelled**[12] by **lack**[13] of sleep, **anxiety**[14] and **frustration**[15], **inevitably**[16] lifted.

To **submit**[17] to this riddle's secrets was not an option. Instead, she **unfurled**[18] the **flimsy**[19] parchment she and Dylan had so often **pored**[20] over these last weeks since she'd **pilfered**[21] it from Sir Robert's **quarters**[22]. Cad's **brow**[23] creased as she studied the characters, twisting and

1 **cipher** *(n)* a disguised or secret way of writing something. *(s)* cryptograph, code, cryptogram.

2 **ponder** *(v)* think carefully about. *(s)* consider, contemplate, deliberate. *(ant)* disregard.

3 **symbol** *(n)* a mark or character that represents something. *(s)* sign, ideogram.

4 **elude** *(v)* avoid or escape. *(s)* evade, dodge. *(ant)* embrace.

5 **scour** *(v)* look or search thoroughly. *(s)* scrutinise, study, inspect. *(ant)* overlook.

6 **stump** *(v)* cause to be at a loss. *(s)* baffle, bewilder, confuse, confound, mystify. *(ant)* clarify, explain.

7 **exhaustion** *(n)* extreme mental or physical tiredness. *(s)* fatigue, weariness. *(ant)* vigour.

8 **impair** *(v)* damage or weaken. *(s)* reduce, lessen, decrease. *(ant)* improve, increase.

9 **judgement** *(n)* the ability to make decisions or come to conclusions. *(s)* sense, intelligence. *(ant)* recklessness.

10 **parchment** *(n)* prepared animal skin with a papery appearance used in ancient writing. *(s)* vellum, scroll.

11 **rash** *(adj)* acting without consideration of the outcome. *(s)* hasty, reckless, impulsive. *(ant)* careful, prudent.

12 **fuel** *(v)* power or inflame. *(s)* feed, provoke, stimulate, encourage. *(ant)* deplete.

13 **lack** *(n)* the state of being without or deficient. *(s)* need, want, dearth. *(s)* abundance.

14 **anxiety** *(n) a* worried and nervous feeling. *(s)* apprehension, unease, disquiet. *(ant)* calmness, reassurance.

15 **frustration** *(n)* the feeling of being upset at something that one is unable to change. *(s)* exasperation. *(ant)* satisfaction.

16 **inevitably** *(adv)* in an inevitable (unavoidable) way. *(s)* certainly, definitely. *(ant)* doubtfully.

17 **submit** *(v)* give in to. *(s)* succumb, acquiesce, yield, surrender, defer, buckle, capitulate. *(ant)* defy, resist.

18 **unfurl** *(v)* unroll or roll out. *(s)* open out, unfold, expand. *(ant)* furl, fold up.

19 **flimsy** *(adj)* light and easily damaged. *(s)* fragile, delicate. *(ant)* robust.

20 **pore** *(v)* be absorbed in reading or studying something. *(s)* examine, inspect, scrutinise.

21 **pilfer** *(v)* steal. *(s)* take, rob, thieve, snatch, purloin. *(ant)* give.

22 **quarters** *(n)* accommodation. *(s)* chambers, rooms, apartment.

23 **brow** *(n)* forehead.

turning their **intricate**[1] angles back and **forth**[2] in her head, noting their patterns, similarities and **anomalies**[3].

Neither Cad nor Dylan had dared make a copy for fear of losing the cipher's **accuracy**[4] in **translation**[5]. Both she and Dylan were **adept**[6] in coding and **deciphering**[7], as they'd created their **covert**[8] **communication**[9] language to help keep Cad's secret. **Nevertheless**[10], what she **suspected**[11] to be Sir Robert's **handiwork**[12], had **hitherto**[13] proved unbreakable, and it **infuriated**[14] and **consumed**[15] her too often.

Even in the **current**[16] **unseasonable**[17] warmth, Cad **shuddered**[18], for the parchment **evoked**[19] **ghastly**[20] memories of her ordeal in the oubliette with John. Thank heaven Rhys had found them in time. Thinking of that **gruesome**[21] place turned her **queasy**[22].

Weeks had passed, yet the man they'd left **unconscious**[23] in the oubliette, the man who'd

---

1 **intricate** *(adj)* detailed and complicated. *(s)* complex, elaborate. *(ant)* plain, simple.

2 **forth** *(adv)* forward in direction (or time). *(s)* onwards, ahead. *(ant)* back.

3 **anomaly** *(n)* something that is different to normal. *(s)* oddity, irregularity. *(ant)* normality.

4 **accuracy** *(n)* correctness or precision. *(s)* certainty, exactitude. *(ant)* inaccuracy.

5 **translation** *(n)* the act of making something understandable, especially another language.

6 **adept** *(adj)* skilful or proficient. *(s)* competent, adroit, deft. *(ant)* inept.

7 **decipher** *(v)* succeed in understanding or identifying something. *(s)* decode, decrypt. *(ant)* cipher.

8 **covert** *(adj)* not openly displayed or acknowledged. *(s)* secret, concealed. *(ant)* obvious, overt.

9 **communication** *(n)* the exchange of information. *(s)* reporting, transmission.

10 **nevertheless** *(adv)* all the same. *(s)* however, even so, nonetheless.

11 **suspect** *(v)* believe in the existence or truth of something without proof. *(s)* assume, think, suppose. *(ant)* know.

12 **handiwork** *(n)* something made or done by someone. *(s)* design, creation, work, craft, action.

13 **hitherto** *(adv)* until this point. *(s)* previously, formerly, beforehand, yet, before, thus far. *(ant)* henceforth.

14 **infuriate** *(v)* anger greatly. *(s)* enrage, inflame, exasperate. *(ant)* soothe, calm.

15 **consume** *(v)* strongly affect or overwhelm with a feeling. *(s)* dominate, overpower, control. *(ant)* abandon.

16 **current** *(adj)* in the present. *(s)* ongoing. *(ant)* past.

17 **unseasonable** *(adj)* (of the weather) unusual for the time of year.

18 **shudder** *(v)* tremble unwittingly *(s)* shiver, shake, quiver, convulse.

19 **evoke** *(v)* bring something to the conscious mind. *(s)* induce, arouse, awaken, recall. *(ant)* suppress.

20 **ghastly** *(adj)* causing great fear or horror. *(s)* grim, dire, harrowing, hideous. *(ant)* pleasant.

21 **gruesome** *(adj)* causing horror. *(s)* grisly, hideous, ghastly, macabre. *(ant)* pleasant.

22 **queasy** *(adj)* feeling slightly sick (nauseous) or uneasy. *(s)* odd, unsettled. *(ant)* well.

23 **unconscious** *(adj)* not awake or aware of one's environment. *(s)* asleep, comatose. *(ant)* conscious.

beaten Bryn Davis so badly, had not reappeared. Perhaps he had **perished**[1], but she doubted that. Someone, an **accomplice**[2], the monk with the long, **slim**[3] fingers, had more likely moved him.

'Dylan,' Cad whispered to her sleeping friend. 'Dylan, wake up. You must see this.' But he didn't **stir**[4].

'Dylan,' she hissed, not wanting to wake Rhys, who'd shown no interest in the cipher and seemed ocean deep in sleep.

Nor did she want to disturb the snoring Fishy curled at the foot of Rhys's bed. She smiled **affectionately**[5] at her friends, both two-legged and four.

'Dylan,' she said, **prodding**[6] him.

He shot up. 'Ouch! Don't do that!' Dylan grumbled, clearly readying himself to pepper Cad with **objections**[7].

But, smoothing over the moment, Cad pressed her finger to her lips as she nodded towards Rhys, then shook her head. A **jab**[8] with her hairpin was the one thing that could **rouse**[9] Dylan, who slept like the dead. 'I need you to look at something with me, now.' Cad's heart raced: as if the shadows had come to life, she'd spotted something promising **scrawled**[10] on the parchment.

'Yes, yes. But, do not wake me with that hairpin again, ever.'

Not **burdened**[11] by **conscience**[12], Cad nodded in agreement, a look of **compliance**[13] on her face, but they both knew she would jab him again, and probably tomorrow if need be.

---

1 **perish** *(v)* die, especially suddenly. *(s)* expire, depart, pass away. *(ant)* live, survive.

2 **accomplice** *(n)* a person who helps another commit a crime. *(s)* co-conspirator, collaborator, abettor.

3 **slim** *(adj)* not fat. *(s)* slender, lean, thin. *(ant)* fat, stubby.

4 **stir** *(v)* move slightly. *(s)* disturb, budge. *(ant)* still.

5 **affectionately** *(adv)* in an affectionate (fond) manner. *(s)* benevolently, agreeably. *(ant)* unkindly.

6 **prod** *(v)* poke with something. *(s)* jab, push, nudge.

7 **objection** *(n)* complaint. *(s)* disagreement, protest. *(ant)* approval.

8 **jab** *(n)* a quick, sharp blow. *(s)* prod, dig, stab, push, nudge.

9 **rouse** *(v)* bring out of inactivity. *(s)* stimulate, prompt, provoke, arouse. *(ant)* calm, appease.

10 **scrawl** *(v)* write in a hurried way. *(s)* scribble.

11 **burden** *(v)* cause worry, hardship or distress. *(s)* afflict, overload. *(ant)* relieve.

12 **conscience** *(n)* one's internal moral sense of right and wrong. *(s)* integrity, morality. *(ant)* immorality.

13 **compliance** *(n)* the action of complying (agreeing) to or with something. *(s)* obedience, concurrence. *(ant)* refusal.

'Get the sticks,' Cad said, nodding to where she knew Dylan had hidden the pouch she'd fashioned from old leather **scraps**[1].

Dylan rubbed his eyes, and with a yawn, reached beneath the bed's **slats**[2] where the tiny twigs they'd **painstakingly**[3] **whittled**[4] into **delicate**[5] markers, so they could repeatedly **replicate**[6] the cipher, lay **stowed**[7] away from **prying**[8] eyes. He passed the pouch to Cad, who removed the tiny **indicators**[9] that would **reconstruct**[10] and **deconstruct**[11] the mysteries of the cipher as and when they needed them. Cad knew the puzzle held the secret to the castle's **treachery**[12]. If it was the last thing she ever did, she would find who had **conspired**[13] with her mother, Siân, and her uncle, Dewi, to steal the Gwalch Gem bracelet and trick Llywelyn into killing his dog, Gelert.

Cad knelt, and Dylan **crouched**[14] beside her. With **diligence**[15], she laid out the thin sticks, **mimicking**[16] the parchment's symbols, twisting and turning the tiny twigs to **imitate**[17] the cipher's markings, until they might spot a sign that would unlock its secrets.

'Dylan. I think I saw something in my dreams. The code lined up for me. I'm almost there. What lies on this parchment is **crucial**[18], of that I am sure.'

---

1 **scrap** *(n)* a small piece of something, especially one that is leftover. *(s)* morsel, bit.

2 **slat** *(n)* a thin narrow piece of material such as wood, especially one that overlaps with another.

3 **painstakingly** *(adv)* done in a painstaking (careful) way. *(s)* thoroughly, diligently, meticulously. *(ant)* carelessly.

4 **whittle** *(v)* carve wood into an object. *(s)* pare, trim, shave, model.

5 **delicate** *(adj)* fine in structure. *(s)* dainty, frail, fragile. *(ant)* strong, durable.

6 **replicate** *(v)* make a copy of. *(s)* duplicate, reproduce, recreate.

7 **stow** *(v)* store, pack or keep neatly in a specific place. *(s)* stash, secrete, deposit. *(ant)* unload, remove.

8 **prying** *(adj)* looking or enquiring too closely. *(s)* inquisitive, curious, probing. *(ant)* disinterested.

9 **indicator** *(n)* something that shows or represents something. *(s)* gauge, symbol, signal.

10 **reconstruct** *(v)* make or form again. *(s)* restore, reassemble, rebuild. *(ant)* deconstruct.

11 **deconstruct** *(v)* take something apart. *(s)* dismantle, unravel, interpret. *(ant)* construct.

12 **treachery** *(n)* a breach of trust. *(s)* betrayal, deceit, disloyalty, dishonesty. *(ant)* loyalty, honesty.

13 **conspire** *(v)* make harmful secret plans with. *(s)* plot, scheme, collude.

14 **crouch** *(v)* to lower the body by bending one's knees. *(s)* squat, shrink, huddle. *(ant)* stand.

15 **diligence** *(n)* careful and persistent effort or work. *(s)* rigour, conscientiousness, zeal. *(ant)* laziness, carelessness.

16 **mimic** *(v)* resemble or imitate (copy or behave like). *(s)* mirror, impersonate, simulate. *(ant)* differ from.

17 **imitate** *(v)* copy or simulate. *(s)* mirror, resemble, replicate. *(ant)* differ from.

18 **crucial** *(adj)* of absolute (complete) importance. *(s)* critical, vital, key. *(ant)* trivial.

Dylan rubbed sleep from his eyes, used to Cad's **obsession**[1] with breaking the code. She often woke him at night, or dragged him from **chores**[2] when she thought she was close to **resolving**[3] the cipher's mystery.

'And I think Sir Robert is more involved than he lets on,' said Cad for the thousandth time since **swiping**[4] the parchment from his rooms. 'You lie with dogs, you rise with fleas,' she muttered under her breath, unable to shake the distrust she **harboured**[5] towards her father's **associate**[6].

'Cad, do you not find this **somewhat**[7] tiresome now?' asked Dylan, **irritation**[8] creeping into his voice. 'We have puzzled over this for weeks,' he moaned, 'to no **avail**[9].'

Cad ignored him, **rummaging**[10] through all **viable**[11] explanations in the hope of finding a straw to cling to. If Sir Robert was worried about his lost cipher, he **concealed**[12] his **concern**[13] well. He'd **uttered**[14] not a word since its theft, and no one seemed to be searching for it. Cad wondered if he thought it lost. Cad often asked herself why she'd taken it, and she wasn't sure of the answer, but something had **rattled**[15] her when she'd seen it and with her father **absent**[16] she'd acted on her **hunch**[17].

To keep it safe, Cad ensured the parchment remained hidden within the secretly sewn folds of

---

1 **obsession** *(n)* something one cannot stop thinking about. *(s)* passion, fixation. *(ant)* apathy.

2 **chore** *(n)* a task, often a household one. *(s)* job, work, errand, duty, drudgery.

3 **resolve** *(v)* find a solution. *(s)* solve, answer, fathom, unravel. *(ant)* mystify.

4 **swipe** *(v)* take without permission or payment. *(s)* steal, thieve, pilfer.

5 **harbour** *(v)* hold a thought or feeling in the mind. *(s)* nurture, foster.

6 **associate** *(n)* a business partner or companion. *(s)* ally, comrade, supporter.

7 **somewhat** *(adv)* a little but not a lot. *(s)* a bit, rather, quite, slightly. *(ant)* extremely.

8 **irritation** *(n)* the state of feeling impatient, annoyed or slightly angry. *(s)* exasperation, chagrin. *(ant)* delight.

9 **avail** *(n)* benefit or use. *(s)* advantage, reward, purpose, gain, profit. *(ant)* uselessness.

10 **rummage** *(v)* search in a haphazard (disorganised) way. *(s)* root, scrabble, dig.

11 **viable** *(adj)* capable of working or being. *(s)* feasible, possible. *(ant)* impossible.

12 **conceal** *(v)* hide or disguise. *(s)* screen, shroud, cloak, veil, camouflage. *(ant)* reveal, uncover.

13 **concern** *(n)* worry. *(s)* anxiety, disquiet, apprehension, unease. *(ant)* indifference, serenity, calm.

14 **utter** *(v)* speak. *(s)* say, express, breathe.

15 **rattle** *(v)* make someone nervous, uneasy, or annoyed. *(s)* unnerve, perturb, ruffle. *(ant)* calm.

16 **absent** *(adj)* not present. *(s)* out, gone. *(ant)* present.

17 **hunch** *(n)* an intuitive feeling or idea. *(s)* impression, suspicion, guess, notion. *(ant)* certainty.

her **garments**[1] along with myriad other **miscellanies**[2]. Being raised as a **noble**[3] girl at Cadwaladr Castle until the age of seven, had **sealed**[4] her **embroidery**[5] skills. But to this castle's **inhabitants**[6], who **assumed**[7] she was a **pageboy**[8] on knight's training, her expert **stitching**[9] skills remained **purposely**[10] hidden: boys didn't sew – much to her **chagrin**[11].

'This is the part that **baffles**[12] me,' Dylan **muttered**[13], **defeated**[14], the pinprick to his **rear**[15] now clearly **forgiven**[16] as he ordered the sticks into rows of symbols. 'See, just here.' He pointed to the patterns. 'The missing link is this one; I'm sure of it.'

Cad nodded. 'Mmm. I'm not so sure,' she replied, rearranging the pattern, hoping that might **prime the pump**[17], much to Dylan's irritation judging by the look on his face.

'You're such a bossyboots,' he **chided**[18], watching her **deftly**[19] move the tiny twigs into various positions, her face fixed in **concentration**[20].

Cad stared, her eyes narrowing in thought. She fiddled some more, but then shook her head, and in a **fit of pique**[21], **swiped**[22] at the pattern of sticks, destroying their arrangement.

---

1 **garment** *(n)* an item of clothing. *(s)* clothes, outfit, attire, dress.
2 **miscellany** *(n)* a group or mixture of different items. *(s)* assortment, variety. *(ant)* uniformity.
3 **noble** *(adj)* of high birth or rank. *(s)* aristocratic, patrician. *(ant)* humble, peasant.
4 **seal** *(v)* establish or conclude something in a definite way. *(s)* clinch, complete.
5 **embroidery** *(n)* the craft of sewing fabric in a decorative manner.
6 **inhabitant** *(n)* a person or animal that lives in a particular place. *(s)* dweller, resident, occupant.
7 **assume** *(v)* presume to be the case without any proof of it. *(s)* suppose, conclude, believe. *(ant)* prove.
8 **pageboy** *(n)* a boy in training for a knighthood, ranking one below a squire in a knight's personal service.
9 **stitch** *(v)* make or mend by sewing stitches. *(s)* sew.
10 **purposely** *(adv)* done with intention. *(s)* deliberately, wilfully. *(ant)* unintentionally, accidentally.
11 **chagrin** *(n)* annoyance or distress. *(s)* disappointment, exasperation, displeasure, irritation. *(ant)* delight, joy.
12 **baffle** *(v)* totally confuse. *(s)* perplex, bewilder, flummox, confound. *(ant)* enlighten, clear up.
13 **mutter** *(v)* say something that is difficult to hear. *(s)* murmur, mumble, whisper. *(ant)* shout.
14 **defeated** *(adj)* beaten. *(s)* conquered, vanquished, overcome. *(ant)* triumphant, victorious.
15 **rear** *(n)* backside. *(s)* bottom, bum, rump, butt, buttocks.
16 **forgive** *(v)* grant pardon to someone (past participle: forgiven). *(s)* excuse, absolve, exonerate. *(ant)* blame, resent.
17 **prime the pump** (phrase) stimulate something to start or continue.
18 **chide** *(v)* tell off, rebuke or scold. *(s)* reprimand, reproach, reprove. *(ant)* praise, applaud.
19 **deftly** *(adv)* in a deft (skilful) manner. *(s)* capably, adroitly, adeptly. *(ant)* clumsily.
20 **concentration** *(n)* the act of focusing all attention. *(s)* awareness, attentiveness. *(ant)* inattention.
21 **fit of pique** *(n)* a sudden feeling of annoyance.
22 **swipe** *(v)* hit or try to hit. *(s)* swing, slap, lash out.

'Why did you do that?' cried Dylan. 'You were close then. I **swear**[1] it.'

'I order and stare at these darned sticks to copy that code so often, I feel I am losing my mind,' she groaned, **frustrated**[2] at her inability to solve this puzzle after such a lengthy study. 'It is so **perplexing**[3]. Maybe Evans knows it is unbreakable, and that is why he **frets**[4] not at losing it,' she added, **dispirited**[5].

Dylan was used to Cad's **outbursts**[6]. He'd known her since birth; she tested his patience at times, but he was already organising the sticks again, applying his excellent eye for **detail**[7].

Resting her **weary**[8] eyes, Cad glanced over at Fishy, who was curled up at the foot of Rhys's bed and **comically**[9] appeared to be headless. Cad immediately relaxed at the sight of her **canine**[10] shadow, the pup she'd rescued from the **moat**[11], who was now, thanks to the meat pilfered from the kitchens on Cad's invisible night **jaunts**[12], a much larger dog than Cad had ever **anticipated**[13] she would be.

Cad stole a look at Rhys, who seemed to be sound asleep, but one never knew with Rhys and his **curious**[14] ways of silently watching and listening when **folks**[15] thought him stupid. Cad knew otherwise; the **taciturn**[16] boy, whom they'd recently **dubbed**[17] 'Lord Nosy', missed little.

---

1 **swear** *(v)* promise. *(s)* vow, affirm, attest.

2 **frustrated** *(adj)* feeling annoyed from being out of control. *(s)* exasperated, irritated. *(ant)* content.

3 **perplex** *(v)* completely confuse. *(s)* baffle, confound, flummox. *(ant)* enlighten.

4 **fret** *(v)* be constantly anxious. *(s)* worry, fuss, agonise, anguish.

5 **dispirited** *(adj)* feeling hopeless. *(s)* disheartened, dismayed. *(ant)* heartened.

6 **outburst** *(n)* a release of strong emotion. *(s)* eruption, flare-up. *(ant)* containment.

7 **detail** *(n)* an individual fact or item. *(s)* particular, circumstance.

8 **weary** *(adj)* extremely tired. *(s)* exhausted, fatigued, shattered. *(ant)* fresh, refreshed.

9 **comically** *(adv)* in a comical (funny or amusing) way. *(s)* hilariously, entertainingly. *(ant)* seriously, solemnly.

10 **canine** *(adj)* relating to or like a dog. *(s)* doggy, doggish.

11 **moat** *(n)* a defensive, water-filled trench surrounding a castle or town.

12 **jaunt** *(n)* a short journey or outing. *(s)* trip, tour.

13 **anticipate** *(v)* expect. *(s)* predict, foresee, forecast, foretell. *(ant)* neglect.

14 **curious** *(adj)* strange. *(s)* odd, unusual, funny, bizarre. *(ant)* ordinary, usual.

15 **folk** *(n)* people. *(s)* persons, individuals, inhabitants, residents.

16 **taciturn** *(adj)* (of a person) quiet. *(s)* untalkative, silent. *(ant)* talkative.

17 **dub** *(v)* give a nickname to. *(s)* entitle, call, label, name, term, tag.

'Look, Cad. Look again closely. Do you see what I'm seeing?' Dylan said, with the **enthusiasm**[1] of a young child.

Cad leaned over the sticks that imitated the cipher on the parchment, a flutter of unexpected excitement rising as she peered at them with such **intensity**[2], her eyes crossed. 'If we could just **identify**[3] these last two symbols, we may **crack**[4] it,' Dylan added.

She **stifled**[5] a groan – Cad knew this, and had for weeks, but was still unable to **fathom**[6] it. Hitherto, Evans's language had **evaded**[7] her. Then just as she was about to gather up the tiny twigs, something caught her eye. She blinked hard. In her mind, the symbols and letters took on beautiful curves like an unfurling **fern**[8], new shapes appearing as the sun streamed into the room, **illuminating**[9] the sticks on the floor before her. Then, like soldiers lining up to march into battle, like an arrow between the eyes, it hit Cad.

'Dylan,' she whispered, her heart **soaring**[10]. 'Dylan, I think I have it—'

But she stopped **abruptly**[11] as the door to their quarters burst open. Without thinking, she **automatically**[12] swiped the twigs beneath the bed and out of view. Cad's face **flushed**[13] with **fury**[14], her chest tightening with **rage**[15]. Bryn Davis, the **senior**[16] **squire**[17] whose **hide**[18] she'd

---

1 **enthusiasm** *(n)* eager enjoyment, approval or interest. *(s)* fervour, zeal. *(ant)* apathy.

2 **intensity** *(n)* the characteristic of being intense (powerful). *(s)* vehemence, vigour. *(ant)* apathy.

3 **identify** *(v)* work out who or what someone or something is. *(s)* establish, recognise, know.

4 **crack** *(v)* solve. *(s)* fathom, decipher, break, decode. *(ant)* encrypt.

5 **stifle** *(v)* restrain a reaction or stop oneself acting on an emotion. *(s)* suppress, repress, curb. *(ant)* encourage.

6 **fathom** *(v)* comprehend after much thought. *(s)* understand, grasp, perceive. *(ant)* misunderstand.

7 **evade** *(v)* avoid or escape. *(s)* elude, dodge. *(ant)* confront.

8 **fern** *(n)* a green flowerless plant which has leafy, feathery fronds.

9 **illuminate** *(v)* light up. *(s)* brighten, lighten. *(ant)* darken, dim.

10 **soar** *(v)* climb or fly rapidly above usual levels. *(s)* ascend, rise. *(ant)* plummet.

11 **abruptly** *(adv)* in an abrupt (unexpected and sudden) way. *(s)* hastily, quickly, immediately. *(ant)* gradually.

12 **automatically** *(adv)* done without thinking about beforehand. *(s)* spontaneously, impulsively. *(ant)* thoughtfully.

13 **flush** *(v)* become red. *(s)* blush. *(ant)* pale.

14 **fury** *(n)* wild anger. *(s)* rage, wrath, outrage, temper, frenzy. *(ant)* calmness.

15 **rage** *(n)* extreme anger. *(s)* wrath, fury, indignation, outrage.

16 **senior** *(adj)* high in rank or status. *(s)* superior, high-ranking. *(ant)* junior.

17 **squire** *(n)* a young noble man serving a knight in exchange for training to be a knight himself.

18 **hide** *(n)* the skin of an animal. *(s)* pelt.

saved from a cruel beating filled the doorway, wearing a **smug**[1] smile that was a work of art. Cad swallowed some ugly words, then swallowed some more.

'You,' he said, pointing at Dylan. 'You're wanted to clean **armour**[2], now.' Then with a look of **utter**[3] **contempt**[4], his eyes turned to Cad. 'And *you,*' he snarled, are in the kitchens, *now*!'

Then Davis was gone. And as if he'd stolen the solution from Cad and taken it with him, the pattern she had clearly seen vanished from before her eyes.

---

1 **smug** *(adj)* having an overly high opinion of oneself. *(s)* self-satisfied, superior, complacent. *(ant)* humble, modest.
2 **armour** *(n)* the metal plates worn to protect the body in battle. *(s)* covering, shield.
3 **utter** *(adj)* absolute. *(s)* total, complete, downright. *(ant)* partial.
4 **contempt** *(n)* the feeling that someone or something is worthless. *(s)* disdain, dislike, scorn. *(ant)* admiration.

LEARN WITH THE CADWALADR SERIES

The Cadwaladr Chronicles: Book 1 – Trap forms part of *The Cadwaladr* integrated education series.

When you have finished *The Cadwaladr Chronicles* series, it's time to move on to the following trilogy, *The Cadwaladr Quests.*

The Cadwaladr Quests series comprises a trilogy of novels, supporting workbooks and vocabulary revision notebooks.

Find all *The Cadwaladr Quests* books online via your local Amazon store.

The Cadwaladr Quests: Book 1 – Tangled Time

Other supporting books:

The Cadwaladr Quests: Book 1 – Tangled Time – Workbook

The Cadwaladr Quests: Book 1 – Tangled Time – Vocabulary Revision Notebook

11+ Vocabulary, Comprehension and Verbal Skills – Workbook 1

*

The Cadwaladr Quests: Book 2 – Race For The Gold

Other supporting books:

The Cadwaladr Quests: Book 2 – Race For The Gold – Workbook

The Cadwaladr Quests: Book 2 – Race For The Gold – Vocabulary Revision Notebook

*

The Cadwaladr Quests: Book 3 (the finale) – Cat's Eye

PARENTS, GET FIVE FREE COMPREHENSION EXERCISES

Parents, to receive your free comprehensions (with answers) based on *The Cadwaladr Chronicles: Book 1 – Trap,* please leave a review for *Trap* on Amazon and email a screenshot to:

freebies@slager.co.uk.

I will add you to my mailing list[1] and send you the comprehensions by email.

1 You can unsubscribe from the mailing list at any time. Further details will be emailed to you as soon as you are added.

REVIEWS, PLEASE!

If you've enjoyed *The Cadwaladr Chronicles: Book 1 – Trap*,
please leave a review on Amazon.
Thank you!

ERRATA AND INFORMATION

To report any **errata**[1], please email: **errata@slager.co.uk.**
If you would like information about new books in *The Cadwaladr Chronicles* series, please visit:

SLAGER.CO.UK

You can stay up to date with S. L. Ager, author of *The Cadwaladr Chronicles* series,
on social media:

facebook.com/SLAgerAuthor
instagram.com/SLAgerAuthor
linkedin.com/in/SLAgerAuthor
pinterest.com/SLAgerAuthor
twitter.com/SLAgerAuthor
tiktok.com/@s.l.ager

1 **erratum** *(n)* an error in writing or publishing (plural: *errata*).

Printed in Great Britain
by Amazon

29802432R00110